GUIDE TO
Fitting Out

by JIM EMMETT

ZIFF-DAVIS PUBLISHING COMPANY

New York

Introduction

My grandfather used to have a word for them: "Thingamajigs."

He had variously owned a lumber schooner and two tugboats and he knew that every job on a ship had to be done right. He and Jim Emmett would have gotten along just fine. Both men would have liked the thingamajigs of sixty years ago and the gadgets of today. Each of them would have had fine tools to show the other. Each of them would have had his own reasons for wanting a vessel to be shipshape before leaving harbor. One would have known more about hemp rope and utilitarian gray paint—the other would have known more about stainless steel, 1960 adhesives, and electricity.

You can guess why my grandfather came into this introduction: it is because a large part of boat care takes old-fashioned knowledge. That is what makes this *Guide to Fitting Out* so valuable. The solid stuff is here.

Of course, it's a far cry from a lumber schooner of the nineteenth century to any of dozens of small pleasure boats Jim Emmett knows inside and out. New materials, better wrinkles for making hatches watertight, and a lot of engineering knowledge go into boat maintenance as Emmett knows it.

The author of this guide just about lives on the water, moving north and south with the seasons. Like those of us who are shorebound half the time, he keeps working at making things, fixing things, improving things.

All boatowners—yes, even wealthy yachtowners—keep their eyes open for the right way to keep the jib sheets from fouling, or a better way to take care of ice-box drainage or ventilation of the cabin. Just watch them when they visit each other's boats in a harbor. The owner shows off his new liquor cabinet, built under the table. The visitor sees a different way to stow charts. Many skippers even keep notebooks. One I know is full of notes, drawings, lists of "fix-it later," and oddments like interesting names for dinghies (a ketch named *Secret* with a dinghy named *Shhh!*).

If you haven't begun your own scrapbook of recipes, instructions, and things to make, let this book be your start. Your main worry will be that the owner of the next boat in the yard will borrow it and be slow to return it.

Perhaps my grandfather wouldn't have gone in for, say, very much varnish, even if he owned one of today's cruising boats. But he would have known the right way to apply it, so that the varnish shone. He would have liked learning how to apply gold leaf. He would have known what to do with a serving mallet.

All the items mentioned in passing in this introduction are in this *Guide*—plus a few hundred more. And a good thing too, for a reader can save hundreds of dollars with the ideas in this book, and have hundreds of hours of pleasure to boot.

JOHN R. WHITING
Irvington, N. Y.

Preface

Most all boatmen are gadgeteers at heart. We're forever making changes to our boats, adding new features and working out ways to make maintenance simpler or its results more satisfying or longer lasting. It's possible that boats may eventually become so standardized, so maintenance free, that an owner will have little choice but to use his boat as it is. Even if so, boating will have lost some of its attraction.

As it is, of course, there is an almost endless number of changes one can make and features that he can add, ranging from the most simple sort to quite serious winter-time projects. Fortunately, most boating enthusiasts are fairly handy with tools, and so often the only encouragement they need to get started on a certain job is having the how-to-do-it information. I hope this book contains just this kind of material.

There are in all 240 different plans for improvements to a boat. Each project is described in a large clearly labeled drawing and accompanying instructional text. Generally, there's but a single project to a page—and never more than two. We have not crammed anything together, but have kept the instructions large and open so that they can be followed as the reader is at his workbench or aboard his boat.

None of these ideas is new or untried. They have all appeared in my Gadgets department in *Rudder* magazine. (This is now a feature of *Popular Boating*—"Fitting Out with Jim Emmett".) I have selected for publication here only those items which have proved to be the most help to the greatest number of readers.

Look at the list of contents and you'll see that I've taken in the three popular fields—sail, power, and outboards—and with something on nearly every phase of the sport. Many of the projects have resulted from my own experience, which includes building half a dozen boats and reconditioning as many or more used ones. Many of these ideas, however, have come from readers who have been kind enough to use my column as a medium for passing along to others their way of doing a certain job. To these, my thanks for their interest and loyalty over the years and for helping to make this book possible.

I also want to thank those boatowners and also my many boatbuilder and boatyard-owner friends up and down the coast for allowing me to "steal" such worthwhile ideas as I've come across in being aboard their boats or visiting their places. Finally, to *Rudder* goes my gratitude for permission to reuse the material which first appeared in that magazine. Also, to its editor, Boris Lauer-Leonardi, personally for his encouraging me to keep on contributing such material.

My thanks also go to Wm. Taylor McKeown, Editor of *Popular Boating,* who encouraged and helped the planning and assembling of the material for this book.

My only wish is that boatmen will have as much fun in using the ideas here as I've had in going over the accumulated material, trying to decide which projects to use and which to omit in putting this book together.

JIM EMMETT

Contents

GUIDE TO
Fitting Out

CHAPTER 1

Engines

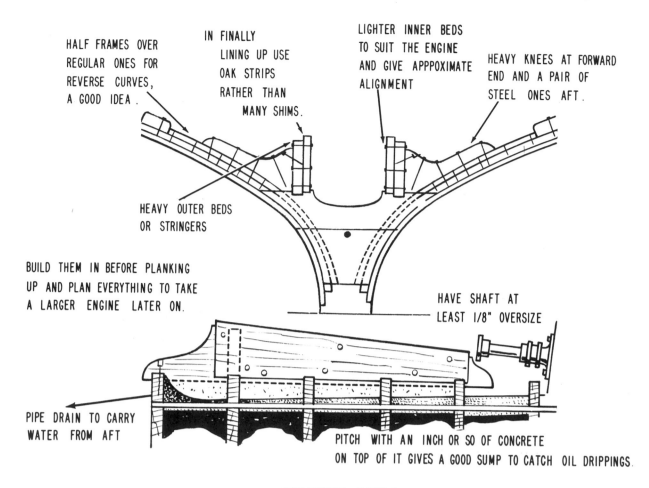

HALF FRAMES OVER REGULAR ONES FOR REVERSE CURVES, A GOOD IDEA.

IN FINALLY LINING UP USE OAK STRIPS RATHER THAN MANY SHIMS.

LIGHTER INNER BEDS TO SUIT THE ENGINE AND GIVE APPPOXIMATE ALIGNMENT

HEAVY KNEES AT FORWARD END AND A PAIR OF STEEL ONES AFT.

HEAVY OUTER BEDS OR STRINGERS

BUILD THEM IN BEFORE PLANKING UP AND PLAN EVERYTHING TO TAKE A LARGER ENGINE LATER ON.

HAVE SHAFT AT LEAST 1/8" OVERSIZE

PIPE DRAIN TO CARRY WATER FROM AFT

PITCH WITH AN INCH OR SO OF CONCRETE ON TOP OF IT GIVES A GOOD SUMP TO CATCH OIL DRIPPINGS.

ENGINE BEDS

If you are planning to build a boat, do not neglect the engine bed. Install it right after the hull framework has been completed and before planking up. It's easier to work through the frames, and the bed can be better secured. Also, if you're wise, plan it to take a larger engine than the one you intend to install. When you eventually have to think about replacing the engine, the chances are that you'll want more power. Should it come to selling, having engine beds and shaft assembly that will allow for the other fellow's putting in a larger engine can be a good selling point.

Apart from having the propeller shaft a good ⅛ inch in diameter larger than required for the engine in mind, and the stuffing box and stern bearing sized accordingly, put in amply heavy outer stringers or beds and space them wide enough apart so that lighter, say 1½-inch, beds will be required, bolted inside them, for mount-

ing your engine. Securing these with carriage bolts to the heavier members leaves them easily removable so that new ones, thicker or thinner, to suit the next engine can be put in their place. Should it be necessary, a considerably larger engine may be just right for the outer stringers.

The deep floor timbers and the knees shown are both good ideas, for there is nothing like well-secured beds to give vibrationless running. I've suggested in the lower sketch the use of pitch with an inch or so of concrete molded over it to give a closed sump for catching oil drippings from the engine. This is the best insurance against a dirty main bilge. Although what is done here will depend largely on the boat's shape and construction, it is a good idea to run a copper tube or pipe in this to carry any chance water from after sections to the main part of the bilge to prevent such water from flowing into the oil sump.

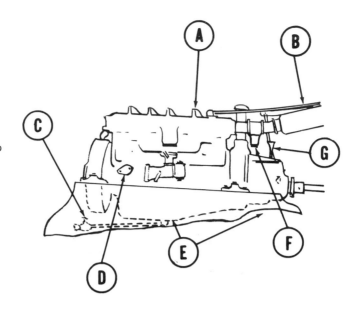

A - REMOVE THE COIL AND MOUNT
ADJACENT TO THE ENGINE—
BUT WHERE IT WILL KEEP COOLER

B— IF THERE IS NOT A TEMPERATURE
CONTROL, FIT A BYPASS LINE WITH
CONTROL TO CARRY COOLING WATER
BACK TO THE PUMP

C— IF SPACE BENEATH PERMITS, FIT
A DRAIN LINE WITH COCK AND PLUG FOR SUMP

D— IF TANK WILL GIVE GRAVITY FEED,
REMOVE FUEL PUMP AND CONNECT
DIRECTLY TO CARBURETOR

E— A PROPER MARINE-TYPE FUEL
STRAINER IS A MUST AND ONE ON
THE WATERLINE WORTHWHILE

F— THERE SHOULD BE A CONDENSATION
TRAP IN THE EXHAUST LINE

G— REVERSE OR REDUCTION GEAR BREATHER PIPES
MAY NEED SCREEN OIL—SPRAY TRAPS

ENGINE INSTALLATION POINTERS

Not all the pointers noted above will apply to every engine or the manner of its installation, but a few of them may prove worthwhile. *A* suggests removing the coil from its conventional position on the engine and mounting it on an adjacent bulkhead or even beneath the deck— any place where it will be dry. Otherwise (particularly on long runs), it is apt to get very hot and give trouble or fail sooner than it rightly should.

B covers the needs of the engine which has no temperature control. Perhaps the easiest installation is a tee fitted in the water-outlet line from the manifold, so that a gate valve can be put in and a hose line led to another tee in the water-intake line. The setting of the valve will then adjust the flow of warm water to mix as desired with the cool from the hull intake to give the desired running temperature of from 150 to 170 degrees.

In few auxiliaries is there sufficient depth beneath the engine to make the sump drain plug usable, but it is often possible to fit an ell and a pipe length as to extend beneath or beyond the front end, where there may be enough depth to use a pan to drain off the old oil.

D is an effort to simplify the installation by getting rid of the fuel pump; this gives you one less accessory that might give trouble. You must first be certain that your tank or tanks will flow by gravity, to the last gallon and under any condition. It has been my experience with several engines that you can safely run the fuel line directly to the carburetor simply by removing the fuel pump and closing its opening with a heavy brass plate and gasket secured by bolts into the pump's mounting holes.

E, a good-sized marine-type fuel strainer and a strainer at the waterline are worthwhile fittings, particularly if the boat is used in shallow or silt-laden waters. *F*, a trap to catch exhaust-line condensation, is something I would not be without.

G, oil-spray traps for a reverse gear with a breather pipe, will often end the nuisance of the rear end of the engine being covered with a film of oil after a long run. Where the fault cannot be traced to an actual oil leak, there is a chance the fumes from a breather pipe, particularly with the oil level high, are laden with oil. It is a simple matter to remove the usual ell from the top of the pipe and fit in its place a reducer with its larger upper end packed with two or three discs cut from ordinary copper-wire screen.

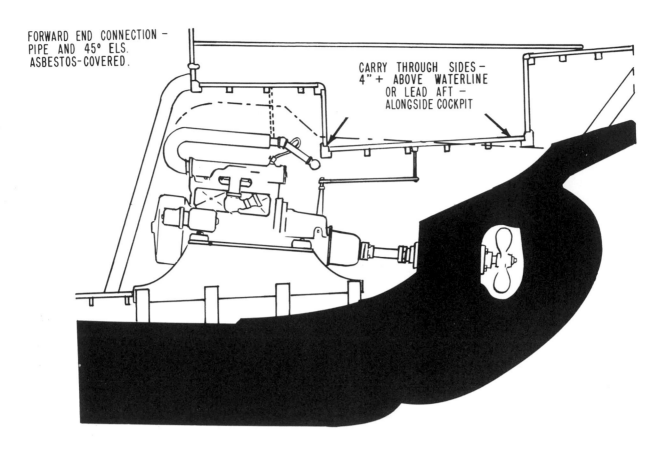

FORWARD END CONNECTION –
PIPE AND 45° ELS.
ASBESTOS-COVERED.

CARRY THROUGH SIDES –
4" + ABOVE WATERLINE
OR LEAD AFT –
ALONGSIDE COCKPIT

FRONT-END EXHAUST CONNECTION

In the average auxiliary, the exhaust line is frequently the most difficult part of installing the engine. Above all, the exhaust line must be laid out so as to drain perfectly. When the engine is not running, neither cooling water left in the line nor outside water, as from following waves, should be able to work its way back into the engine. Back pressure must be avoided. The size of the engine's exhaust connection usually allows for a certain amount of this, but beyond that back pressure not only cuts down the engine's power appreciably but can cause uneven running. Water-cooled parts of the line should run reasonably clear of woodwork; if you can manage it, the whole line should be installed in such a way that its main joints are accessible. It may be necessary to use a large wrench in the event of trouble. Above all, don't overlook the importance of perfectly tight joints. I have been aboard many boats where it would be fatal to remain below in bad weather with

everything battened down and the engine going, for even the best of engine-ventilation systems can backdraft under adverse conditions.

It may help here to make use of the forward-end exhaust connection, now an optional feature on most marine engines. Aboard the ketch in the example shown, a forward-end connection exhausting through the sides gave an efficient installation. Had he wished, the owner probably could have led the line, perhaps from a higher loop, aft alongside the cockpit and through the transom. What caused his problem mainly was the closeness of the cockpit to the engine. Although a water-jacketed copper loop would have been best, this one, lagged with asbestos and made of pipe and nipples· connected by 45-degree elbows, runs coolly enough. Needless to say, the after end of this quite heavy section should be supported in a way that will relieve the strain on the manifold connection.

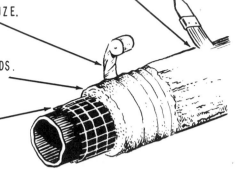

④ PAINT WHILE STILL WET WITH A MIX OF
CEMENT, LIME, AND WATER.
LATER, WHEN SET BY TIME AND HEAT, USE ENGINE PAINT.

③ HOLD BY WINDING WITH SURGICAL GAUZE.

② MOLD ASBESTOS CEMENT IN PLACE WITH YOUR HANDS.

① ENCASE WITH 1/2"-MESH GALVANIZED RAT WIRE
RATHER LOOSE AROUND PIPE
AND TIGHTER ABOUT ELBOWS

COVERING A HOT EXHAUST LINE

Although a water-cooled exhaust line is much preferable to a covered hot one, there is a big difference in cost that many of us must consider. Properly covered, a hot line will not heat the surrounding space too much, and, of course, it will be safe. Nor have I found the pipe to rust out any quicker if covered than if left bare.

A good method of covering is with the use of ½-inch-mesh galvanized rat wire. This helps to hold the asbestos cement in place, the hardest part of the job. Cut this wire in pieces to encase the pipe—rather snug-fitting single wrappings over the elbows and slightly looser ones about the straight sections—so that all will have about the same diameter. Secure them by bending the cut ends of one edge to hook into meshes of the other edge of each piece. I have used so-called asbestos cement, but have found there is not enough cement ingredient in it to adhere well. It is best to add to it or to shredded asbestos or fibers either Portland cement or plaster of Paris. I like the former because lime can then be added to make the mixture adhere even better in molding it in place. Although I have heard of different proportions being used, this does not seem too important. A 10-quart bucket about half-full of the asbestos, enough dry cement to bring it a good two-thirds full, and 2 cupfuls of lime (as used in concrete work) seems about right.

Mix these dry ingredients in the bucket, or better still in a box; then add water and remix thoroughly, until the consistency is such that it can be molded into a ball without falling apart. You may have to add more water to have the mix adhere as you mold it with your hands about the wire-encased line. A mix that is on the soft side can be pressed through the meshes to hold, where a stiffer one cannot. As you work along, covering 5 or 6 inches at a time, hold the under part with one hand while you use the other to wrap it with 1½-inch surgical gauze. With all covered and wrapped, the mess will have set enough so that you can go back over it with your hands to shape more uniformly with the gauze to hold it.

While still wet, paint it with a mixture of three parts cement to one part lime mixed with water to the consistency of thin paint. Wait a day or so and then run the engine. When you are sure the heat of this has thoroughly hardened the covering, paint with engine enamel, if it is in a place that shows.

I have also tried molding this shredded asbestos mixed with plaster of Paris about 1½ inches thick over the bare pipe, holding it by immediately wiring on pieces of smaller mesh (¼-inch rat wire previously cut to shape), and then molding another outer layer of cement over this. While results were good, I think it is the harder way. The lime does seem to give adhesion.

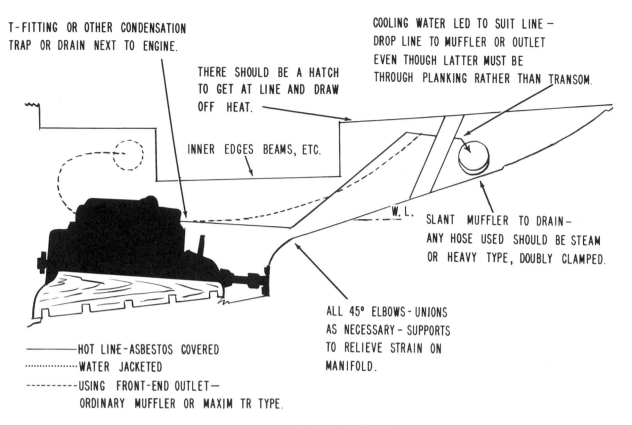

T-FITTING OR OTHER CONDENSATION
TRAP OR DRAIN NEXT TO ENGINE.

THERE SHOULD BE A HATCH
TO GET AT LINE AND DRAW
OFF HEAT.

COOLING WATER LED TO SUIT LINE —
DROP LINE TO MUFFLER OR OUTLET
EVEN THOUGH LATTER MUST BE
THROUGH PLANKING RATHER THAN TRANSOM.

INNER EDGES BEAMS, ETC.

W. L.

SLANT MUFFLER TO DRAIN —
ANY HOSE USED SHOULD BE STEAM
OR HEAVY TYPE, DOUBLY CLAMPED.

ALL 45° ELBOWS - UNIONS
AS NECESSARY - SUPPORTS
TO RELIEVE STRAIN ON
MANIFOLD.

——————— HOT LINE - ASBESTOS COVERED
·················· WATER JACKETED
- - - - - - - - USING FRONT-END OUTLET —
ORDINARY MUFFLER OR MAXIM TR TYPE.

EXHAUST-LINE HINTS

A faulty layout of the exhaust line, especially aboard an auxiliary, can make the best engine a poor performer. Back pressure, water in the engine (either sea water or from condensation), and overheating are common troubles which often can be traced to a badly planned exhaust line. The proper installation, water-jacketed and with a type of muffler that is best suited to the particular setup, usually is expensive, with the result that exhaust lines too often are installed in the cheapest and quickest way. A cheap line can be satisfactory, but it should be considered as a temporary measure, to be used only until the correct layout can be afforded.

A hot line, as shown by the solid line above, will work satisfactorily in climates where the weather is not too hot, or in cases where the engine is not used for long and steady runs, or where there is a hatch aft to draw off the heat on the longer runs. This hot-line exhaust will also work better on slow-turning engines, because a slow-turning engine does not throw off

as much exhaust heat as a high-speed engine.

Water from condensation will accumulate in any exhaust line, so take the precaution of fitting a condensation trap or drain next to the manifold, even though it may be merely an ordinary T fitting with a short nipple and cap— or perhaps a drain cock—to eliminate the necessity of removing the cap. The drain also is useful in checking your line for water when under sail before a following sea; or, the drain can be left open. Unions will be necessary to facilitate assembly.

The usual precautions should be observed: the use of 45-degree elbows to avoid short turns; the line should slant up to a high point well above the waterline, likely aft, and then drop down to the discharge even though the latter might be rather near the water level, which apparently is no great objection so long as the outlet is not submerged when running. Water should be let in so that it will drain, probably beyond the crook or into the muffler, without having to depend on valves or cocks. Strap-iron supports necessary to hold the line and take the strain off the manifold connection should have pieces of ¼-inch asbestos between them and the pipe. Also, woodwork near the line should be protected with a layer or so of this same material, even though the pipe is lagged with asbestos. The commercial clamp-on type of covering with a corrugated asbestos core will not withstand this heat, and if you can get at the line at all, cement will not be difficult to apply. Buy the shredded asbestos and mix with a little plaster of Paris, a tablespoonful to the pound, and enough water to make a very stiff mixture. Mold this with your hands, 1-inch thick and a section at a time. It should stick long enough to allow wiring a jacket of galvanized rat wire over it. With this in place, you can then force more cement through the meshes until the pipe is completely covered and all neatly smoothed down. This line will last fairly long.

When you are able to install a proper and permanent exhaust line, consider not only your present engine but also the possibility of installing a different one later on. When replacing or changing engines, one invariably steps up in power, seldom down, and because a water-jacketed exhaust line that is well made of brass or copper should outlast several engines, it can be made large enough, about ½-inch larger in diameter in anticipation of power increases. I have run across several installations where a well-made line which was originally planned for a small engine was later used for a larger one with resultant trouble due to back pressure. Then too, even with a line of correct size there is a chance of carbon or corrosion at the joints and the outlet which will constrict the line.

Original design or construction of a boat seldom seems to provide for replacement of the exhaust line; when replacement is necessary, rather than run a new line the same as the old one, which perhaps was installed during building, consider some entirely different setup to solve your problem, especially if you can use a Maxim TR type of muffler. In most cases, the cockpit beams are so close to the waterline that it is impractical to install a muffler there, and spaces on either side of the cockpit may be hard to get at or may have tanks fitted. In case you are installing a new engine, it might be well to consider the option of a front outlet.

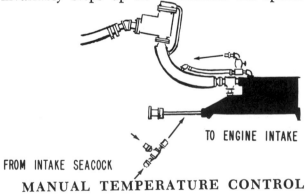

FROM INTAKE SEACOCK   TO ENGINE INTAKE

MANUAL TEMPERATURE CONTROL

When an engine is not equipped with an automatic control to raise its temperature in cold weather, a simple, manually operated device serves well. Such a control does not starve the pump of water, but merely permits enough heated discharge water to lead back to the intake line to raise the temperature of the engine and allow it to run more efficiently. While shown with a typical exhaust layout for an auxiliary, the idea can be used with any similar installation by tapping the discharge line.

Although opening the control valve fully will warm up the engine quickly, I think it is best to set it partly open to let it heat up more slowly. Then, when the temperature gauge shows the usual summer running figure, close the valve to the point which will maintain it. With our engine I have found that merely cracking the valve open will suffice for quite cold weather and that, on a long run, once it is set right further attention is seldom necessary.

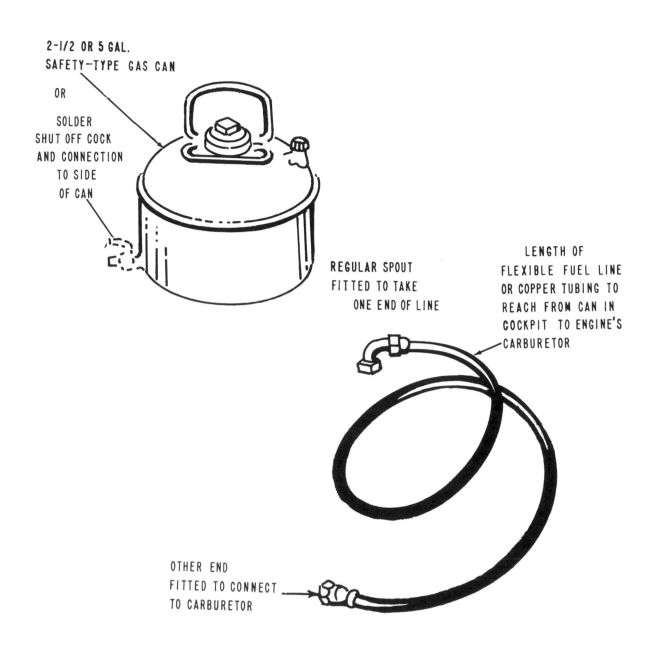

2-1/2 OR 5 GAL.
SAFETY—TYPE GAS CAN

OR

SOLDER
SHUT OFF COCK
AND CONNECTION
TO SIDE
OF CAN

REGULAR SPOUT
FITTED TO TAKE
ONE END OF LINE

LENGTH OF
FLEXIBLE FUEL LINE
OR COPPER TUBING TO
REACH FROM CAN IN
COCKPIT TO ENGINE'S
CARBURETOR

OTHER END
FITTED TO CONNECT
TO CARBURETOR

EMERGENCY FUEL SYSTEM

Charlie Hannibal on the *Tom Breeze* told me about the idea shown above. Simply carry a reserve of gas in a can fitted with either its spout or a cock soldered in its side to take one end of a suitable length of flexible fuel line or even copper tubing. The other end of this line has a fitting that can be quickly connected to the carburetor with its regular fuel line disconnected. This line should be long enough so that in the event of fuel-system trouble in a tight spot (line badly plugged or the fuel pump failing), the can can be chocked up in the cockpit and its line connected directly to the carburetor to feed by gravity.

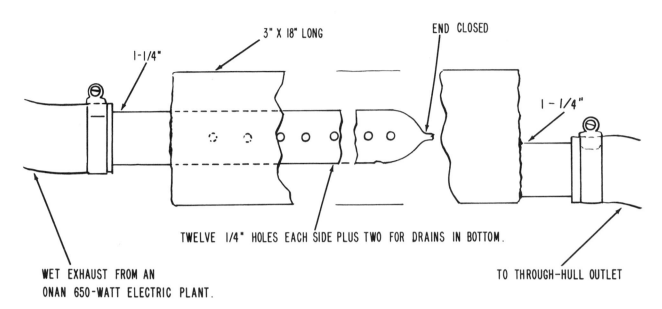

ALL PIPE AND END PLATES ARE OF COPPER BRASS.

3" X 18" LONG

END CLOSED

1-1/4"

1 - 1/4"

TWELVE 1/4" HOLES EACH SIDE PLUS TWO FOR DRAINS IN BOTTOM.

WET EXHAUST FROM AN
ONAN 650-WATT ELECTRIC PLANT.

TO THROUGH-HULL OUTLET

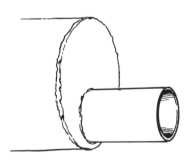

PLATES AND PIPES BRAZED IN

LIGHTING-PLANT SILENCER

One of the quietest running electric plants that I have come across is on Al Robinson's 48-foot Wheeler, *Interlude*. Its exhaust is water-cooled, and the line is a long one, both of which are helpful factors. However, the real reason for its being so quiet is likely the silencer that Al made for it. As shown, this is simply an 18-inch length of 3-inch brass pipe, with brazed end plates holding two pieces of pipe that are the right size for the exhaust hose. The longer inlet pipe has a dozen ¼-inch holes drilled in each side and a couple of drain holes. One has its end merely squeezed closed, while the other is a short stub to take the outlet hose.

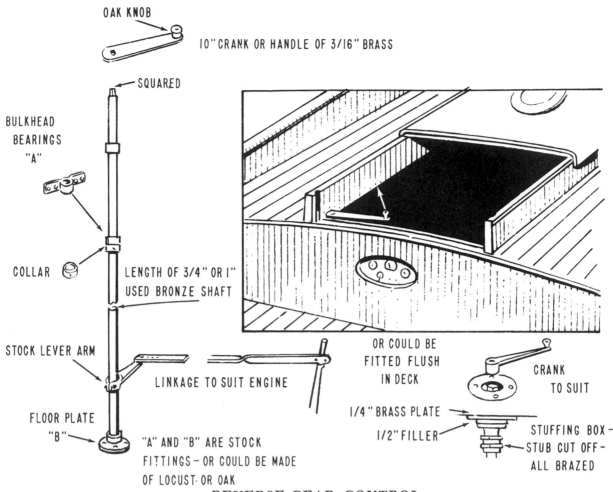

OAK KNOB

10" CRANK OR HANDLE OF 3/16" BRASS

SQUARED

BULKHEAD
BEARINGS
"A"

COLLAR

LENGTH OF 3/4" OR 1"
USED BRONZE SHAFT

STOCK LEVER ARM

LINKAGE TO SUIT ENGINE

OR COULD BE
FITTED FLUSH
IN DECK

CRANK
TO SUIT

1/4" BRASS PLATE

1/2" FILLER

STUFFING BOX –
STUB CUT OFF –
ALL BRAZED

FLOOR PLATE
"B"

"A" AND "B" ARE STOCK
FITTINGS – OR COULD BE MADE
OF LOCUST OR OAK

REVERSE-GEAR CONTROL

If the type of reverse-gear control shown here can be used, it has a number of good points. In the first place, particularly if the owner is making the installation himself, its cost should not run high, since few fittings must be bought. More important, there need be nothing about that will be in the way when not used, and the position usually can be worked out to give the helmsman good vision ahead while he is using the control in maneuvering about a dock. Also, if the installation is properly made, the action is positive, with nothing to go wrong below.

The idea is to provide a well-secured upright shaft with a squared head, so that the crank or handle and the engine's reverse gear lever can be linked up below. In the main sketch, the upper end is shown in the corner of a bridge-deck companionway, where it is kept low enough so that the handle can be used with the cover pulled. However, this type is as often used with the shaft carried through the cockpit deck, close to a side or an end and led through a stuffing-box-type fitting to keep water from below. Or, the whole works can be located centrally and kept flush by using a homemade fitting of a stuffing box with its projecting stub sawed off and brazed to a filler disc and flush plate, as shown. A socket-type handle is then required, but there is the advantage that this can be worked with the foot.

While the location of the throttle control is not shown, it should be carefully thought out in conjunction with the reverse-control arrangement, for one will often want to handle both simultaneously. Both should be located where attention can be given the tiller or wheel at the same time.

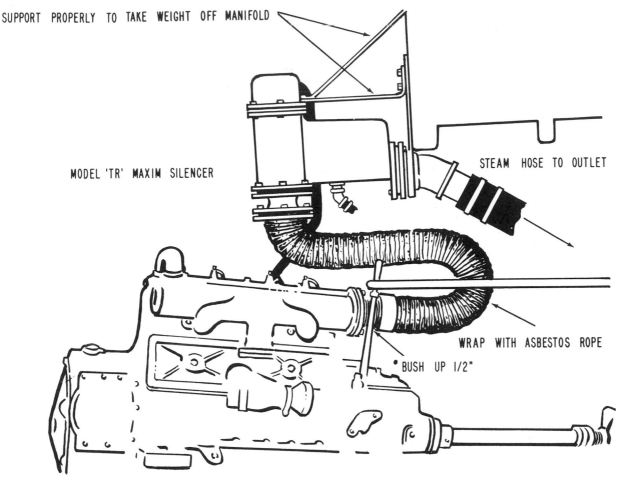

SUPPORT PROPERLY TO TAKE WEIGHT OFF MANIFOLD

MODEL 'TR' MAXIM SILENCER

STEAM HOSE TO OUTLET

WRAP WITH ASBESTOS ROPE

BUSH UP 1/2"

EXHAUST-LINE LAYOUT

This is the most satisfactory exhaust-line lay-out I have ever had. Of course, it can be used only if there is sufficient height over the engine to mount the Maxim TR type muffler used. This muffler, despite its advantages for sailboat installation, does take up a good bit of room and may be difficult to install. In order that its weight may be properly supported, it is usually located astern, generally in the lazarette, since the cockpit is seldom high enough above the waterline for safety. In our case, however, it would have cluttered up the lazarette, and the long length of hot pipe would have been an objection unless an expensive water-jacketed section was used.

As shown, the exhaust line is bushed up ½ inch immediately upon leaving the manifold, to avoid back pressure in this hot section to the muffler. It was purposely bought ½ inch larger than the engine called for to permit this, although I am now sure the size specified for the engine would have been satisfactory. This S curve is made up of stock pipe fittings wrapped with asbestos rope, which has proved satis-factory in keeping the line safe and preventing heat from escaping. Plastering it with asbestos cement would have been another, perhaps neater method, but I believe it is harder on the pipe. A steam hose, all double-clamped, is attached to a long length of pipe to carry the exhaust and its cooling water from the muffler to the outlet through the transom. The weight of the muffler must be taken off the exhaust line and engine manifold by supporting it with stout iron straps, well secured to adjacent wood-work, with holes in their lugs to take the stud bolts in the muffler.

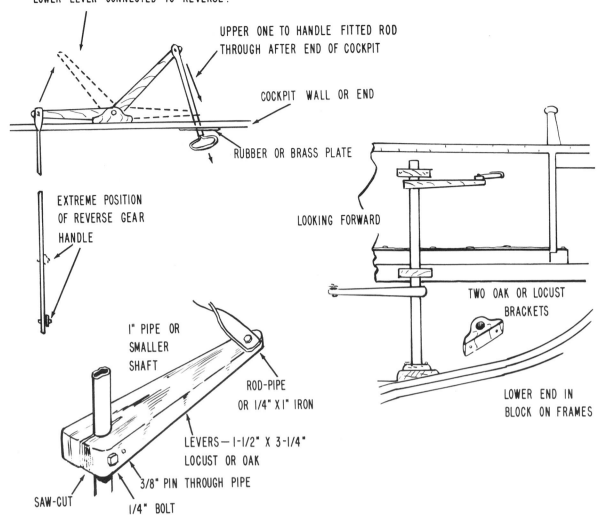

UPRIGHT IN SPACE AFT OF COCKPIT WITH
LOWER LEVER CONNECTED TO REVERSE.

UPPER ONE TO HANDLE FITTED ROD
THROUGH AFTER END OF COCKPIT

COCKPIT WALL OR END

RUBBER OR BRASS PLATE

EXTREME POSITION
OF REVERSE GEAR
HANDLE

LOOKING FORWARD

1" PIPE OR
SMALLER
SHAFT

ROD-PIPE
OR 1/4" X 1" IRON

LEVERS — 1-1/2" X 3-1/4"
LOCUST OR OAK

3/8" PIN THROUGH PIPE

SAW-CUT

1/4" BOLT

TWO OAK OR LOCUST
BRACKETS

LOWER END IN
BLOCK ON FRAMES

REVERSE CONTROL

The objection to the reverse-control lever coming through the cockpit deck by means of a fitting which is hard to keep watertight is avoided in this homemade type. Space abaft the cockpit is required to install the upright and for the levers to work, but the handle through the after end of the cockpit is out of the way, at least, in the ahead position. And in the installation shown, the handhold part of bent rod was threaded to screw in or out of the pipe section as required. Length of the levers must be in keeping with the travel of the reverse-gear handle, and the upright pipe or shaft should be heavy enough so as not to be weakened seriously by holes for through pins or bolts holding levers.

Poor power in reverse can sometimes be traced to more holdback pressure being required on the gear lever than the leverage of the control arrangement can apply. In one case where the usual adjustments failed to remedy this, a ⅜-inch line was led from the lever back through a block in the lazerette and out a hole in the after bulkhead of the cockpit, with a heavy knot in the end of the rope. In a pinch, tension on this line gave the extra pull required.

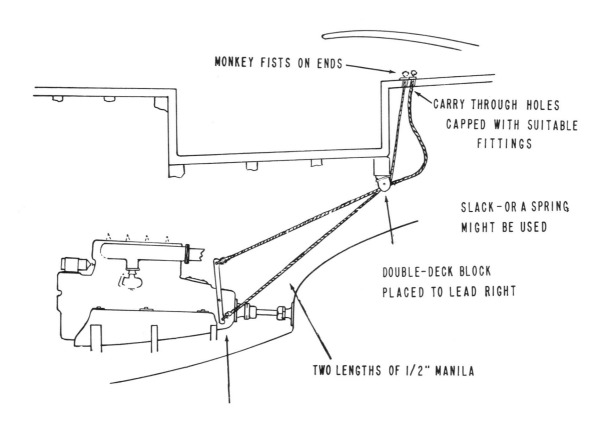

LOCATION OPTIONAL –
BUT NEAR TILLER OR WHEEL

MONKEY FISTS ON ENDS

CARRY THROUGH HOLES
CAPPED WITH SUITABLE
FITTINGS

SLACK – OR A SPRING
MIGHT BE USED

DOUBLE-DECK BLOCK
PLACED TO LEAD RIGHT

TWO LENGTHS OF 1/2" MANILA

SHACKLE TO BAR-TYPE LEVER

ROPE REVERSE CONTROL

Rope-type reverse controls are rigged on Herrick Thompson's schooner *Haligonian*. Herrick avoids having to carry one of the lines forward and then back, as is necessary when both lines are led from the top of a regular reverse lever, by using a bar-type lever instead. Of course, there must be room for the lower end of this to move, but this, along with the lower length of bar necessary, will depend on the particular installation. At any rate, the two lines are led back to a double deck block fastened to have them lead right where wanted—in this case, to the afterdeck. There they are carried through holes and suitable deck fittings to be finished off with monkey fists. When these are down over the holes of fittings which are higher centrally than at the edges, they will let little water below. Of course, these ends could be carried almost anywhere by leading the lines through additional blocks, but here the whole thing is kept simple so that nothing much can go wrong.

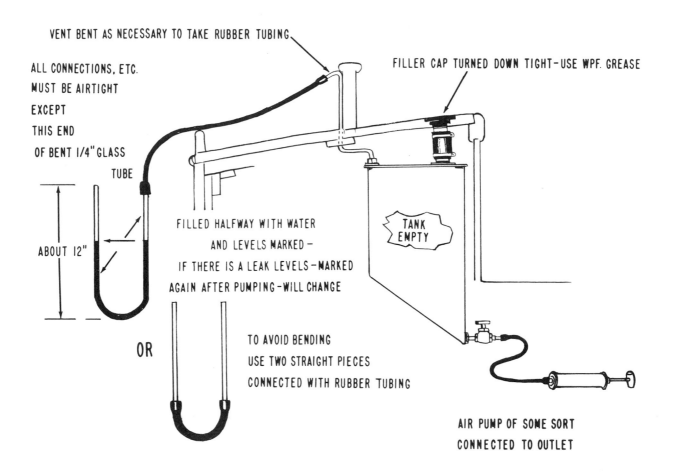

VENT BENT AS NECESSARY TO TAKE RUBBER TUBING

FILLER CAP TURNED DOWN TIGHT-USE WPF. GREASE

ALL CONNECTIONS, ETC.
MUST BE AIRTIGHT
EXCEPT
THIS END
OF BENT 1/4" GLASS
TUBE

ABOUT 12"

FILLED HALFWAY WITH WATER
AND LEVELS MARKED —
IF THERE IS A LEAK LEVELS — MARKED
AGAIN AFTER PUMPING — WILL CHANGE

TANK
EMPTY

OR

TO AVOID BENDING
USE TWO STRAIGHT PIECES
CONNECTED WITH RUBBER TUBING

AIR PUMP OF SOME SORT
CONNECTED TO OUTLET

TESTING FUEL TANKS FOR LEAKAGE

I like this method of detecting fuel-tank leaks because it can be employed without removing the tank and effectively reveals the presence of air as well as liquid seepage, both of which are highly dangerous. Air leaks at the top of a fuel tank are particularly dangerous, as they seldom are immediately suspected as the source of gasoline fumes below deck. It is not easy to detect these fuel-tank leaks and find their sources.

D. V. Gladding had these leaks in mind when he used the method aboard a ketch he bought. One of her fuel tanks had been emptied and disconnected, and he wanted to determine whether this was done because the tank leaked. He devised the method shown here to keep from tearing out structural members of the cockpit in order to remove the tank.

How one rigs up for the test will depend on the particular tank location. In Capt. Gladding's case the piece of ¼-inch glass tubing bent to a

U shape was connected by means of a length of rubber hose to the tank's air vent. Care was taken to see that the filler cap was on tight (waterproof cup grease on the cap's threads will ensure airtightness). Then the outlet line beyond the shutoff was removed and a pump from an old kerosene pressure stove was hooked up there. Finally, having made sure that all connections were perfectly tight, he filled the glass tube about halfway with water and marked the levels. The actual test was made by giving the pump a few strokes to create enough pressure (2 or 3 ounces should suffice) to displace the water columns in the glass tube. The outlet valve was then closed and the new level marked. An inspection half an hour later showed no change, which meant that the tank was perfectly tight. Had there been any escape of air, the level would have changed from the observed marks.

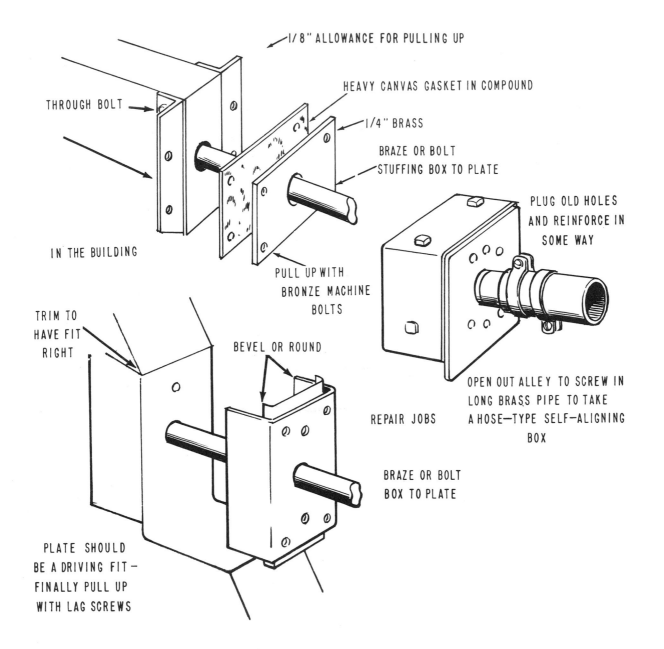

1/8" ALLOWANCE FOR PULLING UP

THROUGH BOLT

HEAVY CANVAS GASKET IN COMPOUND

1/4" BRASS

BRAZE OR BOLT STUFFING BOX TO PLATE

IN THE BUILDING

PULL UP WITH BRONZE MACHINE BOLTS

PLUG OLD HOLES AND REINFORCE IN SOME WAY

TRIM TO HAVE FIT RIGHT

BEVEL OR ROUND

REPAIR JOBS

OPEN OUT ALLEY TO SCREW IN LONG BRASS PIPE TO TAKE A HOSE–TYPE SELF–ALIGNING BOX

BRAZE OR BOLT BOX TO PLATE

PLATE SHOULD BE A DRIVING FIT – FINALLY PULL UP WITH LAG SCREWS

SECURING THE STUFFING BOX

When one or both of the lags holding an inside stuffing box has lost its hold in the wood, or has corroded away, a bad leak results. Ordinarily, it is possible either to put in lags that are longer or heavier enough to hold or to turn the box far enough that fresh holes can be bored. Still, particularly where the fastenings go into end grain, the time will come when the wood has become so chewed up that something else must be tried.

The upper sketch shows a way of fastening which is becoming popular as the original way of securing the box. Or, if there is room alongside to bore for the fastening of the angles, this method could be used for a repair job. The other sketches show ways of correcting extreme cases. Both will reinforce the log—something that is usually necessary to make the job permanent.

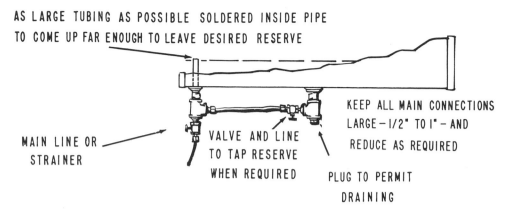

AS LARGE TUBING AS POSSIBLE SOLDERED INSIDE PIPE
TO COME UP FAR ENOUGH TO LEAVE DESIRED RESERVE

KEEP ALL MAIN CONNECTIONS
LARGE — 1/2" TO 1" — AND
REDUCE AS REQUIRED

MAIN LINE OR
STRAINER

VALVE AND LINE
TO TAP RESERVE
WHEN REQUIRED

PLUG TO PERMIT
DRAINING

FUEL-RESERVE TANK

Another advantageous installation is a fuel tank made to fit its location and having two outlets of larger diameter than usual. The main outlet is carried above the bottom of the tank, a frequent practice, but in this case high enough to prevent drawing off the last 5 gallons. Considered as a reserve, this can be tapped when required by another line connected to the main one. Valves are fitted as required, and a drain plug is provided for cleaning the tank. Trouble from water, or sludge which is apt to collect in the reserve, is guarded against by carrying a wire-mesh strainer, through which all gas going into the tank is strained, and by fitting an efficient, large, marine bronze-type strainer in the line. Where fuel is pumped from the top of a tank, it would seem a simple matter to arrange this to leave a reserve which could be drawn from the bottom through another line.

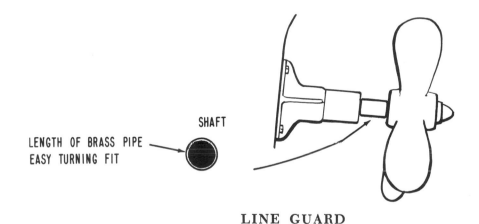

SHAFT

LENGTH OF BRASS PIPE
EASY TURNING FIT

LINE GUARD

The line guard shown above is not sure protection against à stray line's being wound up by the propeller, but the captain of a boat on which I saw one of these told me it at least makes it easier to free the wheel. This guard is simply a length of brass pipe long enough to extend from the stern bearing to the wheel's boss or hub. The pipe's inside diameter should be an easy turning fit on the shaft, and its length should be such that it will not bear on the bearing or hub. In winding up a line, it is usually an easy matter to free the part about the blades of the wheel, but very difficult to unwind or even cut that part jammed around the shaft. As this idle sleeve will rotate on the shaft, a line is not so apt to be picked up, or if it is, the turning sleeve usually permits pulling it free.

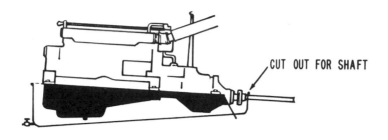

16-20 OZ. COPPER OR ZINC, STAINLESS STEEL

CUT OUT FOR SHAFT

ACTS AS A SHIM

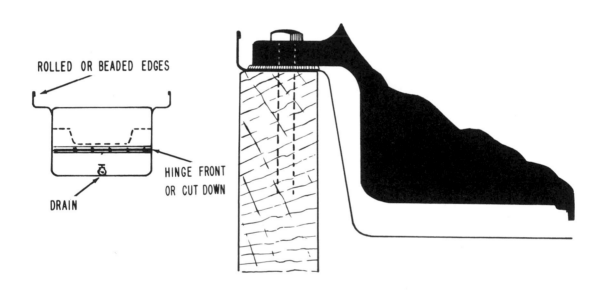

ROLLED OR BEADED EDGES

HINGE FRONT OR CUT DOWN

DRAIN

ENGINE OIL PAN

Jack Avery, in sending me his idea for making an engine oil pan, explains that he has had such pans on several different boats. The time to make one is when the engine is off its beds, using measurements taken off the base of the engine and being sure that ample clearance is left. Sixteen-ounce copper cuts and solders nicely, the hot-rolled type being the softer to work, Avery says. Carry the sides up all around and roll or bead the edges. It is best to have the pan long enough to catch any drippings from the rear end, notching it out there to take the coupling or shaft. For the forward end, it is nice to have the upper part hinged, or to cut it down somewhat for handier swabbing out. However, with the bottom slanted and a drain cock fitted, there should be little swabbing necessary, except possibly for a seasonal cleaning. This is an old and well-known idea, but few boats have such a pan. Certainly, it is the ideal way of keeping oil out of the bilges.

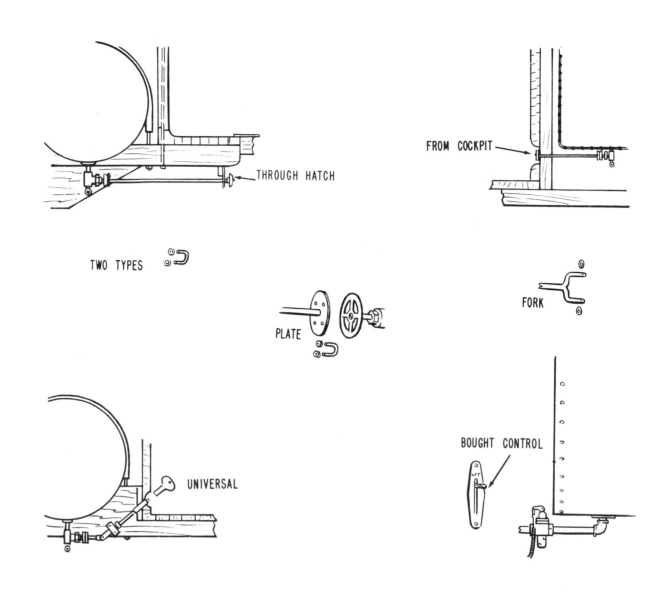

THROUGH HATCH

FROM COCKPIT

TWO TYPES

PLATE

FORK

UNIVERSAL

BOUGHT CONTROL

REMOTE SHUTOFFS

On plans the tanks are usually shown with the shutoff cock or valve where it is easily reached. In the actual boat, the opposite is too often the case. Some change has made the shutoff, or maybe a pair of them, difficult of access. What is sensible, then, is to fit on some sort of remote control.

Naturally, the easiest solution is to use a type which can be bought. If this is not feasible, some way of turning the handle of a proper valve, preferably of the packless or Kerotest type, may be worked out. The top sketch on the left shows the control easily reached through the cockpit engine hatch. In the opposite sketch, where the tank or tanks are higher, the control wheel is let in flush in the cockpit side. I have also seen this idea used with a universal joint in the control line, but when the hookup becomes that complicated, it would seem wiser to buy a proper remote-control unit which provides the valve as well as the control.

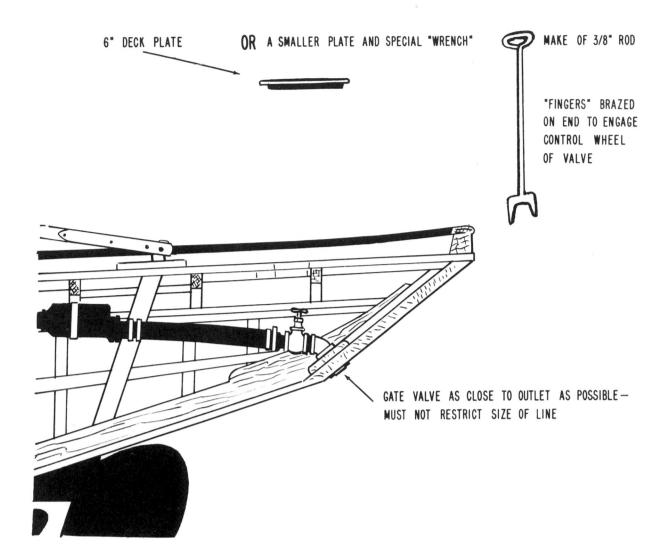

6" DECK PLATE   OR A SMALLER PLATE AND SPECIAL "WRENCH"   MAKE OF 3/8" ROD

"FINGERS" BRAZED
ON END TO ENGAGE
CONTROL WHEEL
OF VALVE

GATE VALVE AS CLOSE TO OUTLET AS POSSIBLE —
MUST NOT RESTRICT SIZE OF LINE

POSITIVE EXHAUST SHUTOFF

Clive Jamieson is responsible for the idea of the positive-exhaust shutoff. There is nothing new about this, but it does give me a chance to point out that this, or a similar arrangement, can often save one much worry and trouble. Theoretically, in a well-planned exhaust line the installation of a shutoff should not be necessary. In actuality, it may not be possible to give the after part of the line enough drop from the high point to render it effectual when one is sailing before a heavy following sea.

An outside plug can be used to keep water out of the engine, but it is hard to get one securely in place on a boat with considerable overhang and the outlet through the planking. More important, perhaps, it is often more difficult to get the plug out when the engine is needed. Despite the usual rag wrapped around the plug, the swelling of the plug can make the job one for the dinghy and quieter waters.

The arrangement is simple, and no directions are necessary for installing. Mr. Jamieson's suggestion for avoiding what can always happen with such a shutoff is a good one. After closing the valve and screwing the deck plate on, the key for the latter is always hung on a hook over the engine's starter button, just in case he forgets.

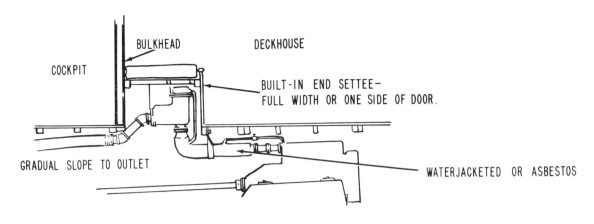

COCKPIT   BULKHEAD   DECKHOUSE

BUILT-IN END SETTEE—
FULL WIDTH OR ONE SIDE OF DOOR.

GRADUAL SLOPE TO OUTLET

WATERJACKETED OR ASBESTOS

MAXIM 'TR' OVERHEAD TYPE MUFFLER

OR

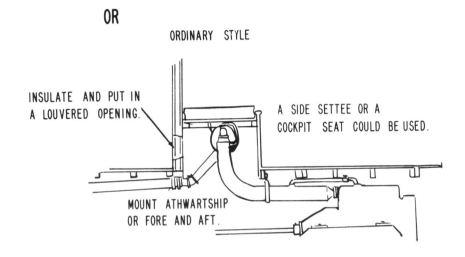

ORDINARY STYLE

INSULATE AND PUT IN
A LOUVERED OPENING.

A SIDE SETTEE OR A
COCKPIT SEAT COULD BE USED.

MOUNT ATHWARTSHIP
OR FORE AND AFT.

MUFFLER COMPARTMENT

The top arrangement was worked out by an owner after his 36-foot power cruiser almost sunk because of a defect in its original exhaust-line layout. The pipe ran in almost-straight lines from the twin engines to the outlets just above the waterline, aft. And as is so often the case with such lines, the mufflers and much of the piping always had salt water remaining in them. What happened was that during the owner's absence, something rusted through. Then, enough water lapped into the outlets and on through to put the stern down. Naturally, the condition worsened quickly and by the time the boat's plight was noticed by someone in the yard, she was flooded.

In planning the new lines, advantage was taken of the short settees on each side of the deckhouse door. By cutting through and reinforcing the deck or floor, two compartments were created for the overhead-type mufflers used. From them, the lines ran with enough slope to be self-draining.

The owner explained that regular-type mufflers could be used, mounted athwartships, as shown in the lower sketch, or fore and aft. Also, a longer side settee or cockpit seat could be used for a muffler compartment. It is only a matter of gaining the foot or more of extra height over what the deckhouse or cockpit floor usually affords.

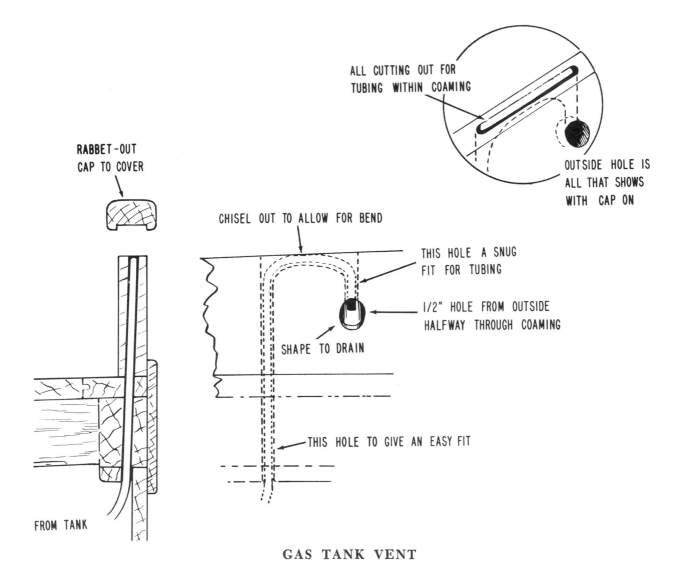

ALL CUTTING OUT FOR
TUBING WITHIN COAMING

OUTSIDE HOLE IS
ALL THAT SHOWS
WITH CAP ON

RABBET-OUT
CAP TO COVER

CHISEL OUT TO ALLOW FOR BEND

THIS HOLE A SNUG
FIT FOR TUBING

1/2" HOLE FROM OUTSIDE
HALFWAY THROUGH COAMING

SHAPE TO DRAIN

THIS HOLE TO GIVE AN EASY FIT

FROM TANK

GAS TANK VENT

The type of tank vent shown here can be used on tanks located alongside the cockpit or in cases where the tube fitting can be brought up there through the coaming. The installation of such a vent is easiest while building, but in many instances it can be undertaken on the finished boat.

The idea is to drill a long hole completely through the coaming and deck adjacent to the tank's vent outlet. This hole can be a loose fit for the tubing to be used, but 4 or 5 inches astern of it another hole should be drilled to a snugger fit. The latter should reach from 2 to not more than 4 inches below the top of the coaming. Chisel out between these to permit the tubing to take an easy bend. Finally, bore a ½-inch hole from outside into the coaming, locating this to connect with the bottom of the last hole bored and going only deep enough to take it in. Clean this out so that it is smooth and slope its lower part to drain. Then paint well, using filler to smooth the boring. Cut tubing to the length required and bend it to permit shoving it through the holes into place. The flaring to connect to the tank must, of course, be done from below. A cap must be used atop the coaming to keep water out.

An improvement might be to make the outside hole into the coaming larger—say 1 inch—to allow for covering it with fine mesh screen as a safety precaution.

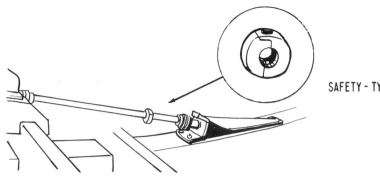

SAFETY COLLAR

If the set screw in the after half of the coupling connecting the tail shaft to the engine is set down properly in a depression drilled for its point, and then is wired or otherwise locked in place, there would seem to be no chance of the shaft backing out. This happens too frequently, however, and quite often aboard boats with the engine apparently well installed. The simplest insurance against this is to fit a collar on the shaft. Indeed, one wonders why it is not standard practice. The split style shown is a stock fitting. Aboard an auxiliary, where a feathering-type wheel with any tendency to take hold suddenly can throw an excessive strain on everything, the collar should be closer to the stuffing box than shown here.

CHAPTER 2

Sails and Rigging

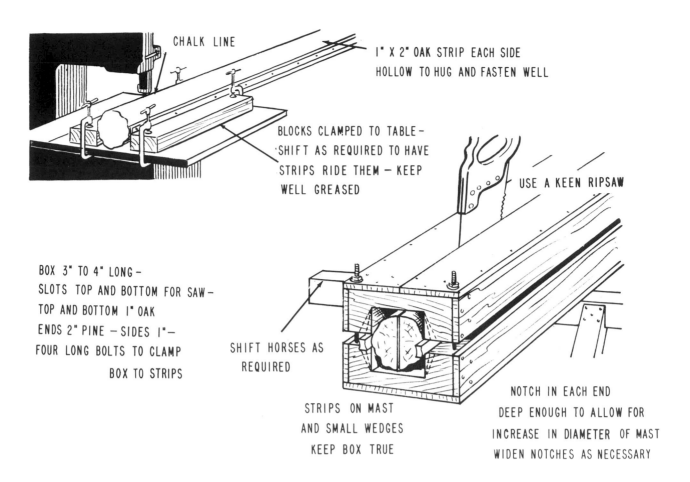

CHALK LINE

1" X 2" OAK STRIP EACH SIDE
HOLLOW TO HUG AND FASTEN WELL

BLOCKS CLAMPED TO TABLE—
SHIFT AS REQUIRED TO HAVE
STRIPS RIDE THEM — KEEP
WELL GREASED

USE A KEEN RIPSAW

BOX 3" TO 4" LONG—
SLOTS TOP AND BOTTOM FOR SAW—
TOP AND BOTTOM 1" OAK
ENDS 2" PINE — SIDES 1"—
FOUR LONG BOLTS TO CLAMP
BOX TO STRIPS

SHIFT HORSES AS
REQUIRED

STRIPS ON MAST
AND SMALL WEDGES
KEEP BOX TRUE

NOTCH IN EACH END
DEEP ENOUGH TO ALLOW FOR
INCREASE IN DIAMETER OF MAST
WIDEN NOTCHES AS NECESSARY

RIPPING A MAST FOR HOLLOWING OUT

After changing one solid mast over to a hollow one, and watching similar operations several times, I feel that the splitting or ripping of the stick (to have the cut perfectly straight) can be the most difficult part of the job. The problem is to keep the cut from spiraling around the stick. With a heavy-enough power saw (upper sketch), you can make an even cut, if you have plenty of help on the ends of the stick to leave you free to do the guiding. Strips attached on each side of the mast and blocks clamped to the saw's table for these to ride on will help prevent the cut from spiraling. However, the taper of the stick and the positions of the blocks must be changed from time to time, with both always shifted in or out an equal distance, as determined from measurements in from the edges of the table. The real guide for the cutting should be a chalked line carefully struck down the stick and penciled in either

before or after positioning the strips—but, in either case, true with them.

Undertaking the job by hand with a ripsaw can make for less chance of something happening to spoil the stick. A ripsaw that is sharp and set to cut evenly can be a pleasure to work with. A saw box as shown in the lower sketch will be a help.

After the mast has been hollowed, no attempt should be made to dress or smooth the sawed faces before gluing the two halves together. Pull off any long spirals of wood left by the saw and use coarse sandpaper lightly to brush away the roughness. Then, select a suitable grade of resin glue for making the joint. When these glues first came out, touching surfaces had to be well-nigh perfect to secure proper bonding, but grades can be bought today that will give perfect holding even with surfaces slightly roughened by the saw.

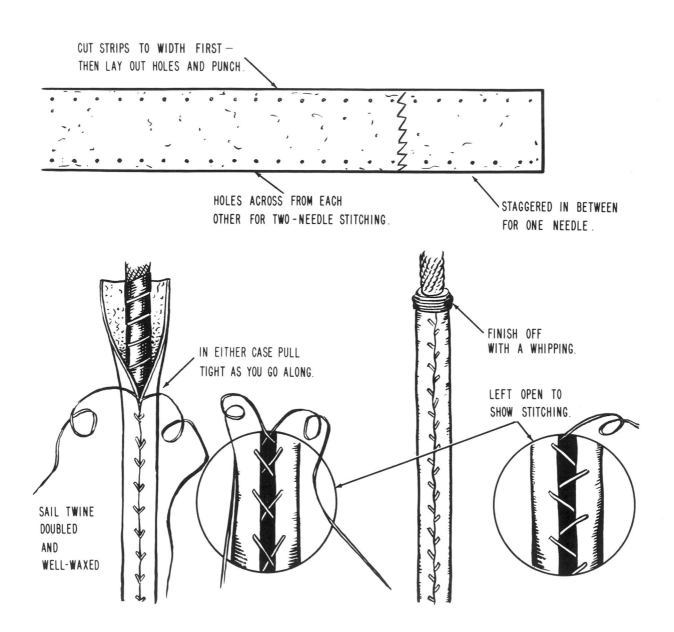

CUT STRIPS TO WIDTH FIRST —
THEN LAY OUT HOLES AND PUNCH.

HOLES ACROSS FROM EACH
OTHER FOR TWO-NEEDLE STITCHING.

STAGGERED IN BETWEEN
FOR ONE NEEDLE.

IN EITHER CASE PULL
TIGHT AS YOU GO ALONG.

FINISH OFF
WITH A WHIPPING.

LEFT OPEN TO
SHOW STITCHING.

SAIL TWINE
DOUBLED
AND
WELL-WAXED

COVERING WITH RAWHIDE

In covering rope or wire with rawhide, a quicker and neater job can be done if a test strip a few inches long is stitched on first. This will not only determine accurately the width required, but will also show how far the holes for the stitches should be from the edges in order to have them pull the leather snugly in place. After this, get out a strip or strips of the required length and mark and punch or prick the holes, using an awl or pricker. They should be exactly opposite one another, if you intend to use two needles for the stitching, and staggered for only one needle, to avoid the covering's twisting-in while it is being put on.

In either case, double the twine and wax it well. A whipping or several neat turns should be put on after the first few stitches have been taken; the other end should be similarly finished when the covering is in place. Finally, apply a coat of one of the mildew-proofing preparations that will at least slow up the leather's darkening.

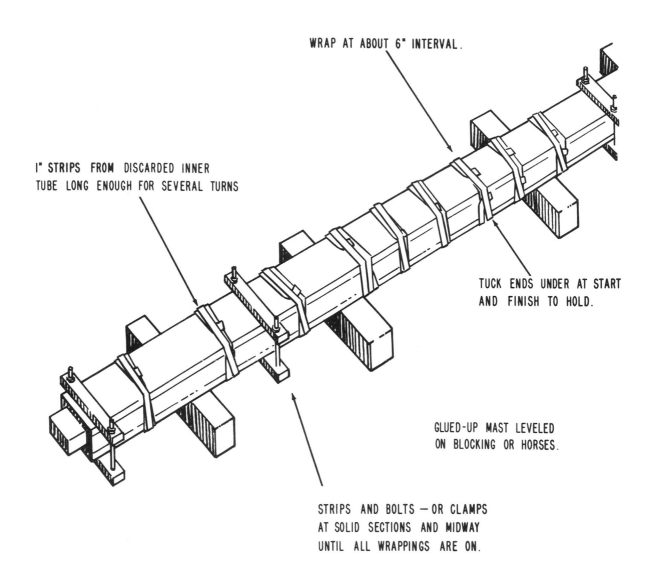

WRAP AT ABOUT 6" INTERVAL.

I" STRIPS FROM DISCARDED INNER
TUBE LONG ENOUGH FOR SEVERAL TURNS

TUCK ENDS UNDER AT START
AND FINISH TO HOLD.

GLUED-UP MAST LEVELED
ON BLOCKING OR HORSES.

STRIPS AND BOLTS — OR CLAMPS
AT SOLID SECTIONS AND MIDWAY
UNTIL ALL WRAPPINGS ARE ON.

GLUING WITH RUBBER STRIPS

George Works has had good luck building four masts by merely using rubber strips rather than the numerous clamps otherwise required to ensure proper bonding of the glue. One-inch-wide strips, 2 to 3 feet in length or long enough to stretch several times around the assembled stick are cut from discarded inner tubes. Gluing up is as usual, except that the assembled mast must be up on horses or on blocks on the floor to permit the wrapping. The usual C-clamps or oak strips and bolts are used at the tenon and other blocked places, and at approximately the half-way point. Starting at the middle and working toward the ends, the mast is wrapped tightly at about 6-inch intervals, your thumb held on the end as the strip is stretched to near the limit of its elasticity at each turn. Both ends are finally secured by tucking under the last turn. Clamps can be removed as reached. When all wrappings are on, be sure that the stick is level and true on its blocks, using wedges or shims as required to have it perfect. As pressure is uniform, a good gluing job can be expected no matter what the shape or how the parts are fitted.

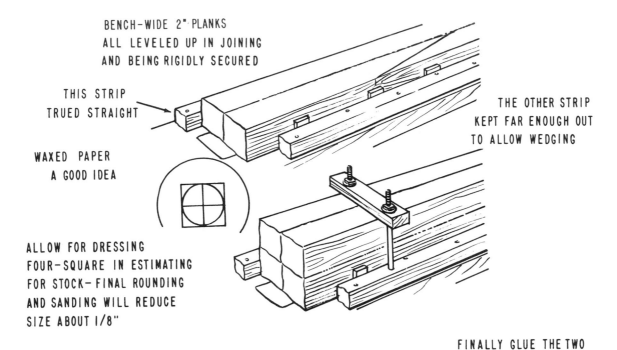

MAKE UP AS
TWO SEPARATE
LAYERS

TRY TO HAVE GRAINS
OF PIECES OPPOSED

BENCH-WIDE 2" PLANKS
ALL LEVELED UP IN JOINING
AND BEING RIGIDLY SECURED

THIS STRIP
TRUED STRAIGHT

THE OTHER STRIP
KEPT FAR ENOUGH OUT
TO ALLOW WEDGING

WAXED PAPER
A GOOD IDEA

ALLOW FOR DRESSING
FOUR-SQUARE IN ESTIMATING
FOR STOCK-FINAL ROUNDING
AND SANDING WILL REDUCE
SIZE ABOUT 1/8"

FINALLY GLUE THE TWO
TOGETHER

GLUED-UP SOLID MAST

Pete Brice writes that several years back he made a glued-up solid mast for his cutter that has remained perfectly sound along its glue lines and has kept its straightness. His method is rather unusual and has several advantages. He mentioned that 4-by-8-inch spruce, bought in the rough, was used. The rough timber was split on an edge saw and then dressed four-square to 3½ inches on a planer to give a trifle over the desired diameter. Each quarter piece had its butt marked so that in assembling, the grains of the touching members could be opposed. This prevents warping and is sufficient reason for gluing up a stick rather than using a solid piece. Scarphs or joints were then cut and all were built up on the floor, as they would be in the finished job.

The bench, in the meantime, had been built up perfectly straight and level as shown. One of the bench strips merely took the numerous wedges used. Clamps could have been used instead, or even bolts and pull-up pieces, but this

wedging method is simple and can be relied on, if the side strips are large enough and well secured.

When the two layers were glued up and the squeezed-out glue removed, they were glued together. For this part of the job, holes were bored in the strips of the bench to take the usual hold-down bolts with their crossbars. Naturally, the edges of the two layers were kept perfectly in line.

Rather than putting any taper in the stick in this making-up process, the excess wood was cut away later, using a Skill-saw along guide strips.

With this four-piece method, weight can be saved by running the pieces through a jointer to cut what is wanted off one corner, thus obtaining a stick that is hollow, except for where filler pieces have been glued in making up. Pressure for the bonding of the glue must then be very carefully applied to have it fall evenly on the narrower edges being glued.

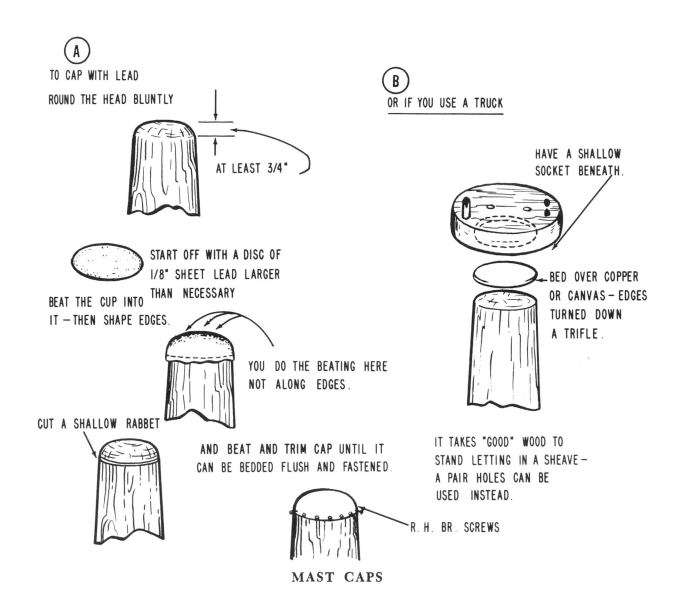

A

TO CAP WITH LEAD

ROUND THE HEAD BLUNTLY

AT LEAST 3/4"

START OFF WITH A DISC OF
1/8" SHEET LEAD LARGER
THAN NECESSARY

BEAT THE CUP INTO
IT – THEN SHAPE EDGES.

YOU DO THE BEATING HERE
NOT ALONG EDGES.

CUT A SHALLOW RABBET

AND BEAT AND TRIM CAP UNTIL IT
CAN BE BEDDED FLUSH AND FASTENED.

R. H. BR. SCREWS

B

OR IF YOU USE A TRUCK

HAVE A SHALLOW
SOCKET BENEATH.

BED OVER COPPER
OR CANVAS – EDGES
TURNED DOWN
A TRIFLE.

IT TAKES "GOOD" WOOD TO
STAND LETTING IN A SHEAVE –
A PAIR HOLES CAN BE
USED INSTEAD.

MAST CAPS

If the end grain of the head of a mast is left unprotected, rot is pretty sure to get in its work. Certainly, if the stick is a round one, there is no reason why this cannot be avoided, and the surest way is to use an old-fashioned lead cap. If this is done neatly, it will be inconspicuous on a painted stick and not out of place on a varnished one, although in the latter instance it must be painted buff or sand color. There is no great trick to this, except in the shaping of the cap, where the idea is to beat the lead over the rounded head in such a way as to stretch it and work the cup in. Do not attempt it by tapping the edges.

If a wood cap is used instead, do not fit the type which gives a smaller pole or head coming up through it and do not merely set a solid truck atop the head. A socket at least ¼ inch deep should be cut, or, better still (as the truck is apt to check), sandwich in a disc of copper with its edges turned down a trifle or even a piece of canvas. This latter can be depended upon, along with the actual bedding, to keep water from the end grain. Thoroughly seasoned wood must be used to avoid checking, and even then it is a good idea, after shaping, to boil the piece in linseed oil, particularly if the disc is pierced by a sheave socket or even a pair of holes for a flag halliard. Then, treat the entire head of the stick with an approved marine wood preservative before fastening in place.

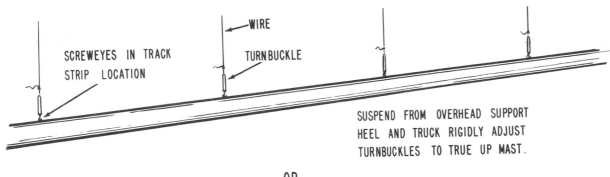

SCREWEYES IN TRACK
STRIP LOCATION

WIRE

TURNBUCKLE

SUSPEND FROM OVERHEAD SUPPORT
HEEL AND TRUCK RIGIDLY ADJUST
TURNBUCKLES TO TRUE UP MAST.

OR

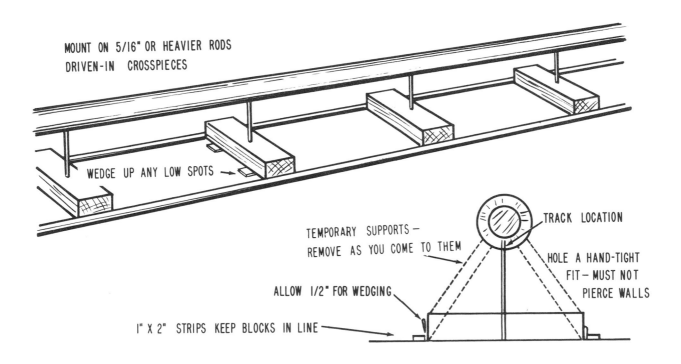

MOUNT ON 5/16" OR HEAVIER RODS
DRIVEN-IN CROSSPIECES

WEDGE UP ANY LOW SPOTS

TEMPORARY SUPPORTS —
REMOVE AS YOU COME TO THEM

ALLOW 1/2" FOR WEDGING

1" X 2" STRIPS KEEP BLOCKS IN LINE

TRACK LOCATION

HOLE A HAND-TIGHT
FIT — MUST NOT
PIERCE WALLS

SECURING A MAST FOR "FIBERGLASSING"

Covering masts with fiber glass is becoming quite popular. Those who have done it tell me that one of the big difficulties is to get the mast in the clear for easy access. The work should all be done at one time. Also, for the job to be entirely satisfactory, it must be done with the mast held perfectly true or straight.

So far, I have found two ways of getting around this difficulty. Both take advantage of the usual strip or spline, which takes the sail track and is removed for the job. In the first method, heavy screw eyes are put in the mast along the line of the holes left after removing the strip. These take wires which suspend the mast overhead. The other way is to mount the mast on upright rods or pipes, holes for which are bored along the line of holes for the track strip.

In either case, it is an easy matter to steady the mast by securing braces to its ends.

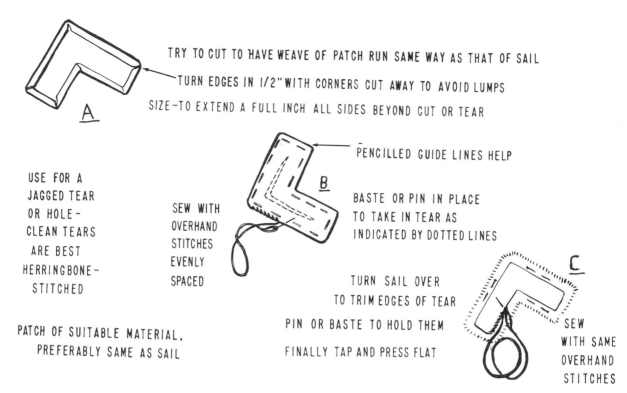

TRY TO CUT TO HAVE WEAVE OF PATCH RUN SAME WAY AS THAT OF SAIL

TURN EDGES IN 1/2" WITH CORNERS CUT AWAY TO AVOID LUMPS

SIZE-TO EXTEND A FULL INCH ALL SIDES BEYOND CUT OR TEAR

A

PENCILLED GUIDE LINES HELP

B

BASTE OR PIN IN PLACE
TO TAKE IN TEAR AS
INDICATED BY DOTTED LINES

USE FOR A
JAGGED TEAR
OR HOLE -
CLEAN TEARS
ARE BEST
HERRINGBONE-
STITCHED

SEW WITH
OVERHAND
STITCHES
EVENLY
SPACED

TURN SAIL OVER
TO TRIM EDGES OF TEAR

PIN OR BASTE TO HOLD THEM

FINALLY TAP AND PRESS FLAT

C

SEW
WITH SAME
OVERHAND
STITCHES

PATCH OF SUITABLE MATERIAL,
PREFERABLY SAME AS SAIL

SAIL PATCH

For a real repair job on a light sail, a patch applied with a sewing machine seems the only way—hand sewing is apt to pucker. The light fabric and stitches close to the edges never seem to have much hold. However, with the heavier sails used on cruising boats, the edges of a clean tear or cut can be satisfactorily herringbone-stitched. If a tear is jagged, or if the canvas alongside is too weak to hold stitches well, a properly applied hand patch is stronger than a machine-sewed one. It is always a good idea to carry aboard a piece of matching canvas for just such an emergency. The patch should be shaped to the tear, allowing 1 inch or 1½ inches (as in Figure A) beyond the damage to take in sound fabric. In cutting the patch, have the weave of the fabric match that of the sail. Turn in the edges at least ½ inch and miter or cut away the corners to avoid lumps at these points. Use a few temporary stitches on all sides of the tear. Do not draw the edges together unnecessarily, but flatten the canvas adjacent, and then place the patch correctly to take in the damage as planned.

Draw pencil lines as an aid to locating the patch and as a guide for the stitching (see *B*). Then pin or baste it down. Use a sail needle in keeping with the weight of the canvas, No. 17 being about right size for the average sail. Thread the needle with good sail twine which has been doubled, well-waxed, and twisted slightly for the sewing. Don't knot the ends but, commencing at one corner, leave about 1 inch of the twine protruding from the first stitch, carrying this under the next few stitches to hold it. Use overhand stitches, neatly made and evenly spaced, with just enough tension on them to hold the patch securely, yet not enough to draw or pucker the job.

With the patch stitched on, tap the stitches flat (the handle of a heavy knife will do). Then, turn the sail over and trim away the edges of the damaged part, so that about ½ inch of the fabric can be turned under all around (as in *C*). The corners should be cut just enough to permit folding under. This turned-under edge should be well within the turned-in edge of the patch. Pin or baste to hold, and sew with the same careful overhand stitches used on the patch. Finally —stretch, tap, and press the whole thing flat.

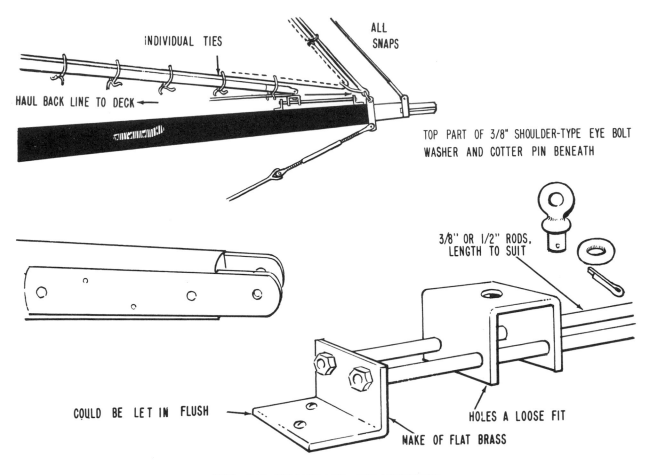

INDIVIDUAL TIES

ALL SNAPS

HAUL BACK LINE TO DECK ←

TOP PART OF 3/8" SHOULDER-TYPE EYE BOLT
WASHER AND COTTER PIN BENEATH

3/8" OR 1/2" RODS,
LENGTH TO SUIT

COULD BE LET IN FLUSH ←

MAKE OF FLAT BRASS

HOLES A LOOSE FIT

JIB OR STAYSAIL TRAVELER

Where a full-length boom is used on a head-sail of any size—and for shorthanded cruising it has several advantages—one is apt to lower the sail without slacking off the clew outhaul. A jackline is often used to take the place of the first few snaps up the stay, but where this must be long, it has a tendency to foul and is pretty sure to require occasional adjusting, particularly in wet weather.

To get away from these faults, and to obtain a better-setting sail, a traveler can be used at the forward end of the boom; and if it is made as shown here, it can be self-tending. This type, for which Howard Chapelle gave the dimensions in designing our schooner, is better suited to a small boat than the single iron bar common on commercial boats. In lowering, the slide runs forward of its own accord on the two rods; in hoisting, it slides aft. The only difficulty is to get the length of travel right—that is, the

length the rods must be to allow the sail to hoist and lower easily and, with the sail up, to have the slide riding the rods very close to where they are held by the after-end fitting.

These rods should be ¾ or ½ inch to avoid bending. This can best be done by throwing the twisting strain of the working sail where the rods are supported. With our rig, their length is 2½ feet. The right length was found by starting out with longer rods and shortening them to suit. The two L-shaped end fittings which are secured to the bowsprit, and the U-shaped slide with its hole to take the fitting on the end of the boom, can be 3/16- or ¼-inch by 1½- to 2-inch flat brass, heated for bending to shape. One hardly needs the haul-back line shown, but it does help to avoid the strain on the rods by keeping the slide well aft with the sail hoisted. It is made fast to a small cleat and cast off before lowering the sail.

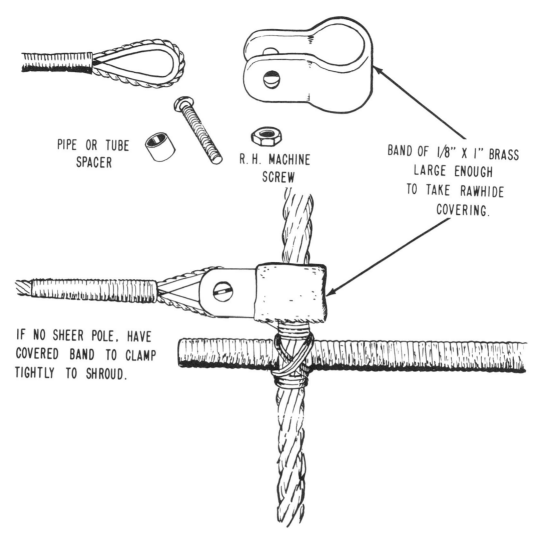

PIPE OR TUBE
SPACER

R. H. MACHINE
SCREW

BAND OF 1/8" X 1" BRASS
LARGE ENOUGH
TO TAKE RAWHIDE
COVERING.

IF NO SHEER POLE, HAVE
COVERED BAND TO CLAMP
TIGHTLY TO SHROUD.

LIFELINES

Where permanent lifelines are led between the shrouds without stanchions, as on a schooner or ketch, it is a good idea to make them in three sections for each side rather than in one long length. Then, in laying at a dock, only one section of the lifeline need be detached. A type of fitting easy to fasten and detach should be used on the one end, a Coleman-type hook; or, if really tight lines are desired, a pelican hook should be used in preference to a shackle. The permanent end of each length then can be best secured with a clamplike band, as shown above, for the usual marline lashings are not to be depended on. They are not apt to be renewed

until one fails and so can destroy the very purpose of such a safeguard. Nor do they look attractive.

If a leather serving is used, this must be allowed for in getting the size of the band right. If there is something like a sheer pole to hold the line at the height wanted, the leathered band can be a loose fit; otherwise, it must be made to clamp the shroud tightly when taken up by the machine screw. The pipe or tube spacer then should give just enough space between the jaws so that the thimble-fitted end of the lifeline is free to work, especially when the other end is detached.

BAGGY WRINKLE

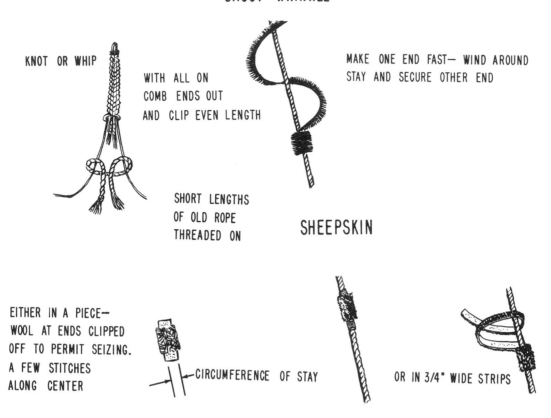

KNOT OR WHIP

WITH ALL ON
COMB ENDS OUT
AND CLIP EVEN LENGTH

MAKE ONE END FAST— WIND AROUND
STAY AND SECURE OTHER END

SHORT LENGTHS
OF OLD ROPE
THREADED ON

SHEEPSKIN

EITHER IN A PIECE—
WOOL AT ENDS CLIPPED
OFF TO PERMIT SEIZING.
A FEW STITCHES
ALONG CENTER

CIRCUMFERENCE OF STAY

OR IN 3/4" WIDE STRIPS

CHAFING GEAR

Too lavish use of chafing gear, or using it when it is not actually required, may be an affectation. Yet in offshore sailing, chafe is an ever-present menace to your sails and running rigging that certainly must be guarded against. Here, we show how baggy wrinkle is usually made—short pieces of either old or new rope hitched about a loop of marline until the required length is made up. Then, with the marline knotted to hold all in place, the separated strands are combed out and finally clipped off to uniform length. Excess marline left on one end is used to secure the length to the stay at the desired location, perhaps over a serving of friction or adhesive tape to help ensure its staying put; then, with the fuzzy side out of course, wound tightly round and round to give a muff or to pad the desired length, the other end is secured with a seizing. For the average-size boat, and where neatness as well as protection is wanted, ¼- or ⅜-inch manila for the short pieces and ⅛-inch marline for stringing will be suitable, ends clipped to be a full 1-inch long, with the finished muff 2 to 4 inches in length.

Sheepskin makes even neater chafing gear, and the clipped sheepskin lining of a discarded jacket or vest is often saved for this purpose. The muff can be sewn on in a piece as shown, or the skin cut in strips, perhaps spirally in from a large circle to make the strips long enough, and then wound around the stay with ends well secured.

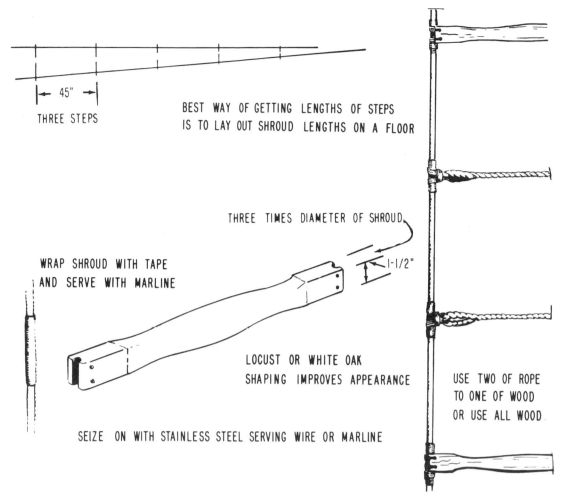

THREE STEPS

45"

BEST WAY OF GETTING LENGTHS OF STEPS
IS TO LAY OUT SHROUD LENGTHS ON A FLOOR

THREE TIMES DIAMETER OF SHROUD

1-1/2"

WRAP SHROUD WITH TAPE
AND SERVE WITH MARLINE

LOCUST OR WHITE OAK
SHAPING IMPROVES APPEARANCE

USE TWO OF ROPE
TO ONE OF WOOD
OR USE ALL WOOD

SEIZE ON WITH STAINLESS STEEL SERVING WIRE OR MARLINE

RATTLING DOWN

Ratlines are a great convenience on a cruising sailboat and are virtually a necessity on a power-boat that is rigged with a mast and other gear for sport fishing. But should they be of rope or wood?

The disadvantage of the traditional rope rat-lines is that they sag under weight. On the other hand, when made of wood they often look rather makeshift. One solution is to combine the two, using two of rope to one of wood and shaping the latter to look right.

As shown, the wood ratlines act as spreaders for the shrouds. Naturally, each must be the correct length for its location. The best way to get the entire set approximately right in this respect is to draw out the length and spread of the rigging on a floor and mark the locations of the rungs. But even so I would leave the final

finishing of one end of each wood rung until it can be tried in its place aloft.

The method of preventing rope or wood rat-lines from slipping is to parcel the wire with friction tape for 2 inches where the ratline will be seized. Then, serve with medium-size mar-line. Finally, seize and hitch on the ratline. If rope is used, daub the serving with Duco house-hold cement; then, before it has had a chance to set, secure with marline, completing by rack-ing with a couple of turns to pull tight. Knots or final hitches should be coated with cement against loosening. For seizing on the wood ones, soft seizing wire is best, preferably of stainless steel. Seize through the holes first, but finish up by serving or winding immediately below to form a sort of shoulder, which will take much of the downward strain off the seizing.

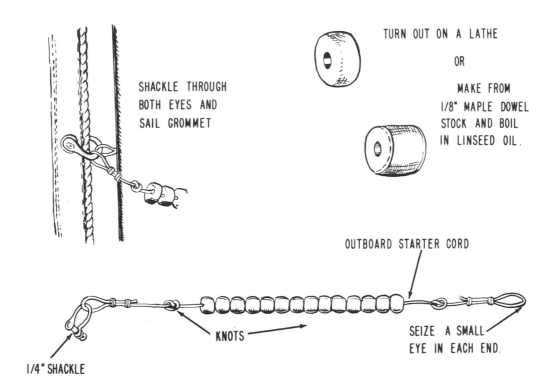

SHACKLE THROUGH BOTH EYES AND SAIL GROMMET

TURN OUT ON A LATHE

OR

MAKE FROM 1/8" MAPLE DOWEL STOCK AND BOIL IN LINSEED OIL.

OUTBOARD STARTER CORD

KNOTS

SEIZE A SMALL EYE IN EACH END.

1/4" SHACKLE

PARRELS

Gaff-headed sail parrels have several advantages over ordinary mast hoops; chiefly, that they will not chafe the mast and will allow the sail to be hoisted or lowered more quickly and with less effort. I believe they also afford a better setting sail. However, to obtain these advantages the parrels must be correctly made and properly rigged.

The parrels or beads themselves will naturally be your first concern. More of them than you think may be required, usually around eighteen to a strop or string, although the number will depend on mast size. They are bead shaped and probably made of lignum vitae. One inch in diameter by ¾ inch thick, with a 5/16- or ⅜- inch hole is a suitable stock size for the average boat. They cost around 4 cents apiece, but can also be homemade. A lathe may be used to turn them out of some suitable wood, preferably well-seasoned locust. They can also be sawn out of 1⅛-inch-diameter maple dowel stock. Those who have used this method speak well of the results and say the dowels should be the same thickness or width (1⅛ inch) and have the

sharp corners well rounded off. In any case, the hole should be accurately drilled, preferably by rigging up some sort of jig. The hole should be a loose fit for the cord or other strop being used, and the outside sharpness should be removed by using a rose bit or larger drill.

Homemade parrels should be treated against checking by boiling for half an hour or so in a container of linseed oil placed in a pan of water.

Although wire strops are sometimes used, they have a tendency to chafe the parrels and mast. A hard-braided line, around 3/16 inch in diameter, is recommended. Outboard starter cord will last 4 or 5 years before becoming dangerously weakened. And if a strop should let go, the sail will hardly be affected until a new one can be fitted. Such cord cannot be spliced, but the end eyes must be seized, preferably with two seizings each, and sewn on. There should be some play among the parrels, but not enough to permit the bare cord to come against the mast. To attach the made-up strops, I have used a small shackle, as shown, to take both eyes.

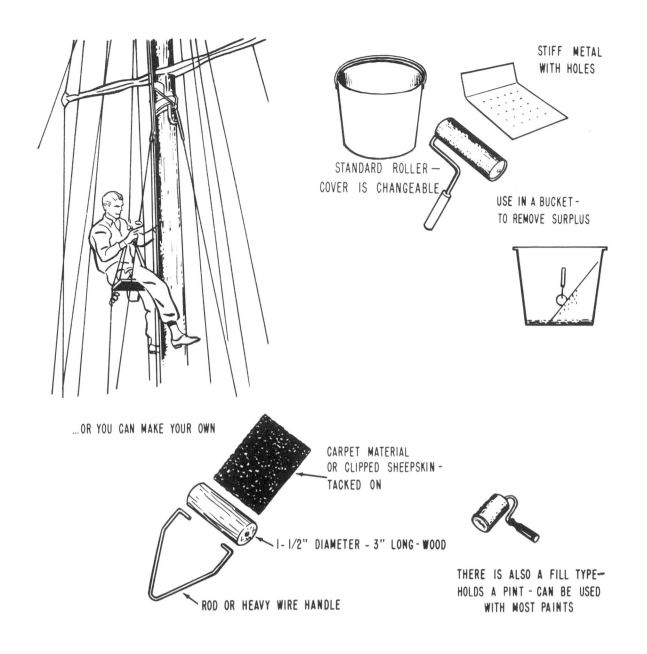

STIFF METAL WITH HOLES

STANDARD ROLLER — COVER IS CHANGEABLE

USE IN A BUCKET — TO REMOVE SURPLUS

...OR YOU CAN MAKE YOUR OWN

CARPET MATERIAL OR CLIPPED SHEEPSKIN - TACKED ON

I- 1/2" DIAMETER - 3" LONG - WOOD

ROD OR HEAVY WIRE HANDLE

THERE IS ALSO A FILL TYPE — HOLDS A PINT - CAN BE USED WITH MOST PAINTS

PAINTING STANDING RIGGING

This roller method is much quicker and far less messy than using a brush or a paint-soaked sponge. Some people use a standard paint roller and some make their own. There is also a fill or reservoir type on the market which is supposed to take oil-base paints, but so far I have not come across anyone who has tried this kind.

The problem is in having your paint with you aloft in handy form for using the roller. A shallow pan can be utilized, placed in a bucket preferably, but a better way is to use the bucket with a sheet of metal with holes in it placed upright, over which you can pull the paint-loaded roller to remove the excess. Each loading of the roller will cover a remarkably long stretch of the wire.

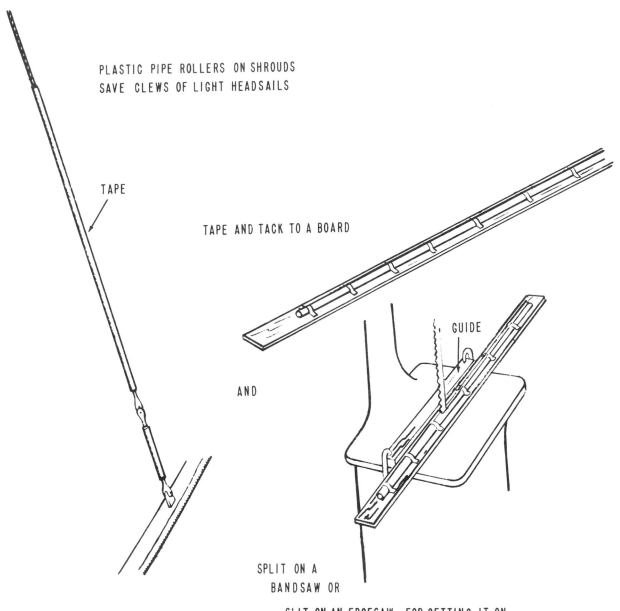

PLASTIC PIPE ROLLERS ON SHROUDS
SAVE CLEWS OF LIGHT HEADSAILS

TAPE

TAPE AND TACK TO A BOARD

AND

GUIDE

SPLIT ON A
BANDSAW OR

SLIT ON AN EDGESAW - FOR GETTING IT ON
USE GLUE ON THE CUTS THEN AND TAPE TO HOLD

PLASTIC-PIPE SHROUD ROLLERS

A very neat set of rollers I saw recently was made of plastic pipe. In showing how they were glued and taped on, the owner explained that he had ripped the pipe lengthwise, using a bandsaw rigged up as shown here. He remarked that, for light shrouds, merely slitting the pipe, as on an edge saw set to cut just through the one wall, might be enough. You could then work it over the wire. In any case, the pipe should be taped and tacked to a piece of old board in order to have the saw cut true.

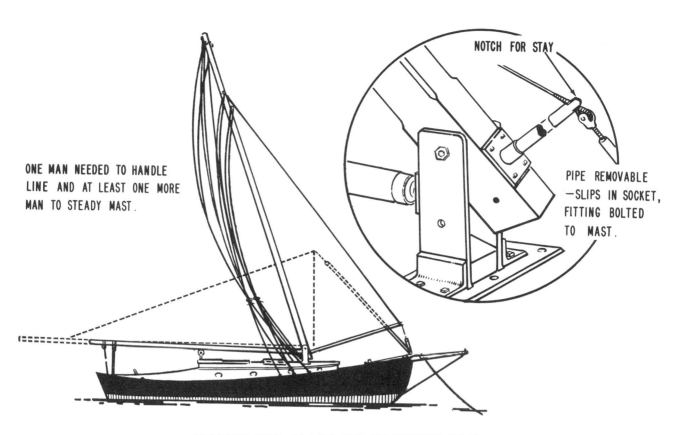

ONE MAN NEEDED TO HANDLE LINE AND AT LEAST ONE MORE MAN TO STEADY MAST.

NOTCH FOR STAY

PIPE REMOVABLE —SLIPS IN SOCKET, FITTING BOLTED TO MAST.

HANDLING MAST IN TABERNACLE

Here is illustrated an idea sent in by Jack Deal. Mr. Deal had his cutter built for extensive cruising, particularly on the Great Lakes, the Finger Lakes, and Lake Champlain, which is the reason why the mast is in a tabernacle.

The stick, he admits, is a large one to handle in this way, but it is not lowered and raised often and he has been able to manage the job without too much trouble. Anyhow, this is much less trouble than taking the mast out, and it is more easily carried.

I have seen an A frame used in somewhat the same way; that is, two steel pipes welded together with a center support to give an A shape. Their heels hinge in fittings on each side inside the chainplates, and the tip is notched to take the headstay or a line to the masthead. However, it was a cumbersome affair and had to be left on shore or kept at the closed bridge for which the owner, who kept his boat well above it, had to raise and lower his mast. Perhaps one of this type could be made so that it could be taken apart for carrying aboard. The single

pipe in a socket as shown here is no trick at all to carry and seems to do the job well.

There can be considerable twist or side strain involved, and since much of this will come on the plate fitting which takes the removable pipe strut, the fitting should be strongly made and well fastened, probably a brass plate with a stub of pipe brazed to it to form the socket and through-bolted rather than screw-fastened to the foot of the mast.

A gallows frame with the usual three notches will allow the boom to be placed in an outside notch to leave the center hollow for the mast. The job can be simplified if the mainsail is removed, a comparatively easy operation if it is sharp headed and has the usual tracks on mast and boom. However, on sizable gaff-headed boats, lowering the mast is not overly complicated. The main thing is to see that nothing can bind. The gaff jaws must be free of the mast and the sail loosely furled. Someone will have to tend the hoops.

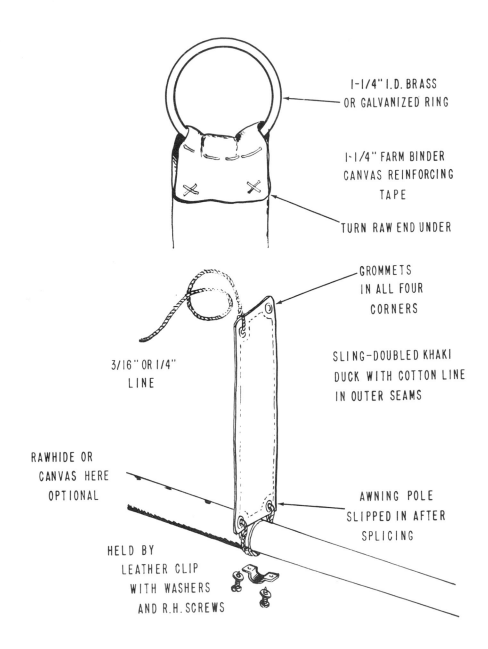

1-1/4" I.D. BRASS OR GALVANIZED RING

1-1/4" FARM BINDER CANVAS REINFORCING TAPE

TURN RAW END UNDER

GROMMETS IN ALL FOUR CORNERS

3/16" OR 1/4" LINE

SLING-DOUBLED KHAKI DUCK WITH COTTON LINE IN OUTER SEAMS

RAWHIDE OR CANVAS HERE OPTIONAL

AWNING POLE SLIPPED IN AFTER SPLICING

HELD BY LEATHER CLIP WITH WASHERS AND R.H. SCREWS

SAIL STOPS AND AWNING SLINGS

The upper sketch shows a convenient type of sail stop. To use it you merely place the stop around the furled sail and pass the plain end through the ring, when it can be pulled up as tightly as you wish and secured by using a slippery hitch.

Brass or galvanized rings for these sail stops (they should be made sufficiently long for tucking in the hitch) can be had from any marine-supply house, but suitable tape is not so easy to find. You need something that will not lose its flatness, more on the order of webbing than tape. The best thing I have found so far is the tape or webbing sold by mail-order houses for reinforcing the canvas on the tables of farm grain binders.

The lower drawing shows an awning sling for use with poles. Only one end need be secured to the pole, as shown, and the line attached to the other end, with the sling in place, can be passed around the pole and through its grommet for securing with a slippery hitch.

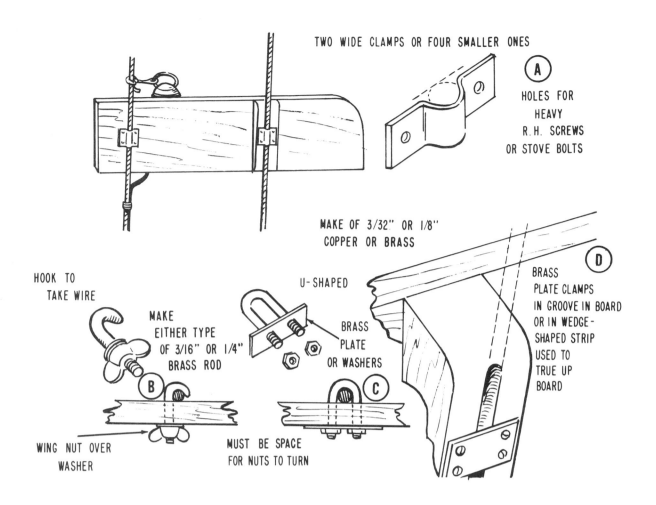

TWO WIDE CLAMPS OR FOUR SMALLER ONES

A

HOLES FOR
HEAVY
R.H. SCREWS
OR STOVE BOLTS

MAKE OF 3/32" OR 1/8"
COPPER OR BRASS

HOOK TO
TAKE WIRE

U-SHAPED

D

MAKE
EITHER TYPE
OF 3/16" OR 1/4"
BRASS ROD

BRASS
PLATE
OR WASHERS

B

C

BRASS
PLATE CLAMPS
IN GROOVE IN BOARD
OR IN WEDGE-
SHAPED STRIP
USED TO
TRUE UP
BOARD

WING NUT OVER
WASHER

MUST BE SPACE
FOR NUTS TO TURN

LIGHT-BOARD CLAMPS

Light boards are always difficult to keep properly in place, unless you have worked out some good way of securing them to the rigging. Several types of clamps or holders are shown. *A* is a strap bent of 3/32- or ⅛-inch brass or copper; *B* and *C* are bent-rod stock, threaded; and *D* is a simple plate in conjunction with a groove cut in the board. With the *A* type, ½ or ¾ inch will be wide enough for narrow straps, with two holes each for fastenings when four will be wanted for each board. Or, you can rely on a single wider strap with four holes and use only one for each shroud. Copper of this thickness will bend easily to the shape required, while brass will probably require annealing or heating to take the bend without breaking. The bend should be such that there will be a scant ⅛-inch

space left for the fastenings, in pulling tight the holder, to clamp the wire to the board. If screws are used, they should be round-headed and heavy, but if it is impossible to get them heavy enough in the short length probably required, rely instead on round-headed brass stove bolts. In either case, the boards will be easy to remove for painting.

A single-hook-type clamp (*B*) to each shroud will be sufficient to hold quite a heavy board. Wing-type nuts over lock washers are best to use here, for they can easily be taken up on or removed. The U-shaped style (*C*) serves well where the wire is large. *D* is used less often. This calls for a groove in the board, or its backing piece, which should be shallow enough for the brass plate to clamp the wire tightly.

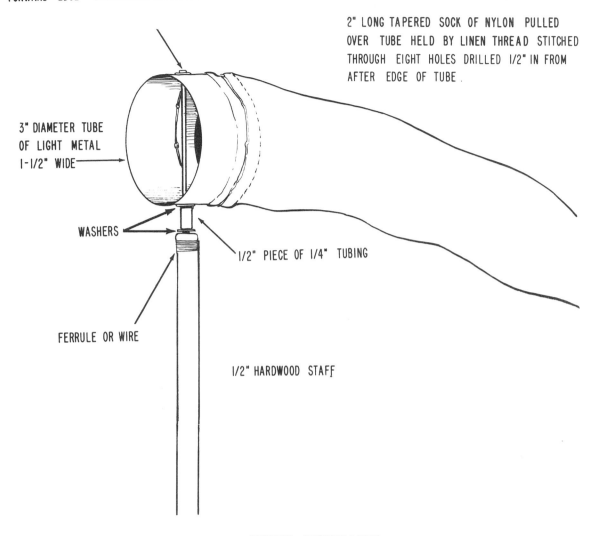

SHAFT— 1/8" ROD BURRED OVER
A WASHER— HOLES FOR IT 1/2" FROM
FORWARD EDGE— EVERYTHING AN EASY FIT

2" LONG TAPERED SOCK OF NYLON PULLED
OVER TUBE HELD BY LINEN THREAD STITCHED
THROUGH EIGHT HOLES DRILLED 1/2" IN FROM
AFTER EDGE OF TUBE.

3" DIAMETER TUBE
OF LIGHT METAL
1-1/2" WIDE

WASHERS

1/2" PIECE OF 1/4" TUBING

FERRULE OR WIRE

1/2" HARDWOOD STAFF

WIND PENNANT

The dimensions for the wind pennant shown here were taken from one given the writer by Capt. Joel Van Sant. It is perfectly made, as is everything that Capt. Joel does, and is so nicely balanced that the stock tails out to the lightest breeze and seldom gets itself fouled.

The metal tube should be light, preferably soldered up from a strip of thin stainless steel or Monel, with the leading edge turned over flat to give stiffness. This turns on a ⅛-inch rod or pin to ride atop the staff on a couple of washers, with a short length of tubing between them and the top burring of the rod over its washer to allow ample play between the parts. The sock, which can be sewn up from any light and strong material, is drawn snugly over the tube, with the raw edge turned under, and is held by waxed linen thread stitched through eight tiny holes drilled ½ inch in from the after edge of the tube. Oak is best for the staff, which should be made long enough to raise the pennant above the mast truck or head, so that it will not foul.

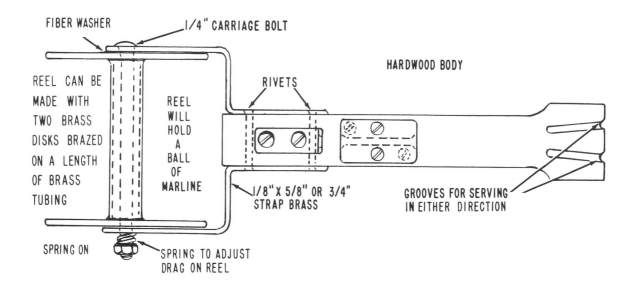

FIBER WASHER   1/4" CARRIAGE BOLT

HARDWOOD BODY

REEL CAN BE
MADE WITH
TWO BRASS
DISKS BRAZED
ON A LENGTH
OF BRASS
TUBING

REEL
WILL
HOLD
A
BALL
OF
MARLINE

RIVETS

1/8" X 5/8" OR 3/4"
STRAP BRASS

GROOVES FOR SERVING
IN EITHER DIRECTION

SPRING ON

SPRING TO ADJUST
DRAG ON REEL

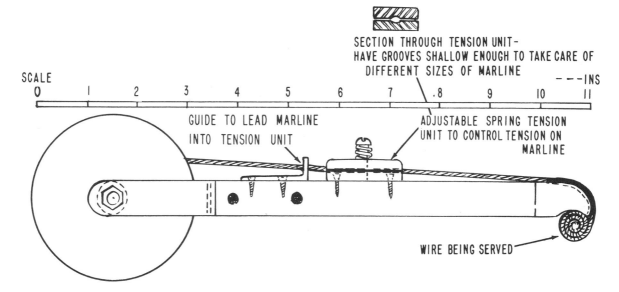

SECTION THROUGH TENSION UNIT-
HAVE GROOVES SHALLOW ENOUGH TO TAKE CARE OF
DIFFERENT SIZES OF MARLINE

SCALE
0   1   2   3   4   5   6   7   .8   9   10   11   — — INS

GUIDE TO LEAD MARLINE
INTO TENSION UNIT

ADJUSTABLE SPRING TENSION
UNIT TO CONTROL TENSION ON
MARLINE

WIRE BEING SERVED

SERVING MALLET

A serving mallet such as Elmer D. Hartley suggested would repay the trouble of making it many times over if one has a new set of standing rigging to make up. Undoubtedly, its owner would be a very popular man about his club, especially at fitting-out time. The sketches show construction clearly and the making of it should be within the capabilities of the average handyman with his ordinary tool kit, because no turning or lathe work is required and the end discs of the reel can be taken somewhere for welding to the tubing. The reel holds a whole ball of marline, and different sizes can be handled if the grooves in the tension unit are not cut too deep. I have noticed in using somewhat similar mallets that one has to get used to the tool, because the tendency at first is to use so much tension as to break the marline.

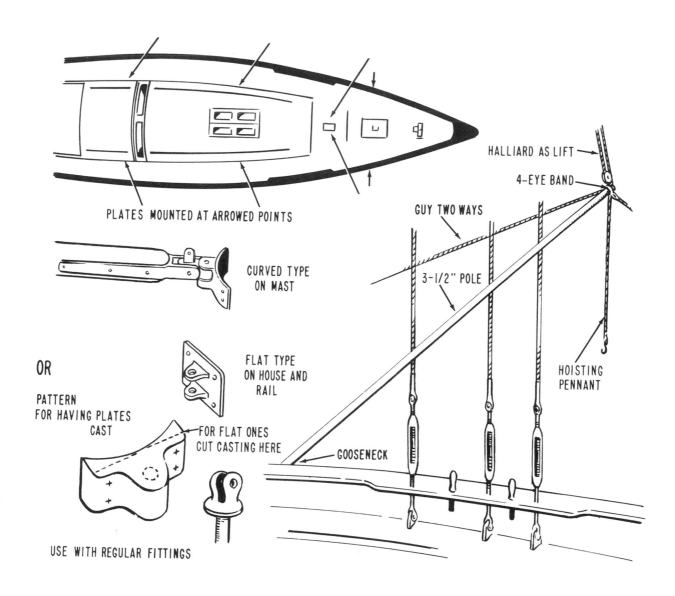

PLATES MOUNTED AT ARROWED POINTS

CURVED TYPE ON MAST

OR

PATTERN FOR HAVING PLATES CAST

FLAT TYPE ON HOUSE AND RAIL

FOR FLAT ONES CUT CASTING HERE

USE WITH REGULAR FITTINGS

GOOSENECK

HALLIARD AS LIFT

4-EYE BAND

GUY TWO WAYS

3-1/2" POLE

HOISTING PENNANT

HOISTING BOOM FITTINGS

While wintering in Florida, the cutter *Orca* does considerable treasure hunting (for fun) off the lower Keys and over in the Islands. She carries a stout spar for hoisting heavy objects, for lifting out the husky tender, and for getting the big anchor on deck. The idea is not a new one, of course, except that, aboard the *Orca*, fittings to take the gooseneck of the boom are located at different strategic points. There's a pair on the mast, naturally, and another pair outside the rail, well forward. Abaft the mast, secured to the sides of the house, are another

two pairs. With the lot it is easy to select the point of lifting that will be best for the job being done.

While standard fittings can be used, the heavy base plates for those on the *Orca* were cast of bronze from a special pattern. As the captain explained, the same pattern can be used for casting the lot, the flat-based ones merely being hacksawed. Or, you can have the foundry man cast curved ones first, and then saw the pattern for casting the flat type.

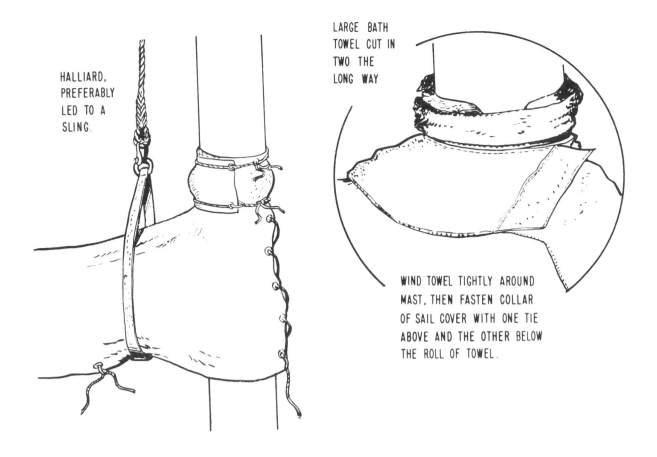

HALLIARD, PREFERABLY LED TO A SLING.

LARGE BATH TOWEL CUT IN TWO THE LONG WAY

WIND TOWEL TIGHTLY AROUND MAST, THEN FASTEN COLLAR OF SAIL COVER WITH ONE TIE ABOVE AND THE OTHER BELOW THE ROLL OF TOWEL.

KEEPING SAIL DRY

There is nothing new in the idea of using a cloth with a sail cover, but it is shown here for those who may not know about it. It is sometimes condemned when the fault may be in using a cloth that is too small. With something of an absorbent nature, such as an old Turkish towel, you can usually keep your sail near the mast dry—something that is otherwise impossible with even the best-made covers. The cloth can be narrow, not over 1 foot wide, but it should be long enough to go around the mast at least twice and tuck under itself, for the idea is to have the cloth absorb whatever rain water gets by the collar of the cover and thus prevent it from running down the mast onto the sail. Wrap the cloth around after the cover is in place, but before fastening the ordinary collar that is wrapped around the mast; then, secure the collar with one tie above the roll of cloth and the other below it. Where the halliard must be left attached, pull the block or blocks well back into the sail, so as to be away from the mast, and be sure to allow some slack for possible shrinkage; carry the cloth between the halliard and the mast and over it in wrapping it around. This is easier than having to open up the sail near the mast for airing when it may be found that mildew has begun.

Now, if the jib cover has a small collar, wrap the cloth around the stay and its halliard before securing the collar over it. However, don't trust the forward end of a jib cover to keep rain out. The first time you come aboard after a heavy rain, untie the collar to remove its cloth and either allow it to dry or put another one on.

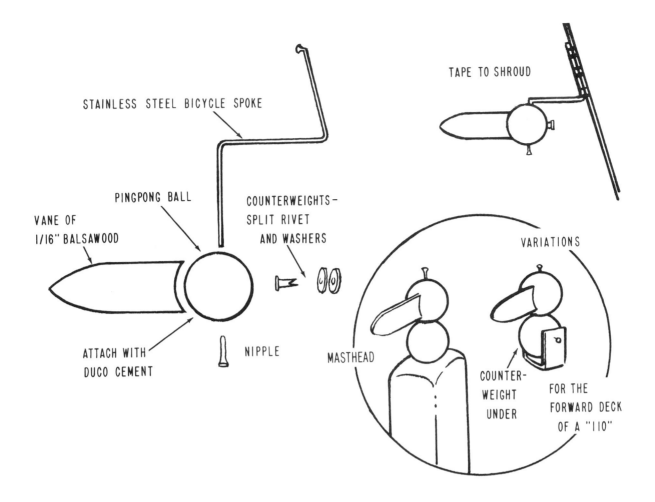

STAINLESS STEEL BICYCLE SPOKE

TAPE TO SHROUD

PINGPONG BALL

COUNTERWEIGHTS-
SPLIT RIVET
AND WASHERS

VANE OF
1/16" BALSAWOOD

VARIATIONS

ATTACH WITH
DUCO CEMENT

NIPPLE

MASTHEAD

COUNTER-
WEIGHT
UNDER

FOR THE
FORWARD DECK
OF A "110"

TELLTALE

Some use yarn, some prefer baby ribbon, and others have worked out their own devices, but if you want an unusually sensitive telltale, the type suggested by George Marsh might be worth trying. Marsh used two of these on the shrouds of his Lawley 15 last year and says that they are not only very sensitive, but will withstand much abuse. There is nothing to foul, and if they are located properly, they should never be touched by a sail. Also, they can be watched by the crew without any danger of neck strain.

The parts required do not cost much and should be easily obtainable. Try to use a stainless steel bicycle wheel spoke; note that it goes through holes drilled in the Ping-pong ball to be held by the spoke nipple beneath. The vane of 1/16-inch balsa wood can be attached easily with Duco household cement. Its slight weight

should be counterbalanced by letting in the rivet on the opposite side and using just enough washers to have the balance right for the ball to spin truly. Paint the vane and ball, if you wish, and tape on the shrouds, as desired.

There is also shown a two-ball type for mounting on the masthead using a short length of spoke, as well as one which Marsh intends to use on the forward deck of his 110. He wanted a telltale which would swing to compensate for the boat's movement. It will be located just behind the fitting on the stem and attached so as to be removable. Note that in this type there is a counterweight beneath the lower ball and that, in both of these two ball telltales, the upper ball should be free to spin on the lower one.

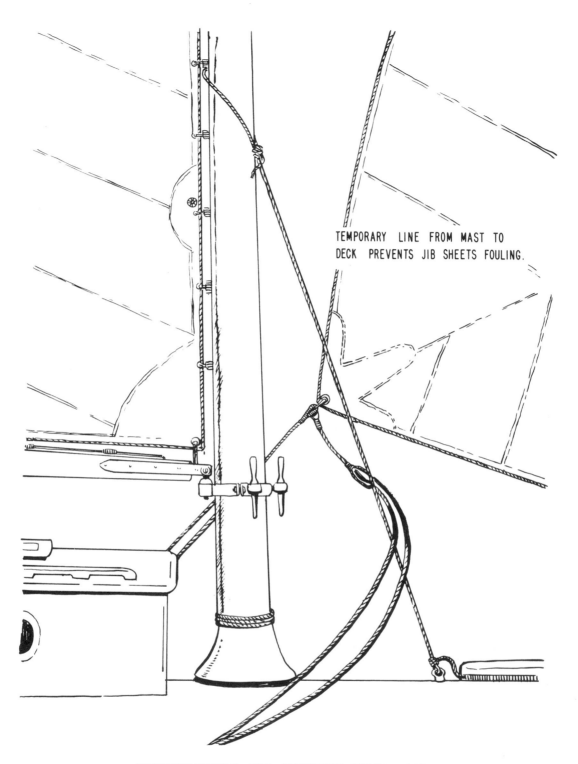

TEMPORARY LINE FROM MAST TO
DECK PREVENTS JIB SHEETS FOULING.

PREVENTING JIB SHEETS FROM FOULING

There is not much to this idea, but where it is practicable it is a pretty sure way of preventing jib sheets from fouling anything on the mast. Of course, if it is found worthwhile, a neater way, and one which will permit lowering the main without having to untie the line, would be to have a small fitting on the forward face of the mast into which the upper end of a line kept for the purpose could be snapped.

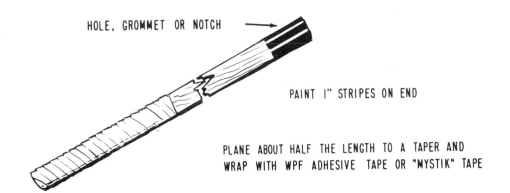

HOLE, GROMMET OR NOTCH

PAINT 1" STRIPES ON END

PLANE ABOUT HALF THE LENGTH TO A TAPER AND
WRAP WITH WPF ADHESIVE TAPE OR "MYSTIK" TAPE

BATTENS

George Marsh has come up with a suggestion for sail battens. He writes that the ash battens he had been using on his 110 class sloops were not entirely satisfactory. So, having acquired a discarded venetian blind in the course of his "junk collecting," he decided to see what could be done with the slats. These, he found, could be split easily with a knife; then, about half the length was planed to a taper, which may be as thin as paper at the end, and all sanded smooth. Finally, this end can be wrapped neatly with waterproof adhesive tape, or Mystik tape which is sold in stationery stores, and painted or varnished all over. Paint stripes on the end (one for short, two for medium, etc.) will speed up sail setting.

I suppose some slats are more suitable than others for this use; those with a natural finish as well as painted ones can be had. George Marsh says those he used were strong enough for batten purposes but that, as they break easily when stepped on, he is starting the season with a good supply.

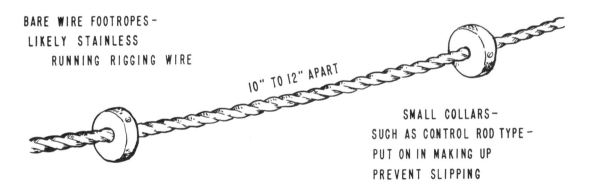

BARE WIRE FOOTROPES –
LIKELY STAINLESS
RUNNING RIGGING WIRE

10" TO 12" APART

SMALL COLLARS –
SUCH AS CONTROL ROD TYPE –
PUT ON IN MAKING UP
PREVENT SLIPPING

WIRE FOOT ROPES

Wire foot ropes for the bowsprit are dependable insofar as strength is concerned, but are too slippery for a safe footing unless served for their entire length. Rather than serving, the ones on the bugeye yacht *Pandora* are of bare stainless steel wire and have tiny collars spaced about a foot apart to keep one's feet from sliding. These have flush-set screws, a type similar to that used on control rods.

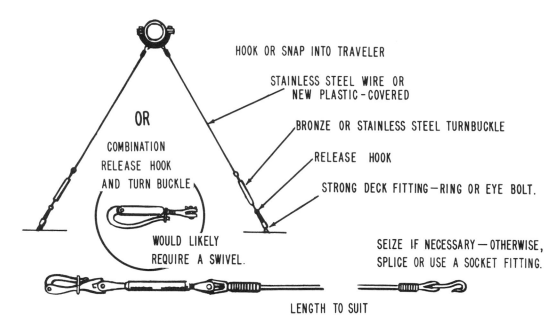

HOOK OR SNAP INTO TRAVELER

STAINLESS STEEL WIRE OR
NEW PLASTIC-COVERED

OR

COMBINATION
RELEASE HOOK
AND TURN BUCKLE

BRONZE OR STAINLESS STEEL TURNBUCKLE

RELEASE HOOK

STRONG DECK FITTING—RING OR EYE BOLT.

WOULD LIKELY
REQUIRE A SWIVEL.

SEIZE IF NECESSARY—OTHERWISE,
SPLICE OR USE A SOCKET FITTING.

LENGTH TO SUIT

BOOM GUYS

Particularly where an upright-type boom support is used, and for offshore work with *any* type of holder except a gallows frame, it pays to have proper boom guys. Rope ones stretch just enough to be a nuisance, so a pair of wire guys is worth having. Stainless steel or plastic-covered wire, made up somewhat as shown here, will prove valuable.

IF REGULAR SAIL CLIPS
ARE NOT AVAILABLE, USE
GALVANIZED ROPE THIMBLES
OR BRASS SAIL-TYPE CUT
WITH A HACKSAW

OPEN TO GO ON
AND THEN CLOSE

THIMBLES REPLACE CLIPS

Marline lashings holding a sail to its slides have a bad habit of chafing through and letting go at inopportune times, and regular sail clips cannot always be had. Rope thimbles, either the galvanized-iron split type or brass sail ones cut through with a hacksaw, are satisfactory. With the latter it is best to try out one of a lot before buying the required number, not only to have a size that, when opened, will go through the grommet and eye of the slide, leaving the bolt rope fairly free, but also to see if the particular thimbles will withstand opening and later closing. All of the galvanized type will and so will most of the brass ones.

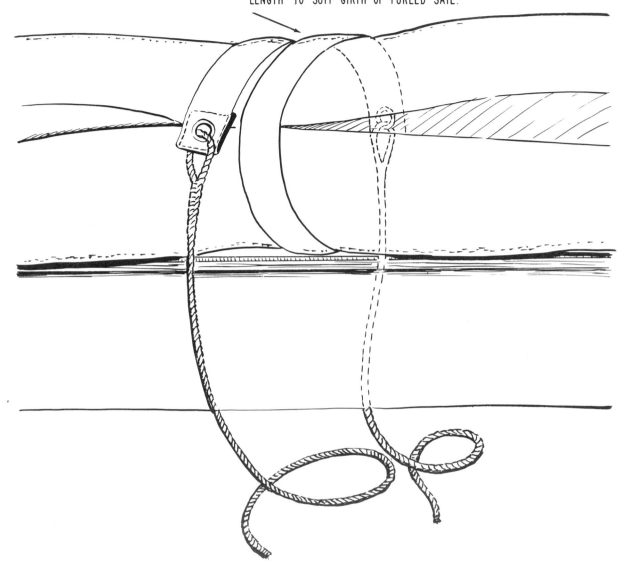

1-1/2" WEBBING — GROMMET AND LANYARD ON EACH END —
LENGTH TO SUIT GIRTH OF FURLED SAIL.

FINALLY SECURE BENEATH BOOM
WITH A SLIPPERY HITCH.

SAIL GASKET

Another simple idea is shown above. If this type of sail gasket is made the correct length for the girth of the furled sail, it is quick and easy to use and will hold the sail neatly atop the boom. Some make them in different lengths, while others have all of them long enough to suit the bulkier parts of the furled sail and elsewhere make an additional pass about the sail to keep the ends well up. Occasionally, a single lanyard is used, but a pair seems to make it easier to position the sail properly atop the boom.

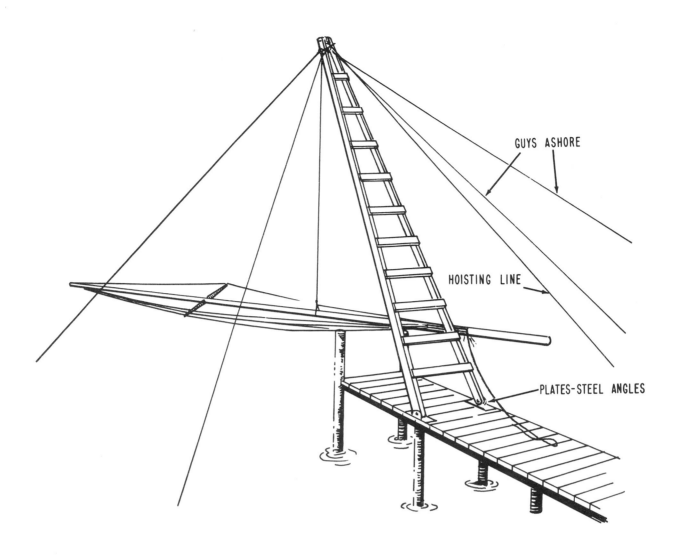

GUYS ASHORE

HOISTING LINE

PLATES-STEEL ANGLES

MAST HOIST

Guy Penniker writes that his small sailing club has been using a pair of legs, made as shown, very satisfactorily for a couple of years now for stepping and unstepping the masts of members' boats. He explained that this is merely an improvement over their original use of a long ladder, guyed out over the end of the dock, which permits them now to handle masts for boats up to 30 feet. With several fellows helping it's an easy matter to set the legs up or to lower them for storing ashore. Guy well and always test before actually using, Mr. Penniker cautions.

CHAPTER 3

Steering

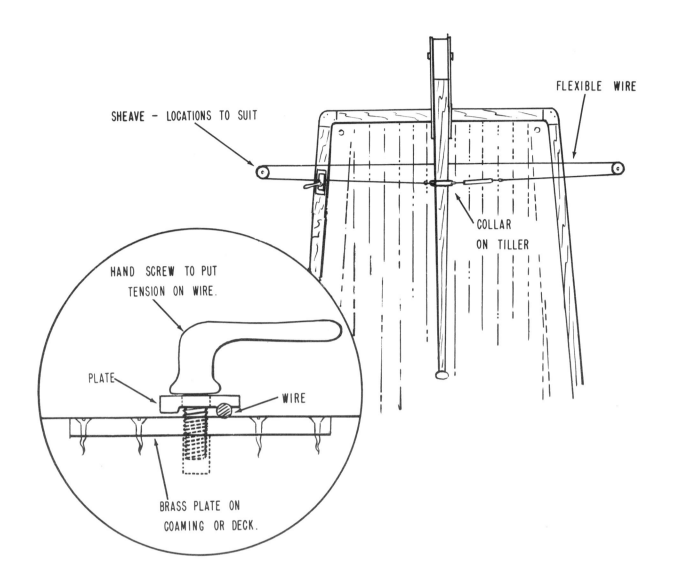

SHEAVE — LOCATIONS TO SUIT

FLEXIBLE WIRE

COLLAR ON TILLER

HAND SCREW TO PUT TENSION ON WIRE.

PLATE

WIRE

BRASS PLATE ON COAMING OR DECK.

TILLER LOCK I

I have come across a number of variations of the idea shown here, for practically every boat requires a somewhat different arrangement to suit the location of the tiller in the cockpit. However, the principle is to run the length of flexible wire or tiller cord in a continuous manner through two suitable sheaves or blocks located on the deck or inside the rail to a collar on the tiller. Tension is then applied to the wire

by means of some easily handled screw-clamp arrangement so as either to set the tiller where wanted or to help ease the strain of holding it. It must not be too much in the way. It must also be detachable, so that at least the connection to the tiller can be removed; naturally, such help in steering will only be needed occasionally.

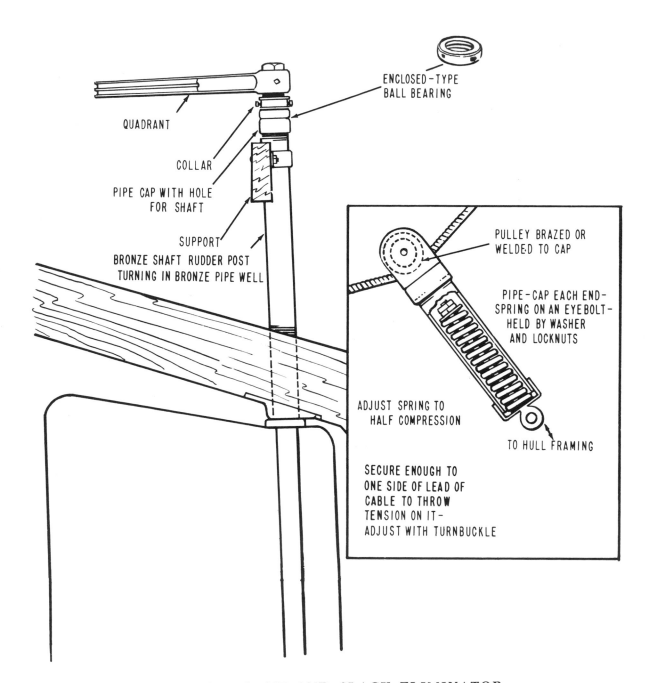

ENCLOSED-TYPE
BALL BEARING

QUADRANT

COLLAR

PIPE CAP WITH HOLE
FOR SHAFT

SUPPORT

BRONZE SHAFT RUDDER POST
TURNING IN BRONZE PIPE WELL

PULLEY BRAZED OR
WELDED TO CAP

PIPE-CAP EACH END-
SPRING ON AN EYEBOLT-
HELD BY WASHER
AND LOCKNUTS

ADJUST SPRING TO
HALF COMPRESSION

TO HULL FRAMING

SECURE ENOUGH TO
ONE SIDE OF LEAD OF
CABLE TO THROW
TENSION ON IT-
ADJUST WITH TURNBUCKLE

RUDDER MOUNT AND SLACK ELIMINATOR

Particularly with a heavy metal rudder steering is much easier if an enclosed ball bearing can be worked into the rudder assembly. While shown here atop a drilled pipe cap, it will work as well over a stuffing box—so long as the lock nut is turned tight.

The slack eliminator is merely an adaptation of a purchased steering-rope tightener. It is made heavier and has a pulley secured to one end so it can be used to one side of the direct line. This heavy-duty type, made with an eye on each end, can be used within the line.

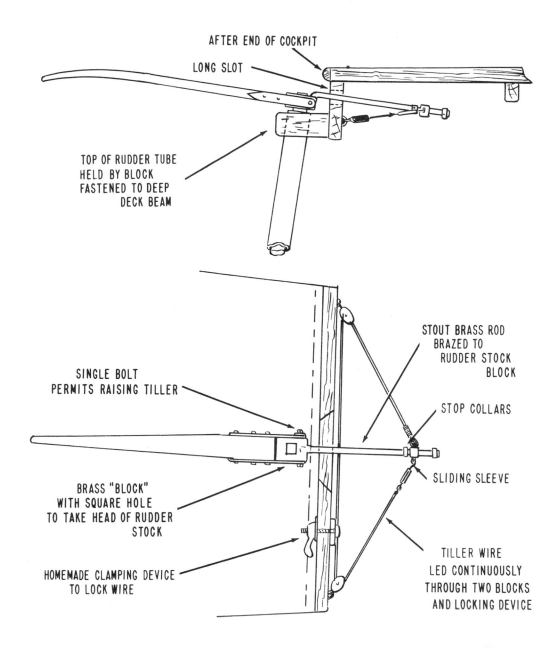

AFTER END OF COCKPIT

LONG SLOT

TOP OF RUDDER TUBE
HELD BY BLOCK
FASTENED TO DEEP
DECK BEAM

STOUT BRASS ROD
BRAZED TO
RUDDER STOCK
BLOCK

STOP COLLARS

SINGLE BOLT
PERMITS RAISING TILLER

SLIDING SLEEVE

BRASS "BLOCK"
WITH SQUARE HOLE
TO TAKE HEAD OF RUDDER
STOCK

TILLER WIRE
LED CONTINUOUSLY
THROUGH TWO BLOCKS
AND LOCKING DEVICE

HOMEMADE CLAMPING DEVICE
TO LOCK WIRE

TILLER LOCK II

Here is an effective method of locking the tiller, either for self-steering while sailing or to prevent the rudder's banging about when the boat is at her mooring. The rudder tube is carried up in the usual way, but has its upper end held by an oak block which is attached to a deep deck beam or heavy after crossmember of the cockpit, thus leaving the head of the rudder stock pretty much in the clear and below the level of the afterdeck. The block of brass with

the squared hole to take the head of the rudder stock permits attaching the brass straps of the tiller with a single bolt, so that the tiller can be raised as desired. To the after end of this block a stout brass rod is brazed, reverse-tiller fashion. The diameter or size of this rod must be in keeping with the size of the boat, and its length and the locations of the stop collars must suit the travel of the tiller.

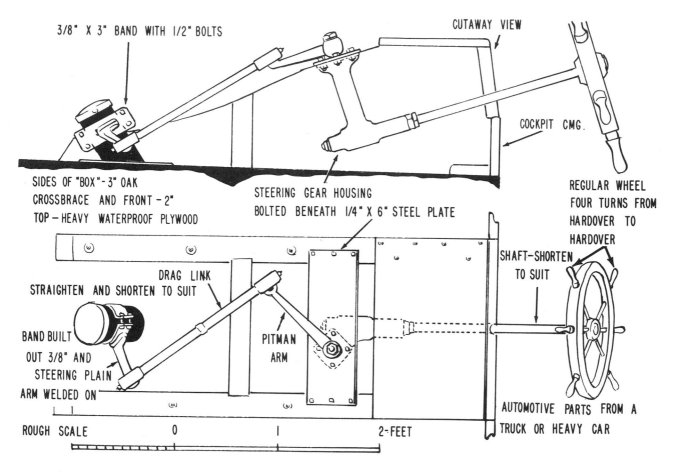

3/8" X 3" BAND WITH 1/2" BOLTS

CUTAWAY VIEW

COCKPIT CMG.

SIDES OF "BOX"- 3" OAK
CROSSBRACE AND FRONT - 2"
TOP - HEAVY WATERPROOF PLYWOOD

STEERING GEAR HOUSING
BOLTED BENEATH 1/4" X 6" STEEL PLATE

REGULAR WHEEL
FOUR TURNS FROM
HARDOVER TO
HARDOVER

DRAG LINK
STRAIGHTEN AND SHORTEN TO SUIT

SHAFT-SHORTEN
TO SUIT

BAND BUILT
OUT 3/8" AND
STEERING PLAIN
ARM WELDED ON

PITMAN
ARM

ROUGH SCALE   0   1   2-FEET

AUTOMOTIVE PARTS FROM A
TRUCK OR HEAVY CAR

STEERING MECHANISM

While it is not often that automotive parts work out well aboard boats, the steerer shown above has proven an exception. As installed at his yard by Al Robinson to replace the tiller on Bob Phelps' 49-foot schooner *Hobo*, it has made steering much easier and free of trouble.

The box was built, as shown, largely to provide rugged support for the mechanism, and it will eventually be improved by raising the height of the sides to make it a regular wheel-box, with the moving parts covered. These parts were bought from a car wrecking place, and include a steering-gear assembly, drag link, pitman arm, and steering plain arm from a 2½-ton Reo truck.

While such parts from another make or from a heavy car might be used, it is necessary to get a type with the pitman arm travel fore and aft. The steering plain arm is welded to the heavy band about the head of the rudder stock and

set away from it ⅜ inch by building the band out. The drag link which connects this to the pitman arm may have to be straightened and also shortened to suit the particular installation. Naturally, the gear housing must be held rigidly as here by being bolted beneath the steel plate, but having the shaft a tight turning fit where it goes through the heavy oak front of the box also helps. The original shaft may be used, shortened to suit, or a length of bronze shafting could be fitted, although machining would be necessary.

A little better than four turns of the steering wheel are required to put the rudder from hard-over to hard-over, during which the action is positive and without looseness or play. Al Robinson gives the cost for all parts, machining, and blacksmith work, but not the labor of actually installing, as between $20 and $25.

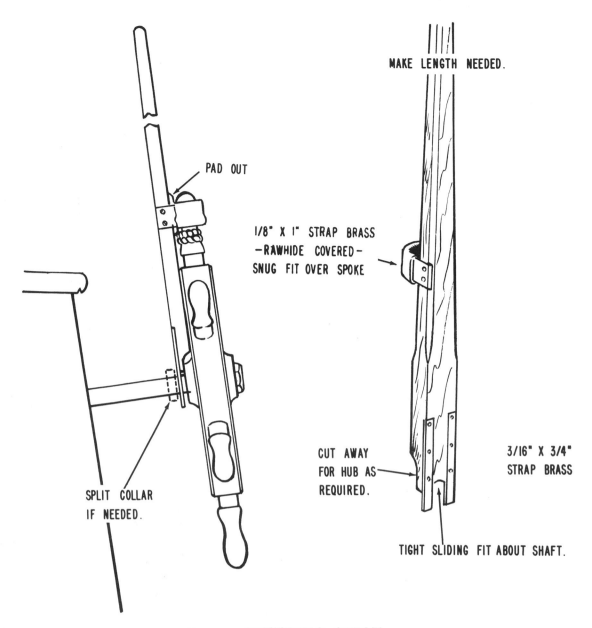

MAKE LENGTH NEEDED.

PAD OUT

1/8" X I" STRAP BRASS
—RAWHIDE COVERED—
SNUG FIT OVER SPOKE

SPLIT COLLAR
IF NEEDED.

CUT AWAY
FOR HUB AS
REQUIRED.

3/16" X 3/4"
STRAP BRASS

TIGHT SLIDING FIT ABOUT SHAFT.

STEERING STICK

Simple ideas are often the best ones. An example of this is the steering stick shown here, which is a handy rig if a boat is so built that one has to stand on a seat or the deck to obtain good vision while under power in a narrow channel.

A stick lashed to the spoke and the hub will suffice, but the type used on the ketch *Sunway* is good because it can be slipped in place on the wheel quickly and as easily removed. The length of the stick should permit comfortable steering from where the helmsman will stand and its dimensions otherwise should suit the wheel and the size of the boat. Ordinarily, the width of the piece will be the combined measurements of the two brass finger pieces and the shaft which they straddle. Then make the thickness, say, 1 inch and taper the width to this at the rounded handle or top. While a strap or lanyard could be attached for making the stick fast about the king spoke of the wheel, a rawhide-covered band as shown, made to an easy sliding fit over the spoke, will require no adjusting.

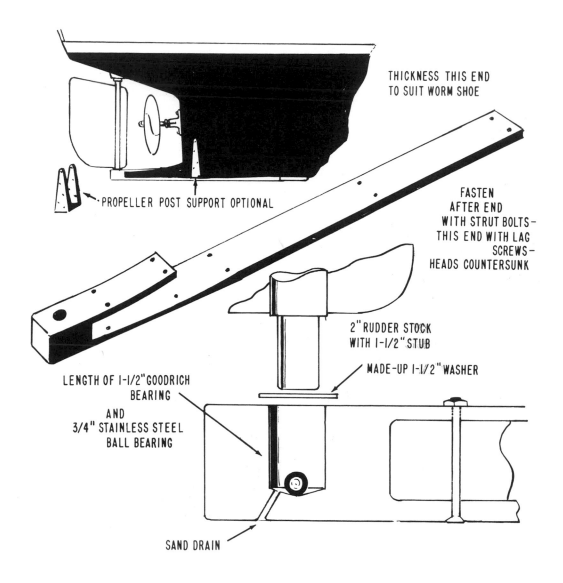

THICKNESS THIS END
TO SUIT WORM SHOE

PROPELLER POST SUPPORT OPTIONAL

FASTEN
AFTER END
WITH STRUT BOLTS-
THIS END WITH LAG
SCREWS-
HEADS COUNTERSUNK

2" RUDDER STOCK
WITH 1-1/2" STUB

MADE-UP 1-1/2" WASHER

LENGTH OF 1-1/2"GOODRICH
BEARING
AND
3/4" STAINLESS STEEL
BALL BEARING

SAND DRAIN

RUBBER BUSHING QUIETS RUDDER

This type of rudder shoe or skeg must be cast from a pattern, but it seems excellent for a heavy powerboat or a motor sailer. As shown, it was made for a 38-footer, measured 5 feet over-all, and was fitted to a 5½-inch-thick keel. The top and bottom parts of its after end were ¾ inch thick and the thickness was gradually increased to 1½ inches to fair in with the worm shoe against which it butted. Six ½-by-4-inch lag screws, with heads countersunk, were used to fasten the main part. Aft, ⅜-inch strut bolts were carried clear through.

The main feature is the rubber bearing used as insurance against that chattering of the heel

of the rudder which often is transmitted through the entire boat. The 3-inch piece of Goodrich bearing is pressed to fit in the hole made to take it. The ball bearing in the socket is centered naturally in the hole made by the drilling necessary to clean out the hole. It takes the weight of the rudder and permits easy turning, but there also is a heavy washer to prevent the stub of the shoulder of the stock from coming entirely on the bearing's bushing. The ⅜-inch drain hole keeps sand from accumulating.

As shown here, the casting weighed 150 pounds and cost $105 to cast in manganese bronze.

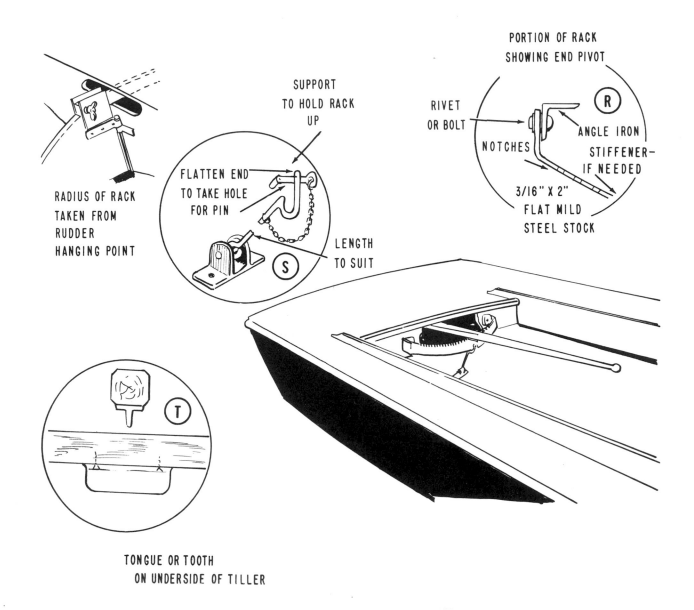

RADIUS OF RACK
TAKEN FROM
RUDDER
HANGING POINT

SUPPORT
TO HOLD RACK
UP

FLATTEN END
TO TAKE HOLE
FOR PIN

LENGTH
TO SUIT

S

PORTION OF RACK
SHOWING END PIVOT

RIVET
OR BOLT

R

ANGLE IRON
STIFFENER -
IF NEEDED

NOTCHES

3/16" X 2"
FLAT MILD
STEEL STOCK

T

TONGUE OR TOOTH
ON UNDERSIDE OF TILLER

TILLER RACK

The tiller rack or comb suggested by E. C. Seibert has at least one advantage over others I've come across—it can be quickly dropped down to be out of the way when not wanted. The whole thing is simple once you have studied his sketches. The radius of the rack is taken from the pivoting point of the rudder, and the tiller itself must be attached to the rudder head in such a way that it can be raised to have the tooth T, which is secured to its underside, clear the notched rack. Mr. Seibert made his parts of steel and then had them galvanized, but since there should not be a great strain on anything, I suppose brass could be used as well. The ends can be held to construction across and beneath the afterdeck, using angles, as in R, and with rivets or bolts to permit pivoting. The support S might be the hardest part to make, as its hooklike end must take the rack, with its tip flattened so that a pin can be passed through a hole drilled in the rack.

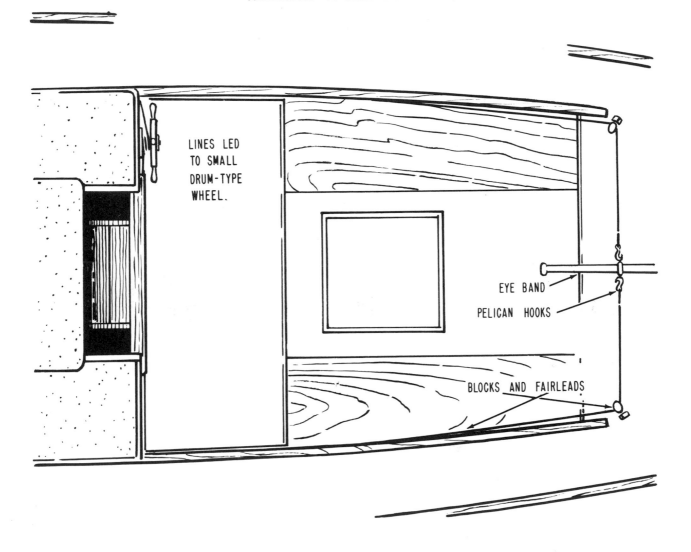

PERCH ON COCKPIT COAMING OR SIT IN
COMPANIONWAY TO STEER UNDER POWER.

LINES LED
TO SMALL
DRUM-TYPE
WHEEL.

EYE BAND
PELICAN HOOKS

BLOCKS AND FAIRLEADS

STEERING ARRANGEMENT

The sloop *Sea Wind* has a steering arrangement that works out very well under power, particularly in running long stretches to and from Florida where her owners, the Du Bois, spend their winters. Lines are led from an eye band about the tiller through blocks and fairleads inside the cockpit coaming to a small drum-type steering wheel mounted on the after end of the cabin to starboard of the companion-way opening. A small pelican hook in each end of the line permits quick and easy attachment to the tiller and quick detachment for regular steering. Perched up on a cushion or seat atop the cockpit coaming, one has good vision ahead. Better still, in cold weather he can steer from the companionway and get the benefit of any heat below.

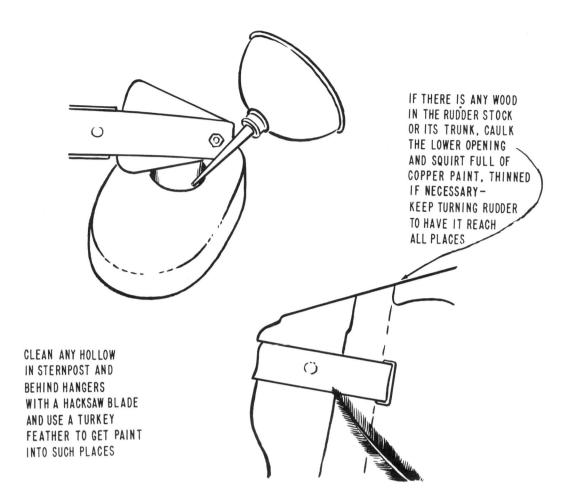

IF THERE IS ANY WOOD IN THE RUDDER STOCK OR ITS TRUNK, CAULK THE LOWER OPENING AND SQUIRT FULL OF COPPER PAINT, THINNED IF NECESSARY— KEEP TURNING RUDDER TO HAVE IT REACH ALL PLACES

CLEAN ANY HOLLOW IN STERNPOST AND BEHIND HANGERS WITH A HACKSAW BLADE AND USE A TURKEY FEATHER TO GET PAINT INTO SUCH PLACES

AVOIDING WORMS

With a wooden rudder stock or trunk one cannot be too careful in avoiding worm infestation. Much the same applies where the rudder stock is bronze but there is a hollow in the sternpost that is not metaled and slots in the wood where the straps or hangers work. About all you can do in the former case is roughly to caulk the lower opening each time you are on the railway and pour or squirt copper paint down from the top. Flood the entire trunk with it as a guard not only against worms but to discourage rot. Swing the rudder back and forth, to try to distribute this to all parts, and leave it in overnight or until it seeps out below. Under any straps use a hacksaw blade to remove barnacles and dirt and scrape off loosened old copper. Then get fresh paint to them. Even a small brush will not reach all such places; the thing to use is a large turkey feather.

CHAPTER 4

Anchor Work
and Mooring

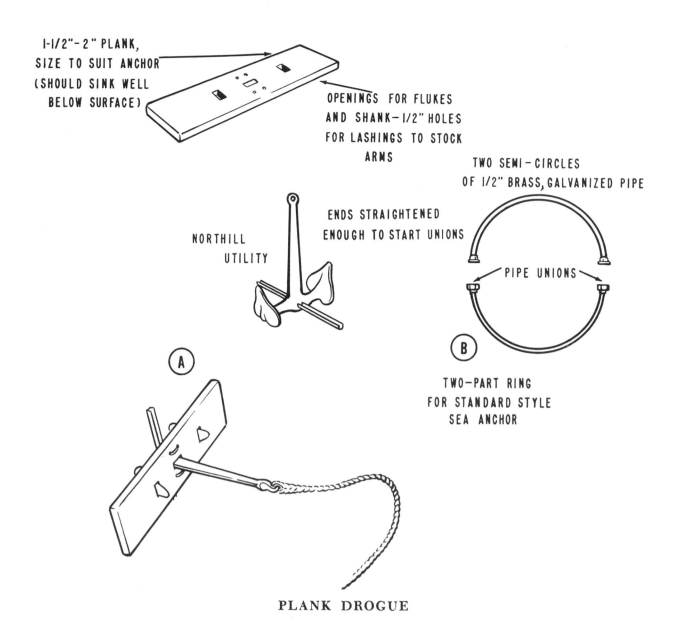

1-1/2"-2" PLANK, SIZE TO SUIT ANCHOR (SHOULD SINK WELL BELOW SURFACE)

OPENINGS FOR FLUKES AND SHANK—1/2" HOLES FOR LASHINGS TO STOCK ARMS

NORTHILL UTILITY

ENDS STRAIGHTENED ENOUGH TO START UNIONS

TWO SEMI—CIRCLES OF 1/2" BRASS, GALVANIZED PIPE

PIPE UNIONS

Ⓐ

Ⓑ

TWO—PART RING FOR STANDARD STYLE SEA ANCHOR

PLANK DROGUE

This plank-type drogue, as used by Captain James of the 38-foot ketch *Sunway*, has several good points. It is hardly meant to take the place of a true sea anchor, but is just an easy-to-make arrangement for such times as it may be needed. While made to suit this Northill utility-type anchor, a plank can be used in somewhat the same way with a kedge. Merely cut holes for the flukes, shank, and lashings, the latter located for making fast to the arms of the flukes. In either case, the outer holes, shown as rectangular, should be shaped to suit the palms or flukes to go through them.

One must experiment with the size of the plank to get it right for the anchor. For best results, the whole thing should ride well below the surface of the water. For his 12-pound Northill, Captain James used a 2 by 10 that was about 4 feet long. Having it longer, up to 6 feet, and thinner, perhaps of 1-inch oak, would give more drag and be more effective, he says. There is a point, though, where you could get too much snubbing action.

B shows a two-part ring idea here that makes for easier stowing of a standard-style sea anchor. The diameter of a ring is usually about 1/10 the waterline of the boat. The two-part ring makes the whole thing occupy about half that space.

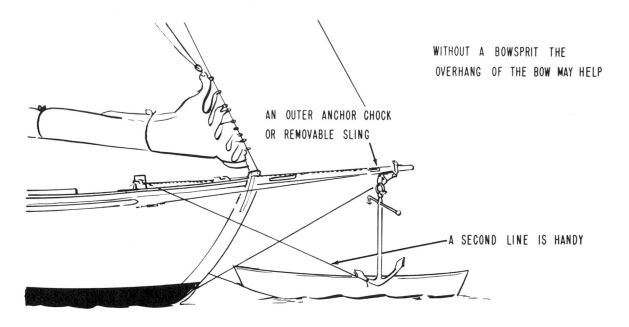

WITHOUT A BOWSPRIT THE
OVERHANG OF THE BOW MAY HELP

AN OUTER ANCHOR CHOCK
OR REMOVABLE SLING

A SECOND LINE IS HANDY

ANCHOR WORK I

"How about a few suggestions for handling a heavy anchor in a small tender?" The reader who sent in this request explained that several times when he had gone aground he had had to get out his 75-pound hook to kedge off. In loading this into an 8-foot pram, as large a boat as he could carry on deck, he usually ended by being just about swamped. Once he almost dropped the anchor through the bottom. But what worried him most was how he and his wife would make out if they ever had to do the job in really rough water.

A year or so ago I could have lost my own boat by this same combination—too small a dinghy for the size of the anchor to be handled. I was aground at about high tide on a lee shore and in water too rough for the little double-ender I was carrying as a tender. Luckily, a passing boat, seeing the fix I was in, floated a line to me and finally hauled me clear. Since then I have been conscious of what can happen in such a case.

Immediately after this experience I switched to a larger tender. Time is often all-important. Usually, the quicker you can make a try at getting your boat off, the more successful you will be. I now carry a 20-pound plow-type anchor and a 200-foot length of ⅝-inch manila stowed

handy in the lazarette. Both are light, but the little anchor digs in and holds out of all proportion to its weight, and the line is kept new. Both can be dumped quickly into the dinghy, then the anchor planted where it should do the most good, and finally the line carried back to the windlass—all without any great trouble even in rough water. Get the longest rope possible.

When that will not do the trick, we use the 75 pounder and a 1-inch line. However, if one is shorthanded, it is foolish to load such an anchor in a small tender by handing it over the side, either amidships, astern, or at the bow. If the boat has a bowsprit, it can be rigged as shown in the illustration. Ordinarily, the bowsprit roller chock is located too far inboard to be helpful, because it is apt to let an anchor of any size hang too close to the water. What is wanted is an outer chock, as shown, for then the anchor can be hauled up enough to permit the tender to work underneath it so that the hook can be lowered in place.

If the boat does not have a bowsprit, there is often enough overhang to allow lowering the anchor into the dinghy. However, a line may be necessary to swing the anchor up enough so that the tender can be maneuvered beneath it.

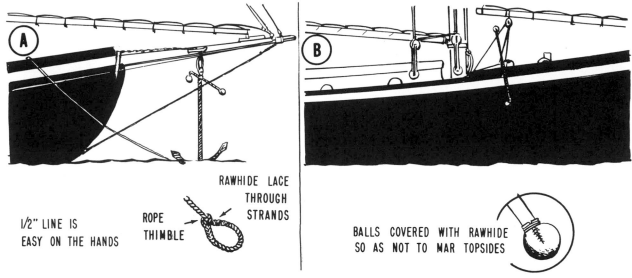

1/2" LINE IS EASY ON THE HANDS

ROPE THIMBLE

RAWHIDE LACE THROUGH STRANDS

BALLS COVERED WITH RAWHIDE SO AS NOT TO MAR TOPSIDES

ANCHOR WORK II

In extended coastwise cruising, one wants anchors, whatever the type, that will hold without one's worrying, especially when away from the boat. This means heavier-than-usual hooks which in turn require better-than-ordinary facilities for handling them, especially in shorthanded going. Generally, the service anchor must be handled an average of, say, every other day. While a good windlass can do the hardest part of the work, the service hook should be kept ready for instant use and provision should be made for washing the anchor clean.

Figure A shows the usual bowsprit setup, with the anchor around 75 pounds in weight—really too heavy to be lashed beneath the bowsprit in heavy going. The roller-type chock should be located just far enough out so that the hook, hauled up just below the water, will not bang against the stem. The chock rail on deck is shod with half-oval iron in order that the anchor can be dragged in over it to rest made-up on deck with the flukes in chocks, each with its lanyard, and another around the stock where it lays over the rail, as in B. If the stock will not foul the headsail sheet, leave it in place. If it must be unshipped, have a key that can be fitted quicker than the usual type. You will notice that the balls of the stock are covered with stitched-on rawhide, with a serving about the stock. These may leave mud marks on the paint, but they cannot mar it. The snaring line is ½-inch stuff, as too light a line is hard on the hands. Since one wants a noose that will stay open in snaring a palm, a rope thimble is spliced in rather than an eye and a rawhide lace is threaded through the strands of the rope at a point that will give a large enough loop, the idea being to swell the line just enough to be a snug fit in the thimble. Have it so that, with the noose once over a palm, a jerk will pull the swollen section through to close the noose.

In A, the anchor (after being washed off) has been hauled up to permit snaring a palm. Now, holding the line with one hand, release a foot or so of chain or rope with the other (one soon gets to know just the right amount) and pull the anchor up outside the bowsprit shrouds, crown first. Keep the flukes and palms clear of the topsides until they are far enough up so that one palm can be hooked over the rail. Hold it there while enough additional slack is given to permit pulling the anchor over and in until its shank can be grasped for finally setting it in its chocks.

Aboard our little schooner a 75-pound yachtsman's-type kedge is handled this way: a Little Giant two-speed windlass is depended on, and the boat hook is used to swish the chain through the water to wash mud out of its links as every 10 feet or so is gotten in. The clean chain drops from the windlass down into its locker, the engine is seldom called on, and the whole job is done without strain or marring of the topsides.

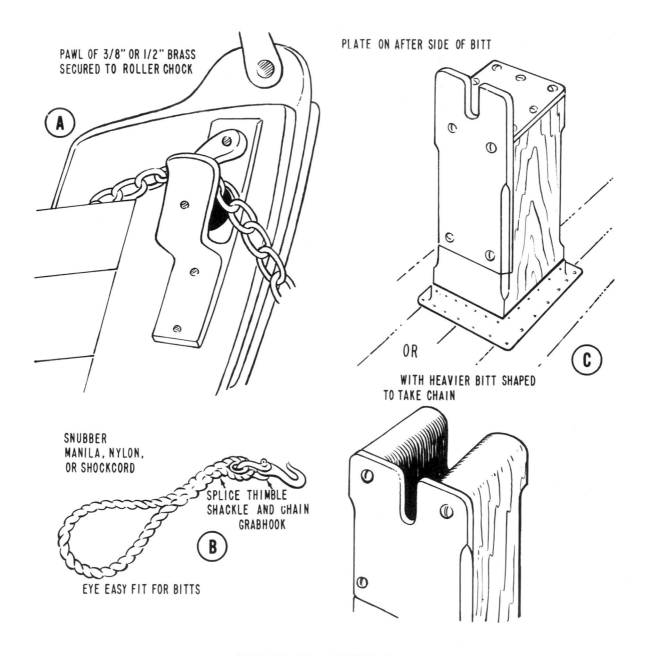

PAWL OF 3/8" OR 1/2" BRASS
SECURED TO ROLLER CHOCK

A

PLATE ON AFTER SIDE OF BITT

OR

C

WITH HEAVIER BITT SHAPED
TO TAKE CHAIN

SNUBBER
MANILA, NYLON,
OR SHOCKCORD

SPLICE THIMBLE
SHACKLE AND CHAIN
GRABHOOK

B

EYE EASY FIT FOR BITTS

CHAIN SNUBBERS I

Pawl-type chain stoppers to handle chains as small as 5/16 BBB can now be had at low prices. One of these suggestions may enable you to improve your boat in this respect.

In *A*, a heavy brass pawl is fitted, by means of a through pin or bolt, to an ordinary bowsprit chock mounted upright on the side of the stem head. The owner told me that it took a good bit of experimenting to get the pawl's size and shape just right. He made a pawl of wood first and used it as a pattern for cutting one in brass.

B is a piece of gear I use on my boat. Riding to the windlass, as we ordinarily do in anchoring, is not a good idea, so when it blows hard enough we hook the snubber to the chain and drop the eye over the pair of bitts, then easing off on the windlass enough so that the bitts take the strain. Either version of *C* is good for a man who prefers to use chain but has no windlass. I suppose one could ride to the plate on the bitt, but it is meant mostly for getting the anchor.

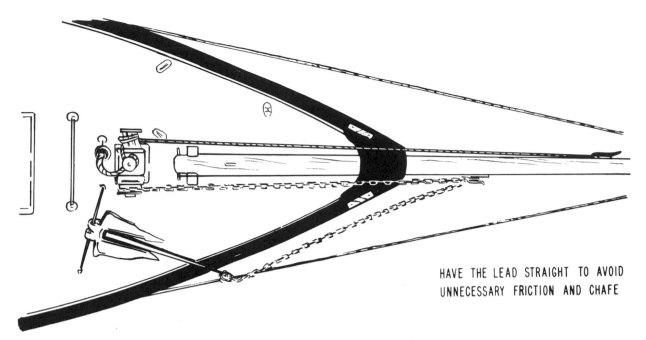

HAVE THE LEAD STRAIGHT TO AVOID
UNNECESSARY FRICTION AND CHAFE

USING A STRAIGHT LEAD

The breaking out of the hook is not an easy job, due principally to the almost right angle of conventional bow chocks. Even the roller-style chock mounted out on the bowsprit does not help as much as it should, if the chain on its way back to the windlass drags hard against the chock, bitts, or other fittings. Therefore, a direct line pull, to approach as closely as possible the ideal setup shown in the illustration above, is worth installing.

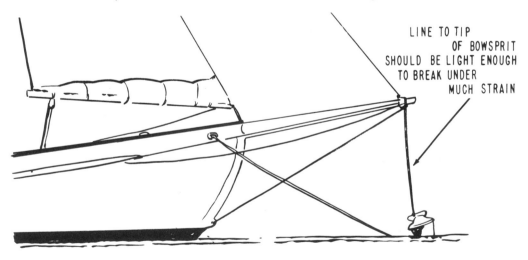

LINE TO TIP
OF BOWSPRIT
SHOULD BE LIGHT ENOUGH
TO BREAK UNDER
MUCH STRAIN

LIGHT LINE

To keep a boat with a bowsprit from nudging its mooring buoy or can in calm weather, H. M. Mossler of the ketch *Holiday* suggests a line led to the tip of the bowsprit. The line should be light enough to break if too much strain is thrown on it, and it need not be as taut as shown. There should be some slack, but not enough to have the can reach the bow or lower bobstay.

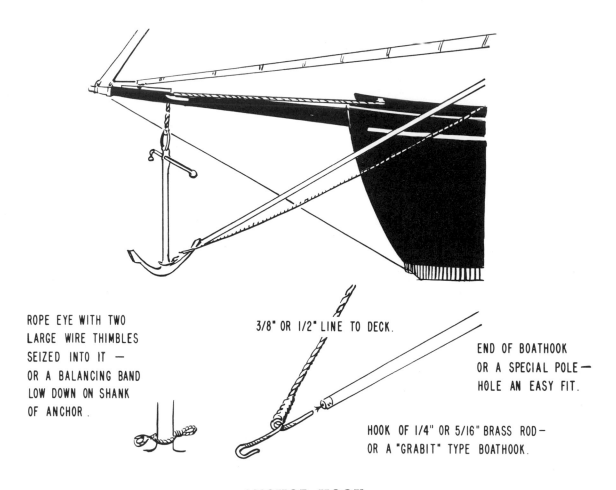

ROPE EYE WITH TWO
LARGE WIRE THIMBLES
SEIZED INTO IT —
OR A BALANCING BAND
LOW DOWN ON SHANK
OF ANCHOR.

3/8" OR 1/2" LINE TO DECK.

END OF BOATHOOK
OR A SPECIAL POLE—
HOLE AN EASY FIT.

HOOK OF 1/4" OR 5/16" BRASS ROD—
OR A "GRABIT" TYPE BOATHOOK.

ANCHOR HOOK

Not the least part of the job of hoisting a sizable anchor aboard when under way may be getting a line over one of its flukes so that it can be hauled up on deck without scarring the topsides. An iron cat hook that could be used with the old-type kedge will not catch on the fluke of the popular nonfouling kedge, and the usual plan is to snare it with a short length of line. But after the anchor has been left to drag in the water a while to wash bottom dirt off and then been hoisted up on a bowsprit chock (or even from the regular bow chock), its flukes generally still are just about awash, and your noose is repeatedly washed away especially if there is any bobble of a sea.

I recently noticed an improvement on this snaring method. A piece of 5/16-inch brass rod was bent, after annealing, to form a hook, an eye, and a short shank, the latter an easy fit in a hole bored in the inboard end of the boat hook. Low down on the shank of an anchor a rope eye with two large wire-rope thimbles or sail-type thimbles seized in was permanently secured, although I suppose a balancing band would do as well, if fastened at that point with its rings toward the flukes (not across from them).

Or, if one is using a new lightweight-type anchor, a short loop could be spliced into the eye usually provided in the head. Whatever is used is caught with the hook; then a tension is kept on the deck line as the handle is pulled free. The line is led clear, usually outside the whisker stays, and hauled in as the cable or chain is slacked off from the bitts or windlass until the anchor is finally pulled in over the rail and onto the deck. I have found that, where the anchor is of substantial weight, the line used to handle it should be at least ⅜ inch in diameter; too small a line is hard on the hands.

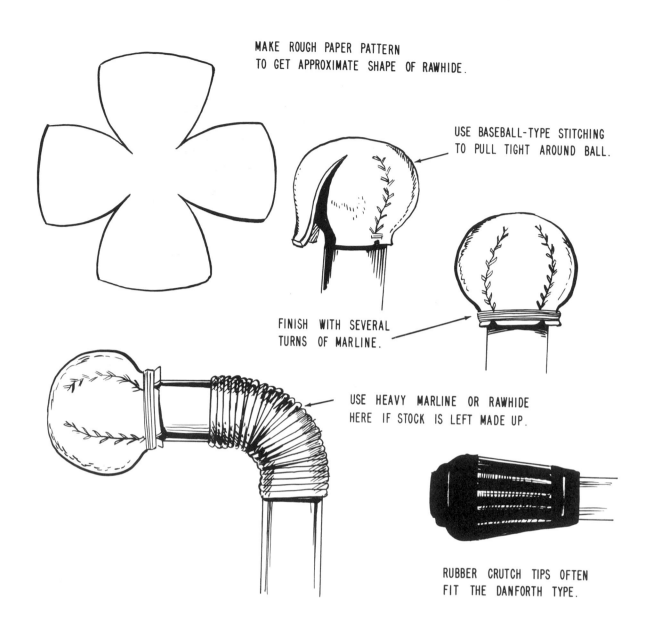

MAKE ROUGH PAPER PATTERN
TO GET APPROXIMATE SHAPE OF RAWHIDE.

USE BASEBALL-TYPE STITCHING
TO PULL TIGHT AROUND BALL.

FINISH WITH SEVERAL
TURNS OF MARLINE.

USE HEAVY MARLINE OR RAWHIDE
HERE IF STOCK IS LEFT MADE UP.

RUBBER CRUTCH TIPS OFTEN
FIT THE DANFORTH TYPE.

PROTECTING THE TOPSIDES

Rawhide stitched over the ball on the stock of any of the kedge-type anchors, as above, will permit hauling the hook aboard by sliding it against the topsides without marring the paint. It is possible by using the cat hook or retrieving line to keep the flukes clear to hold this protected ball against the side of the boat, thus affording easier anchor handling. Oddly enough, this hide covering and its stitching will more than last a season of ordinary use before requir-

ing renewing, and even then can serve as a pattern for replacement, the hardest part of the job. I'd even cover both balls where the anchor is kept with the made-up stock, and then use heavy marline about the turn so that bringing the anchor in either way will not harm the paint. The Danforth type can often be similarly protected by finding crutch or chair tips, preferably of nonmarking rubber, to fit.

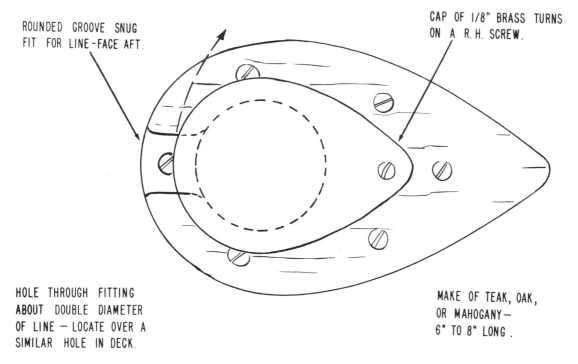

ROUNDED GROOVE SNUG
FIT FOR LINE-FACE AFT.

CAP OF 1/8" BRASS TURNS
ON A R.H. SCREW.

HOLE THROUGH FITTING
ABOUT DOUBLE DIAMETER
OF LINE — LOCATE OVER A
SIMILAR HOLE IN DECK.

MAKE OF TEAK, OAK,
OR MAHOGANY —
6" TO 8" LONG.

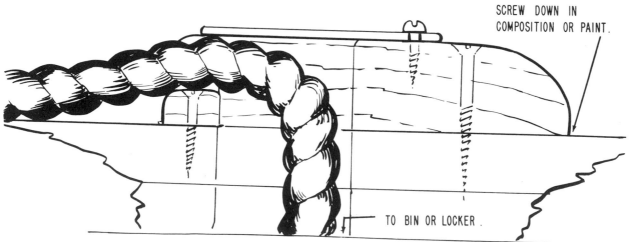

SCREW DOWN IN
COMPOSITION OR PAINT.

TO BIN OR LOCKER.

ROPE NAVELS

This rope deck pipe or navel permits getting the anchor cable or line out and still makes a fairly watertight fitting. The size should suit the diameter of the line used, and the rounded notch aft should be a snug fit for it with about ½ inch of wood left beneath. The center hole should be large enough for the line to pull through easily, and the brass cap or plate should be large enough to cover it and a good part of the line in its groove. For the usual 1- or 1⅛-inch line, the fitting can be made of 1½-inch stuff—seasoned oak, mahogany, or teak, preferably streamlined about as shown, with the opening to face aft so that not too much water will enter.

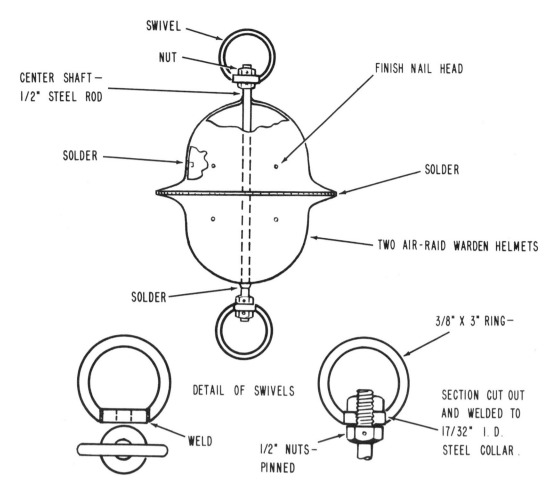

SWIVEL

NUT

CENTER SHAFT —
1/2" STEEL ROD

FINISH NAIL HEAD

SOLDER

SOLDER

TWO AIR-RAID WARDEN HELMETS

SOLDER

3/8" X 3" RING —

DETAIL OF SWIVELS

WELD

1/2" NUTS —
PINNED

SECTION CUT OUT
AND WELDED TO
17/32" I. D.
STEEL COLLAR.

SURPLUS HELMET BUOY

R. J. DeLucia has used two Civilian Defense air-raid-warden helmets, bought as surplus at around 50 cents each, to make a mooring buoy that should support a weight of 35 pounds. The helmets were stripped of their insides and then the paint was cleaned away from around the points to be soldered—the holes left from removing the crown rivets, the brims, and a patch at the top of the crown.

The crown rivet holes were plugged with finishing nails, with all but their heads cut off, and these soldered in.

A hole was punched in each crown for the center shaft. Note how the metal about these holes is dished out to give the solder a better hold. This is best done by drilling the holes on the small side, then using the point of a carpenter's plumb bob or similar instrument to force the metal out, gradually enlarging the

hole until the shaft will pass through. Because this shaft is the stress member of the buoy, it should be steel rod stock, not less than ½ inch in diameter and preferably galvanized.

The sketch shows how the ends are made up with two nuts each to hold the swivels, for which Mr. DeLucia suggests using galvanized steel rings 3 inches in diameter and of ⅜-inch stock, cutting out a section of each to have it take a 17/32 inch I.D. steel collar to which it is welded. Holes drilled to permit pinning all nuts should, of course, allow both swivels to turn. In assembling, the center shaft is inserted and a nut at each end turned down over a short stub of pipe to clamp the brims of the helmets tightly together for soldering their joint. The pipes are removed and the center shaft soldered; then, the ends can be made up and, the nuts having been pinned, the buoy is ready for painting.

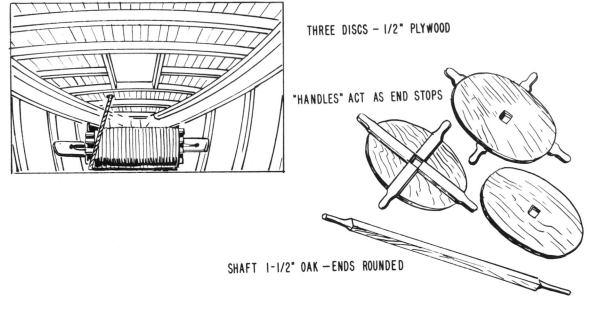

THREE DISCS – 1/2" PLYWOOD

"HANDLES" ACT AS END STOPS

SHAFT 1-1/2" OAK – ENDS ROUNDED

LENGTH AND DIAMETER TO SUIT FOREPEAK

3/4" X 1-1/4" OAK SLATS

ANCHOR RODE REEL

John Davis sent along a sketch of a reel he has installed in the forepeak of his 38-foot ketch for holding the rode of his storm anchor. It is good on three counts. First, the 1¼-inch manila line is kept in better condition, if only because the air can get to it. Second, space is saved, since the reel occupies room that otherwise would hardly be used. Finally, the line is quickly available when wanted. As Davis says, a heavy line such as this is a nuisance to stow; ordinarily, it deteriorates more from storage than from actual use. You will not need your spare anchor often, but when you do it may be in a hurry and you do not want to have to unkink 20 or more fathoms in getting it up from below.

The idea is to provide a reel which will fit right up in the eyes of the forepeak, with its ends held free to turn by wooden blocks or metal fittings secured to a pair of frames or the hull ceiling. Incidentally, this slatted type is to be preferred to a solid reel because of the ventilation it affords.

As Davis describes its use, he threads the line down through the deck plate while his wife below revolves the reel, by means of its end handles, to wind the line evenly. In his case, the reel is a good 2 feet in length and 10 inches in diameter, so the 30 fathoms of line used require but three layers of turns. The larger the reel is, both as to length and diameter, the fewer the layers and the better for the line.

The round ends of the axle or shaft should turn rather stiffly in their fittings; if the reel turns too easily, there is more chance of the line's becoming fouled.

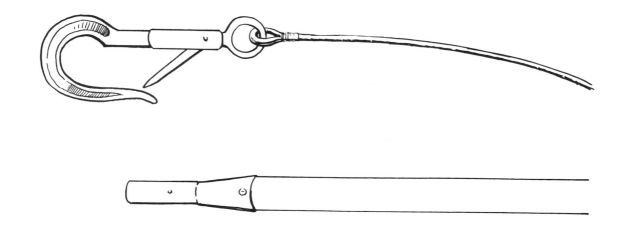

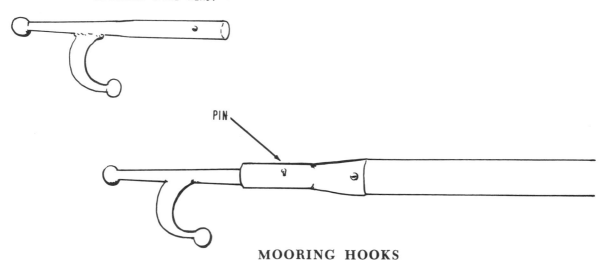

WITH A REMOVABLE SPARE HEAD.

MAKE OF EVERDUR ROD — BRAZE ON HOOK
SECTION AND FILE TO FORM THE BALL POINTS.

PIN

MOORING HOOKS

Any boat used from a mooring should have aboard a Grabit boat hook, which will hook the buoy or float and, by disengaging the handle, leave the boat fast to the mooring by the line that is attached to the hooked head. This type of boat hook is shown above, not as a suggestion for making your own, but to show a spare removable head which I came across in North Carolina. The regular head is patented and must be bought (indeed there would be no economy in trying to make your own), but the owner, who had a nice little cutter, had made

this spare to avoid having to carry a regular boat hook as well as his Grabit one. Everdur rod in a size to fit in the socket of the handle was used, with the curved hook part brazed to it; then, the two ball points were formed by grinding and filing. This was held in place with a cotter pin, although it is likely that some simpler method could be worked out.

An even better idea is sometimes used with this type of boat hook: Fitting a longer **handle, with the Grabit type hook or head on one end of it and a regular boat-hook head on the other.**

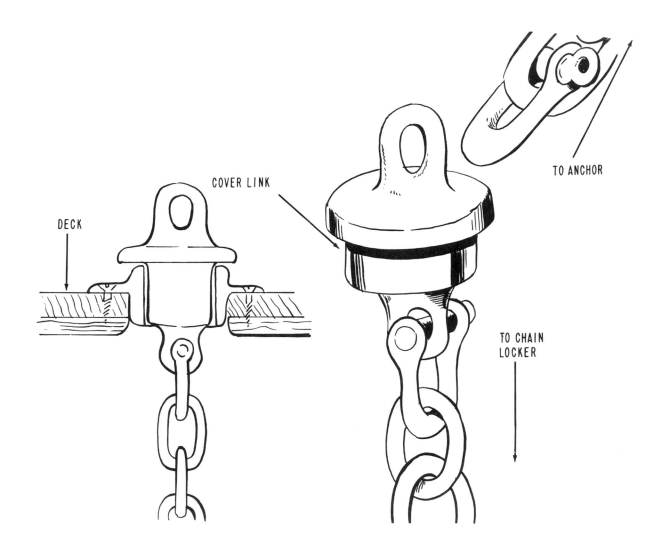

DECK

COVER LINK

TO ANCHOR

TO CHAIN
LOCKER

CHAIN-PIPE COVER

Georges Hofmann sent me the idea sketched here, with the following information on it: "I used this chain deck-pipe extensively in Europe for many years and found it the most reliable and handiest for small cruising and racing boats. The edges of the pipe are well rounded so the chain can slide in and out easily, and the cover, which is a link of the chain, never gets lost, closes the pipe efficiently, and prevents the end of the chain from dropping into the locker be-

low. To anchor, just connect the anchor to the cover and let the whole thing go overboard. The fitting is cast of bronze and is sometimes chromium plated, but the cover must be strong enough to take a strain equal to the breaking load of the chain."

This would seem a worthwhile fitting for some manufacturer to bring out, either in suitable bronze or galvanized iron.

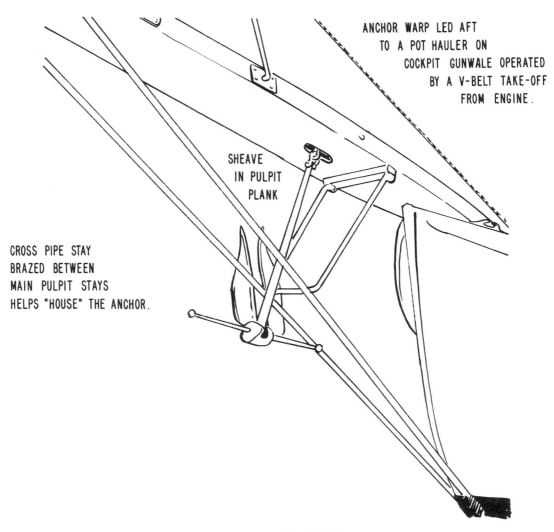

ANCHOR WARP LED AFT
TO A POT HAULER ON
COCKPIT GUNWALE OPERATED
BY A V-BELT TAKE-OFF
FROM ENGINE.

SHEAVE
IN PULPIT
PLANK

CROSS PIPE STAY
BRAZED BETWEEN
MAIN PULPIT STAYS
HELPS "HOUSE" THE ANCHOR.

PULPIT HOUSING

Anchor work aboard the average cruiser is difficult and sometimes dangerous. It is also rough on the boat's topsides. However, Russell Lake has simplified the whole thing aboard his sport fisherman *Buckaroo;* first, by using the pulpit and its rigging for handling and housing the anchor; and, second, by having his engine do the hauling.

Apparently the only fitting added to the regular pulpit is the U-shaped pipe stay, extended from the pulpit's plank and brazed to the two main pipe stays. This is placed to carry the proper lead and naturally to suit the location of the sheave fitted slot forward of it. The anchor line or rode is led between the main supporting stays, forward of this cross-stay and over

the sheave, and then aft to the cockpit. Here, a Westhaver pot hauler placed on the coaming just abaft the wheel and operated by a V-belt takeoff from the engine does the hauling.

Mr. Lake is naturally enthusiastic about how the arrangement has worked out, for the anchor can be hauled or let go without the necessity of going forward. Either the flukes or the stock of the Danforth anchor are bound to catch in the stays when it comes home (as shown above), and there seems no way of its fouling. The boat lays better to her anchor when the rode is led forward of the stem in this way. Mud is not brought aboard and the topsides are not chafed as in the usual handling.

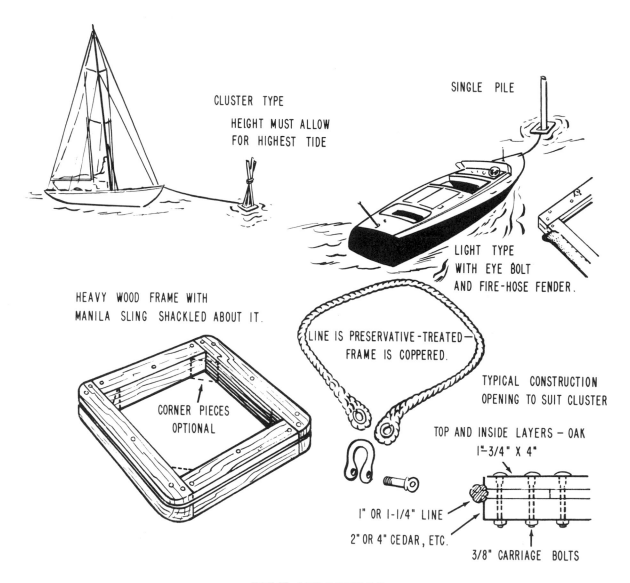

CLUSTER TYPE
HEIGHT MUST ALLOW
FOR HIGHEST TIDE

SINGLE PILE

LIGHT TYPE
WITH EYE BOLT
AND FIRE-HOSE FENDER.

HEAVY WOOD FRAME WITH
MANILA SLING SHACKLED ABOUT IT.

LINE IS PRESERVATIVE-TREATED—
FRAME IS COPPERED.

CORNER PIECES
OPTIONAL

TYPICAL CONSTRUCTION
OPENING TO SUIT CLUSTER

TOP AND INSIDE LAYERS — OAK
1"-3/4" X 4"

1" OR 1-1/4" LINE

2" OR 4" CEDAR, ETC.

3/8" CARRIAGE BOLTS

PILE MOORINGS

As a friend in Virginia points out, pile moorings have a fine reputation for holding. Naturally, the main requirement is to have the pile, or cluster of them, put in correctly: by a pile driver rather than by hand. His, a cluster of three with the heads wired together, was put in by one of the pound-net fishermen there using the rig they drive their long stakes with. So far the mooring has held his boat during three really had blows, despite the exposed location. The mooring yoke or frame used is both strong and convenient. As the sketch shows, it is simply layers of 4-inch-wide oak

bolted to heavy cedar the same width, with a groove in which a sling of 1¼-inch-diameter manila is shackled after splicing and stretching. Wetting shrinks this tightly in place when it acts as a fender for the frame, in addition to being a precaution should the frame fail.

I have also shown a simpler frame, as often used with a single pile. This type is often fendered with old fire hose and has an eyebolt with ring for the pennant. But here, too, it would be a good precaution to carry a chain or wire around the frame to shackle it into the ring.

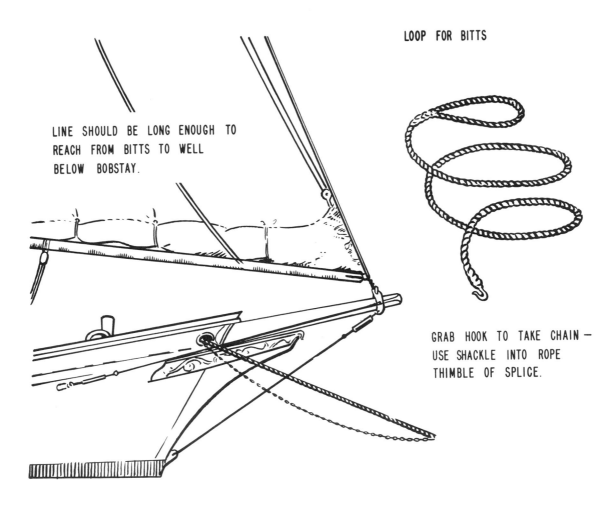

LOOP FOR BITTS

LINE SHOULD BE LONG ENOUGH TO
REACH FROM BITTS TO WELL
BELOW BOBSTAY.

GRAB HOOK TO TAKE CHAIN —
USE SHACKLE INTO ROPE
THIMBLE OF SPLICE.

CHAIN SNUBBERS II

I have always carried aboard my boat a short length of heavy manila with a loop spliced in one end and a chain or grab hook in the other. It is used when anchored in a breeze to drop over the bitts with the hook into the chain just ahead of the windlass, so that the strain can be taken off its wildcat. On the *Sea Adventurer*, there is an improvement on this which is merely a longer length of line with the same loop and hook, the idea being to hook into the anchor chain well below the bobstay, then slacking off the chain enough to ride to the line and so avoid one fault of chain, its rasping across the bobstay. One could serve the line at such points of chafe, but it is simpler to make up a new one as required; and should the line let go, no harm would result because the chain would merely take up on the bitts or windlass to which it is attached.

CHAPTER 5

Lines,
Fenders,
and Cleats

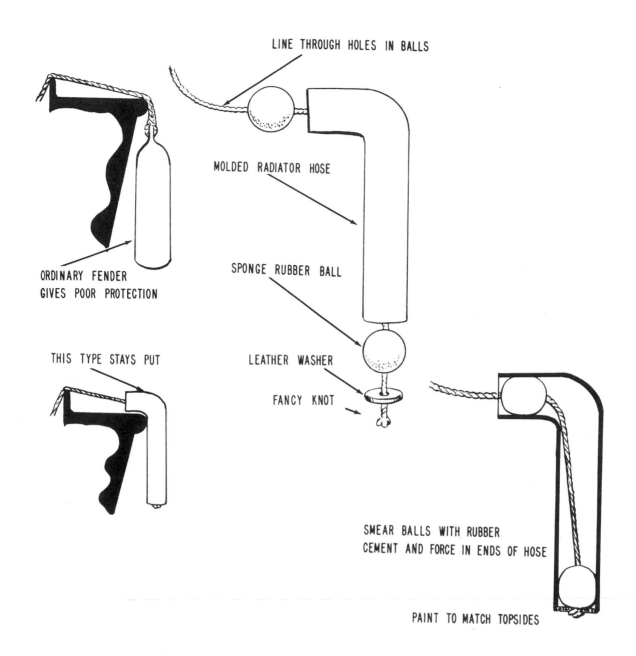

LINE THROUGH HOLES IN BALLS

MOLDED RADIATOR HOSE

SPONGE RUBBER BALL

ORDINARY FENDER
GIVES POOR PROTECTION

THIS TYPE STAYS PUT

LEATHER WASHER

FANCY KNOT

SMEAR BALLS WITH RUBBER
CEMENT AND FORCE IN ENDS OF HOSE

PAINT TO MATCH TOPSIDES

SMALL-BOAT FENDERS I

An idea obtained from George Marsh is shown here. It is a small-boat fender that gives protection where most needed, right at the gunwale, and can be kept in place easily. The molded radiator hose can be bought in different shapes and sizes at filling stations, and the sponge rubber balls can be had in a fair range of sizes at a dime store. A large-enough size should be used so that the ball must be crowded in the hose; or, if the balls are too large for the hose, grind them down with coarse sandpaper. The lanyard is worked through a hole cut in one of the balls, and that end is finished off with a stout leather washer and a fancy knot. The line is threaded through the hose, and the other ball is put on. Both are smeared with rubber cement and crowded into the hose; then the line can be worked into place and the cement allowed to set. Finally, the fender is painted the desired color.

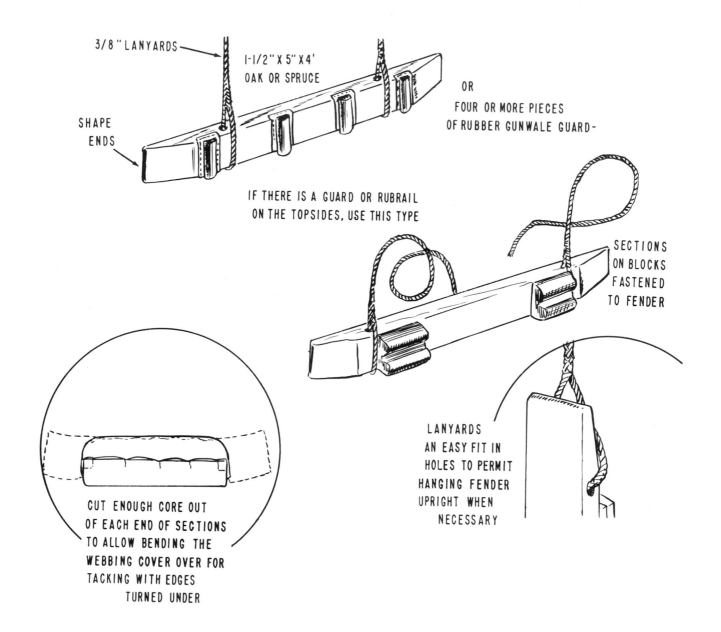

3/8" LANYARDS

1-1/2" X 5" X 4'
OAK OR SPRUCE

SHAPE
ENDS

OR
FOUR OR MORE PIECES
OF RUBBER GUNWALE GUARD—

IF THERE IS A GUARD OR RUBRAIL
ON THE TOPSIDES, USE THIS TYPE

SECTIONS
ON BLOCKS
FASTENED
TO FENDER

CUT ENOUGH CORE OUT
OF EACH END OF SECTIONS
TO ALLOW BENDING THE
WEBBING COVER OVER FOR
TACKING WITH EDGES
TURNED UNDER

LANYARDS
AN EASY FIT IN
HOLES TO PERMIT
HANGING FENDER
UPRIGHT WHEN
NECESSARY

SMALL-BOAT FENDERS II

The difference between this type of fender and others is that sections of rubber gunwale guard, the half-round shape, are used to pad the plank. These are either tacked directly to it, or if the boat has a guard or rub strip on her topsides, the sections are secured to short blocks fastened to the fender plank.

The least-worn parts of a discarded dinghy guard (often found about boat yards) are worth saving, for such pads will retain their resiliency and not get hard and unyielding as will kapok-filled ones. The heavy outside covering can be easily scrubbed clean. The trick in working with this rubber guard stock is to cut enough of the rubber core out of each end of the section so that the heavy webbing or canvas can be carried over the edge of the fender plank or its block and then all edges turned under for fastening with heavy copper tacks. The lanyards should be an easy fit in their holes, so that even when wet and swollen their leads can be changed to hang the fenders upright instead of in the usual horizontal manner.

THREAD THIS END DEEPER AND
FILE SHARP AFTER FORCING THROUGH —
CUT OFF TO TAKE NUT.

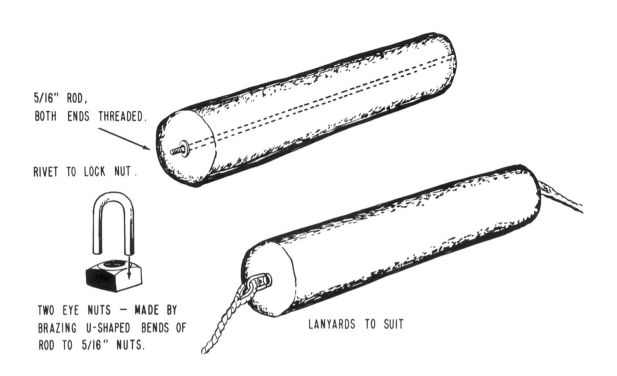

5/16" ROD,
BOTH ENDS THREADED.

RIVET TO LOCK NUT.

TWO EYE NUTS — MADE BY
BRAZING U-SHAPED BENDS OF
ROD TO 5/16" NUTS.

LANYARDS TO SUIT

RECONDITIONING FENDERS

As John Haynes wrote me, one frequently finds, floating or cast up on shore, large canvas and cork-type fenders which are in perfect condition except for having lost their lanyards. Occasionally, I have tried to make them usable again by opening up an end, inserting a loop of line, and then sewing it up again. However, throwing all the strain on one end is always too much for the canvas to stand for long. I have also sometimes wondered why such fenders are not made with a length of flexible wire right through them, with the rope lanyards spliced

into eyes in the ends. Mr. Haynes' idea is somewhat along that line. It is easier to drive or coax a length of rod through than a heavy wire. Then, it is a matter of holding the rod there and using something to take the lanyards. Eye nuts of galvanized iron can be bought. His homemade brass eye nuts will not rust. It is a simple matter to rivet the ends of the rod enough to lock the nuts. Using washers under them is a good idea, if the grommets are quite large. The rod does not make the fender too stiff, he says, and the cork filling continues to keep it resilient.

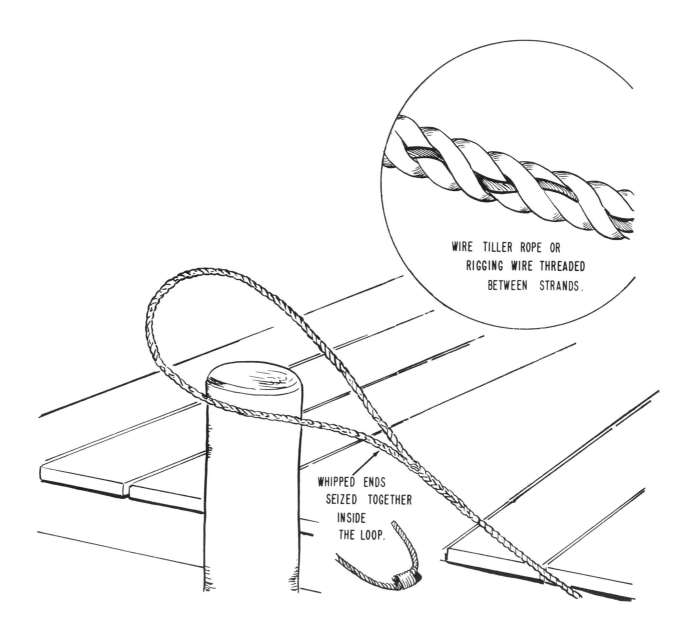

WIRE TILLER ROPE OR
RIGGING WIRE THREADED
BETWEEN STRANDS.

WHIPPED ENDS
SEIZED TOGETHER
INSIDE
THE LOOP.

STIFF DOCK LINE

If your boat is large enough to justify carry-ing dock lines of fairly large-diameter rope, their end loops will, if properly made up when being spliced in, stay open of their own accord to make it comparatively easy to ring the head of a pile in docking. But where lighter lines are used, with the usual tendency of the loop to stay closed, try having one dock line made up especially for this purpose. Thread a length of wire tiller rope or rigging wire, of a diameter sufficient to stiffen the rope, between the strands of the loop part, the ends brought together and seized one over the other, as shown. One can then open the loop with his hands before using the line and be pretty sure that it will stay open.

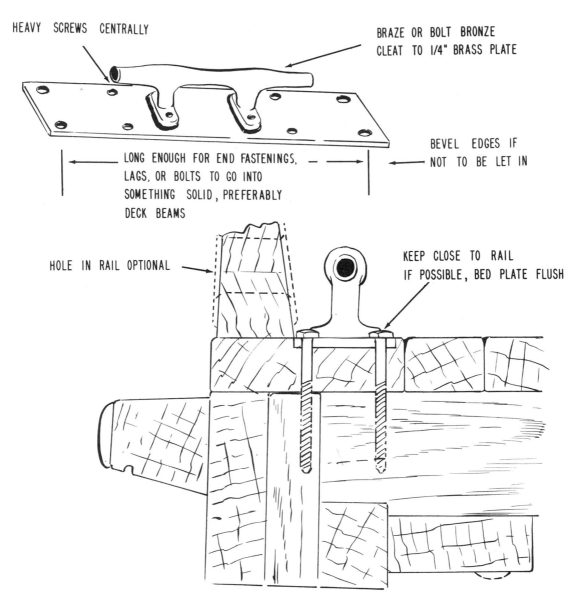

HEAVY SCREWS CENTRALLY

BRAZE OR BOLT BRONZE
CLEAT TO 1/4" BRASS PLATE

LONG ENOUGH FOR END FASTENINGS,
LAGS, OR BOLTS TO GO INTO
SOMETHING SOLID, PREFERABLY
DECK BEAMS

BEVEL EDGES IF
NOT TO BE LET IN

HOLE IN RAIL OPTIONAL

KEEP CLOSE TO RAIL
IF POSSIBLE, BED PLATE FLUSH

DOCKING CLEATS

Where heavy deck fittings which are apt to be subject to considerable strain are added to a boat, it is often difficult to fasten them to hold well. An outstanding example is amidships cleats, which are so handy for handling a boat about docks. Even bolts through the covering board and a block beneath will eventually work sufficiently to permit the cleat to shift slightly under strain and, of course, pave the way for rot. The situation is particularly bad where the covering board is of soft wood, or with a canvas-covered deck and the usual tongue-and-groove decking.

A way of getting around the trouble is shown above. Some variation to suit the particular job can be used. Here, as used aboard the little schooner *Reliance,* the strain of the amidships cleats is distributed over a considerable area by having them brazed to stout brass plates. However, dependence is largely put on the end fastenings—lags—which go through into solid wood beneath. Bedding the plates flush makes for a neat job, but for a canvas-covered or ply-wood deck, the plate would have to be mounted on top, with the edges beveled or rounded.

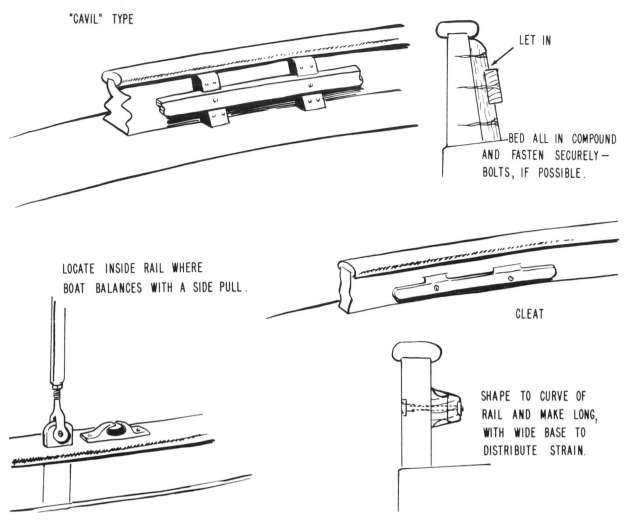

"CAVIL" TYPE

LET IN

BED ALL IN COMPOUND
AND FASTEN SECURELY —
BOLTS, IF POSSIBLE.

LOCATE INSIDE RAIL WHERE
BOAT BALANCES WITH A SIDE PULL.

CLEAT

SHAPE TO CURVE OF
RAIL AND MAKE LONG,
WITH WIDE BASE TO
DISTRIBUTE STRAIN.

'MIDSHIP CLEATS

Docking is greatly simplified if there is a place to make a line fast at a point where the boat about balances with a side pull—usually about one-third the distance back from the bow. One can then bring the boat into the dock broadside (not have it come in bowsprit first, as with a line to the forward bitts) by going ahead and then reversing the engine to take in gradually the slack about the cleat. If the boat has timberheads taking the rail, it is a simple matter to secure real cavils at this point on each side. Ordinary cleats attached inside the rail can hardly be secured strongly enough to take the considerable up-strain apt to be put on their fastenings.

The idea should be to spread the pull of the cleat over a considerable area, as in the two examples shown above. Here, the cavil type should have its uprights at least 4 inches apart and its bar notched in. The cleat type should have a broad and long base, or preferably two bases, as shown; if at all possible, it should be secured with carriage bolts, heads flush outside the rail, nuts over washers inside—countersunk, too, if the thickness of the wood permits. If neither type is practical, an open or stern-style chock on the rail cap just ahead of the forward rigging helps some, as the line can be led through it even though it must be made fast to the regular bitts. A hook, large enough to take the line and secured by a spliced loop to the head of the chainplate (although not shown) can be used in much the same way.

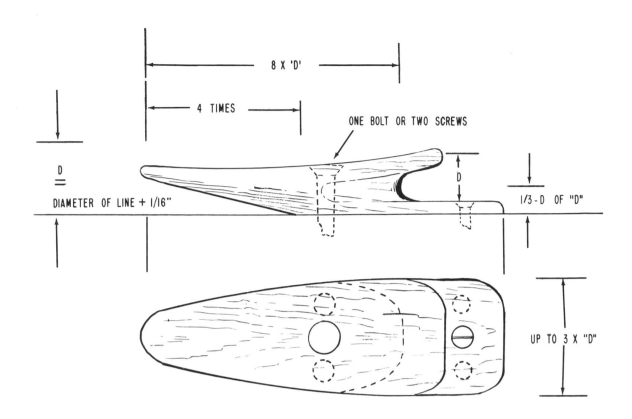

JAM CLEAT

If it is made properly for the line to be used, this cleat will hold well, yet release instantly. Use seasoned locust, osage orange, mulberry, ironwood, or good oak, and boil the completed cleat in linseed oil. The first job is to cut the block to size and lay out the profile shape. Bore a hole for the rope channel and then saw out from it toward the tail end. Finally, saw or cut the taper in the tail. From there on it is largely a matter of working by eye and feel, using files and, finally, sandpaper. Fasten securely, preferably with stove bolts. Or, if the width permits, use heavy screws in pairs.

CHAPTER 6

On Deck

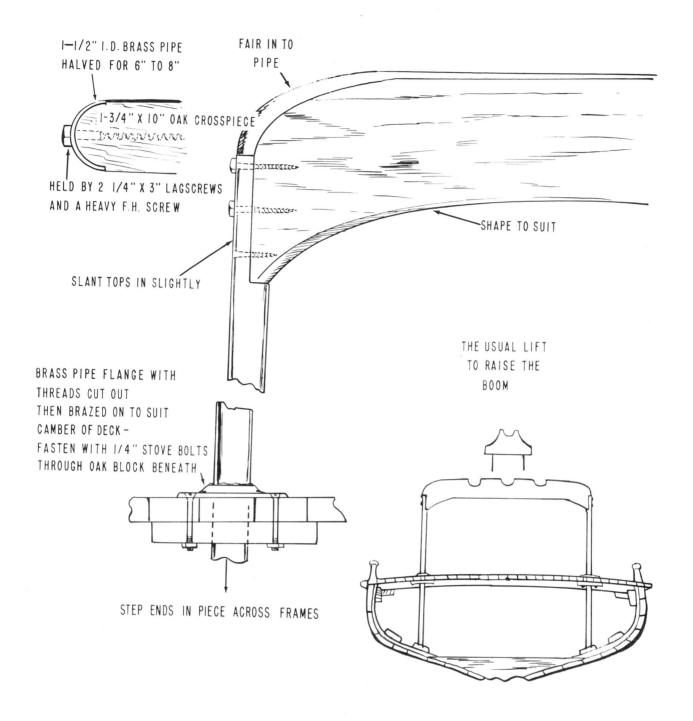

I—1/2" I.D. BRASS PIPE
HALVED FOR 6" TO 8"

FAIR IN TO
PIPE

I-3/4" X 10" OAK CROSSPIECE

HELD BY 2 1/4" X 3" LAGSCREWS
AND A HEAVY F.H. SCREW

SHAPE TO SUIT

SLANT TOPS IN SLIGHTLY

THE USUAL LIFT
TO RAISE THE
BOOM

BRASS PIPE FLANGE WITH
THREADS CUT OUT
THEN BRAZED ON TO SUIT
CAMBER OF DECK —
FASTEN WITH 1/4" STOVE BOLTS
THROUGH OAK BLOCK BENEATH

STEP ENDS IN PIECE ACROSS FRAMES

BOOM GALLOWS

This is a boom gallows with ends that will not catch the mainsheet. The uprights should be brass pipe (in preference to galvanized) and of a diameter in keeping with the boat—from, say, 1 inch inside diameter to the conservative maximum shown for fairly large boats, 1½ inches). The plank for the crossbar should be wide enough to permit shaping the top and bottom edges about as shown. Its thickness should be the same as the outside diameter of the pipe used for uprights. End fastenings which go into the end grain should be amply long, preferably with a couple of lag screws and one heavy, flatheaded wood screw at each end.

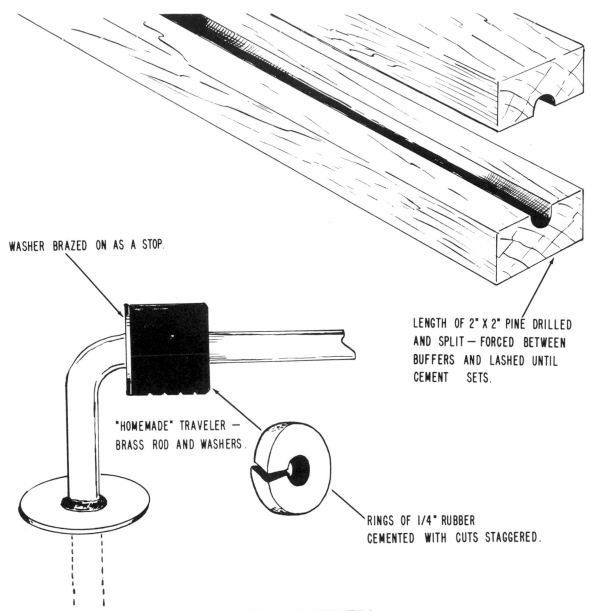

WASHER BRAZED ON AS A STOP.

LENGTH OF 2" X 2" PINE DRILLED
AND SPLIT — FORCED BETWEEN
BUFFERS AND LASHED UNTIL
CEMENT SETS.

"HOMEMADE" TRAVELER —
BRASS ROD AND WASHERS.

RINGS OF 1/4" RUBBER
CEMENTED WITH CUTS STAGGERED.

BUFFER FOR TRAVELERS

The traveler buffer shown in the drawing is used by Karl Hendon aboard his ketch *Dreamer*. He made up his own travelers of Everdur rod, brazing on the washers or plates as deck flanges, with the smaller ones acting as stops for the buffers. For a traveler already in place on a boat, however, the buffers could be held by the bends in the ends of the traveler. The ¼-inch rubber is easy to obtain. The rings can be cut out and split as shown. Enough of them are then slipped onto the traveler and finally bonded with rubber cement. Be sure that the cuts are staggered as for packing a stuffing box gland.

For the cement to hold properly, reasonable pressure must be applied until it has set up. Mr. Hendon suggests using a length of 2-by-2-inch stuff, either drilled for its length and split on a saw or split and the matching hollows roughly gouged out. The idea is to cut the pieces to a certain length so that, when they are forced between the cemented-up buffers and held together with lashings, a fair amount of pressure will be applied.

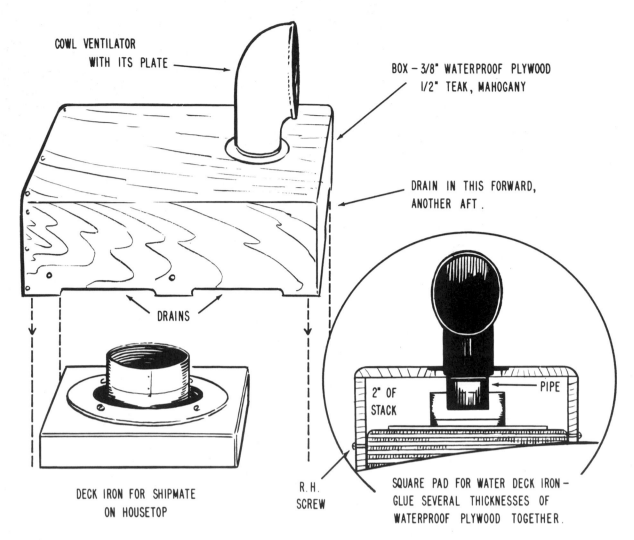

COWL VENTILATOR WITH ITS PLATE

BOX – 3/8" WATERPROOF PLYWOOD 1/2" TEAK, MAHOGANY

DRAIN IN THIS FORWARD, ANOTHER AFT.

DRAINS

DECK IRON FOR SHIPMATE ON HOUSETOP

R.H. SCREW

2" OF STACK

PIPE

SQUARE PAD FOR WATER DECK IRON – GLUE SEVERAL THICKNESSES OF WATERPROOF PLYWOOD TOGETHER.

DECK IRON VENTILATORS I

Here, the water deck iron on the housetop for the Shipmate's stack is utilized as part of a Dorade-type ventilator, to be used in hot weather when the range is not required, with the stack below removed and the smokehead off. The pad necessary to level up the deck iron has been made square to permit better fastening of the box, the excess length of which is kept ahead of it in order that the cowl ventilator can be placed there. One can use a short stub of stack to keep the air intake into the cabin high enough so that water taken through the pipe outlet of the ventilator will not find its way below. If the pad is high enough, merely have the ventilator's pipe-duct outlet low enough to be below the deck iron's opening. Drains should be cut in the ends of the box and in its high side, about as shown. Four or five round-headed screws are used for holding it to the pad.

Whether you are making a square pad for such an installation—or the usual round one—waterproof plywood is the best material to use because, with it, the pad can be kept small without chance of its checking, the common fault with one cut from a plank. It is seldom that plywood thick enough to suit the camber you are up against can be had locally, but enough layers can be glued together to build up a block of the required thickness. Do all the shaping after the glue has set properly. Fastening down should be done with plenty of liquid marine glue or plastic compound, with screws driven from beneath through the deck or housetop into the pad.

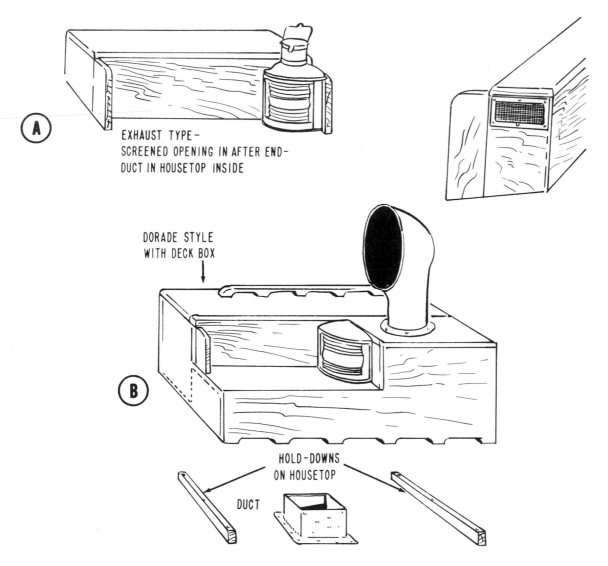

EXHAUST TYPE—
SCREENED OPENING IN AFTER END—
DUCT IN HOUSETOP INSIDE

Ⓐ

DORADE STYLE
WITH DECK BOX

Ⓑ

HOLD-DOWNS
ON HOUSETOP

DUCT

LIGHT-BOX VENTILATOR

An idea I noticed on the *Freedom* is simple enough to class as a gadget rather than a feature of construction. This is the combination light-and-ventilator-box arrangement (Figure *A*), basically a long narrow box without a bottom and with a 3- or 4-inch-deep opening at the top of its after end. A pair of them is used. The outer faces of each take regulation running lights. Each is mounted on the housetop over a duct leading below. The ducts are of the discharge type, a noticeable current of air being sucked up and out. Insect screen, preferably held by a metal frame, can be used over the openings.

A somewhat similar idea, but with even more refinement, is shown in Figure *B*. I saw a pair of such boxes used on a big schooner and believe the idea has possibilities, either as shown or modified to suit a particular installation or boat. For example, the storage-box part could be omitted to keep the size and weight down, but with the ventilator of the intake rather than the discharge type. As shown, the storage box is sealed off from the ventilator part, even having a bottom, and is more or less watertight. The housetop duct leading from below is toward the forward end of the box, as usual. The whole thing is simply secured to hold-down battens and scuppered for drainage.

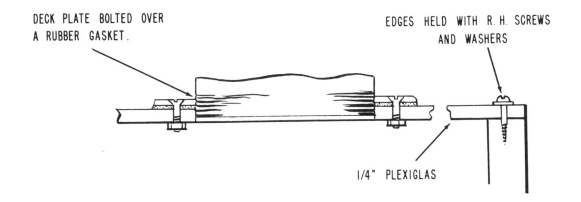

DECK PLATE BOLTED OVER
A RUBBER GASKET.

EDGES HELD WITH R. H. SCREWS
AND WASHERS

1/4" PLEXIGLAS

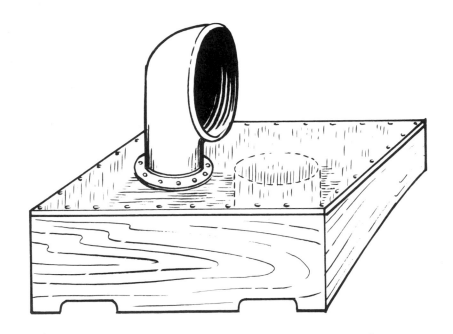

PLEXIGLAS VENT

The idea of using transparent plastic, such as Plexiglas, for the top of a Dorade-type ventilator is a good one. The main advantage is that it will give light below without hindering ventilation or admitting rain or spray. In fastening the deck plate for the ventilator, extra holes should be drilled between those for the plate and then matching stove bolts should be used to pull the plate down over a white rubber gasket or a compound-impregnated canvas. The edges are fastened in the usual way for this material, with round-headed screws through washers and holes drilled to an easy fit to allow for the come and go of the plastic. Since the inside of the box is visible, it should be well made and neatly finished inside. Some dust is bound to get in, so it should be made removable for cleaning.

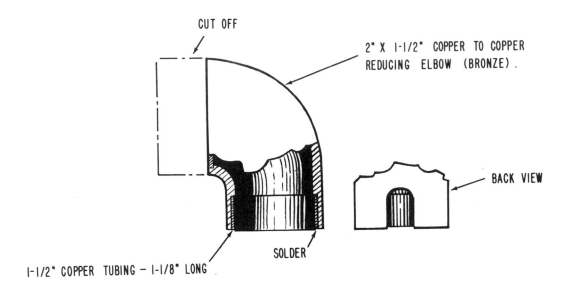

CUT OFF

2" X 1-1/2" COPPER TO COPPER
REDUCING ELBOW (BRONZE).

BACK VIEW

1-1/2" COPPER TUBING — 1-1/8" LONG

SOLDER

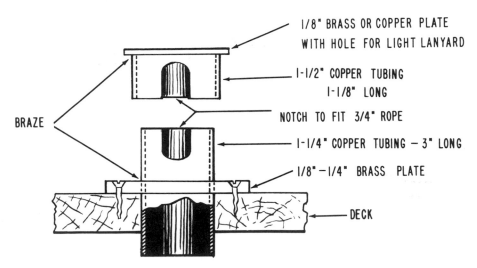

1/8" BRASS OR COPPER PLATE
WITH HOLE FOR LIGHT LANYARD

1-1/2" COPPER TUBING
1-1/8" LONG

NOTCH TO FIT 3/4" ROPE

1-1/4" COPPER TUBING — 3" LONG

1/8" - 1/4" BRASS PLATE

BRAZE

DECK

ROPE AND VENTILATOR PIPE

I like Ralph Keeler's combination rope-and-vent deck pipe idea because of the ventilator top feature. Standard plumbing items and pieces of scrap brass were used to make it. The pipe proper is merely a length of 1¼-inch copper tubing let through a hole worked in a disc of brass plate and brazed there. The cap is a short length of larger tubing, with a plate brazed on top of it and a hole drilled through the projecting edge to take a light lanyard. Both parts have matching notches to take ¾-inch line used with the anchor. A reducing elbow of proper size is used for the ventilator top. It, too, is notched to permit passage of the line.

Note that a portion of the elbow is cut off to improve the shape and that the space inside the other end is fitted with a bit of tubing, soldered in place, to give a proper fit. Brazing brass to copper is not always easy, but heavy copper could be used for the two plates.

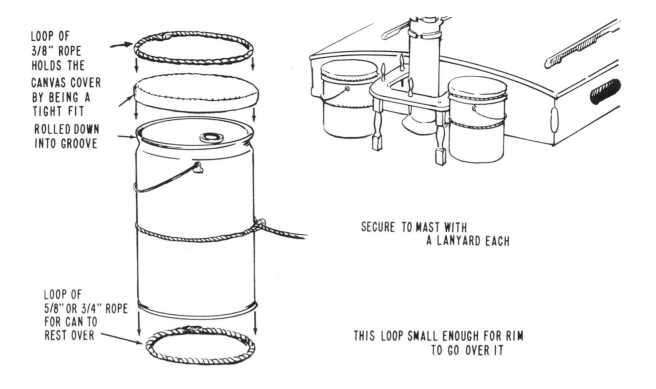

LOOP OF 3/8" ROPE HOLDS THE CANVAS COVER BY BEING A TIGHT FIT

ROLLED DOWN INTO GROOVE

LOOP OF 5/8" OR 3/4" ROPE FOR CAN TO REST OVER

SECURE TO MAST WITH A LANYARD EACH

THIS LOOP SMALL ENOUGH FOR RIM TO GO OVER IT

SPARE GAS

Aboard an auxiliary, with its usually limited cruising range under power, it is best to have some sort of a reserve supply of gasoline along when the engine is to be used frequently, as in following the Intracoastal Waterway. For such a reserve supply, one usually wants something better than a couple of filled cans stowed somewhere about the boat.

For the method shown above, secure a couple of 5-gallon oil cans, the rather common type having a flat top with an indentation or groove below the top rim. Paint the cans, bottoms and all, with engine paint, not only for the sake of appearance but to help avoid rusting. Make a tight-fitting canvas cover for each, with a 2-inch skirt or lip so that water cannot collect on the tops of the cans or find its way inside. Have a round loop or ring of ⅜-inch line, a tight fit, to be rolled down over the cover and fitted into the groove for holding the canvas skirt. Another loop of heavier rope, ⅝ or ¾ inch, is made small enough so that the flange of the bottom of the can will just come over it. When placing the

can on or over this loop, keep the spliced section outboard. This will make up for the camber of the deck and keep the can upright.

The rope holds the can slightly off the deck to avoid chafing or rust-staining the paint. The location shown, a can on either side of the mast or its pin rail with a lanyard from each secured to the mast, is a good one, if it does not prevent handling the halliards. If it does, the cans can be secured on the bridge deck or even inside the cockpit. In any case, the cover and its ring usually act as a fender to guard the surface the can might otherwise chafe.

After having a lighted cigarette stub tossed by a dock bystander burn a hole ⅛ inch deep in the soft cedar of our tender, I sometimes wonder what might have happened had it landed on the top of gas cans carried on deck. The fire hazard involved in such carrying, particularly when one is laying at docks, justifies having such covers fireproofed by giving them several coats of one of the fireproof paints now on the market.

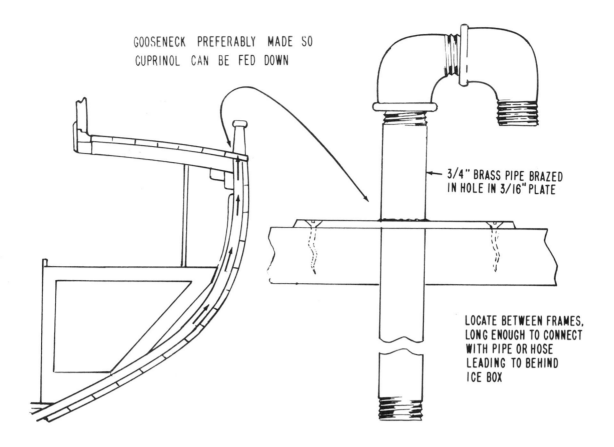

GOOSENECK PREFERABLY MADE SO
CUPRINOL CAN BE FED DOWN

3/4" BRASS PIPE BRAZED
IN HOLE IN 3/16" PLATE

LOCATE BETWEEN FRAMES,
LONG ENOUGH TO CONNECT
WITH PIPE OR HOSE
LEADING TO BEHIND
ICE BOX

HULL VENTILATOR

The hull back of a built-in icebox or refrigerator is a place where much rot gets a start. And while intelligent planning and proper building can lessen the chance of trouble there, it is only common sense to take all possible precautions. For example, on one new boat I saw recently, two small icebox-type ventilators were let into the waterway directly above the space behind the box and connected to it by sheet-metal ducts, with the idea of permitting a flow of outside air. However, a method as good, and one which can often be used on a boat already built, is shown above. I have seen several variations of this; the arrangement must be worked out to suit the particular boat—the icebox and its location and installation and the boat's hull construction or framing. The idea is to have a ventilating fitting, or even a pair of them, in the waterway or close enough to the rail that it will not be in the way. It must be of a type which will not admit water. The pipe gooseneck shown is merely an example; there are many different fittings which could be used. The owner here wanted to be able occasionally to flow some Cuprinol or other marine-type timber preservative down into it. This can be done here merely by turning up the final ell. To render it perfectly watertight involves only screwing on a pipe cap. The important point is to have the lower part of the brazed-in pipe lead behind the sheer clamp to follow down between the frames far enough to permit connection of another pipe or length of hose, which will lead behind the enclosed space back of the box.

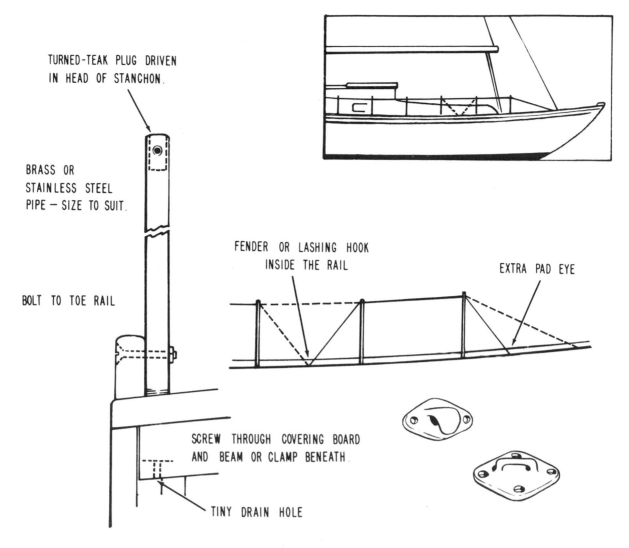

TURNED-TEAK PLUG DRIVEN
IN HEAD OF STANCHON.

BRASS OR
STAINLESS STEEL
PIPE — SIZE TO SUIT.

BOLT TO TOE RAIL

FENDER OR LASHING HOOK
INSIDE THE RAIL

EXTRA PAD EYE

SCREW THROUGH COVERING BOARD
AND BEAM OR CLAMP BENEATH.

TINY DRAIN HOLE

LIFELINE STANCHIONS

Every time I visit Ralph Wiley's yard I come away with a head full of ideas. Ralph's boats have become noted not only for the quality of their construction but also for the novel features he builds into them. Nor are his ideas odd; usually, they are just simpler or better ways of accomplishing certain objectives.

Notice how he has simplified the lifeline stanchions and their fitting, using merely a pipe with its head neatly plugged and lower end threaded for turning through the covering board down into something solid below. Each pipe must be carefully put in, kept erect, and fitted in a watertight way. I have checked such stanchions on boats several years old to find them perfectly

rigid, with no evidence below of water having gone past the threads or even through the small drain hole.

The same sketch shows a simple way of lowering the lifeline for getting on and off the boat at a dock. This method seems to leave the stanchions better supported than where the usual gate is included in the line. As can be seen, it is just a matter of having an extra pad eye aft, located to permit switching the turnbuckle (or possibly a pelican hook) with the line under the hook inside the rail. One can even have an extra hook or so there to give a choice of locations for the gate.

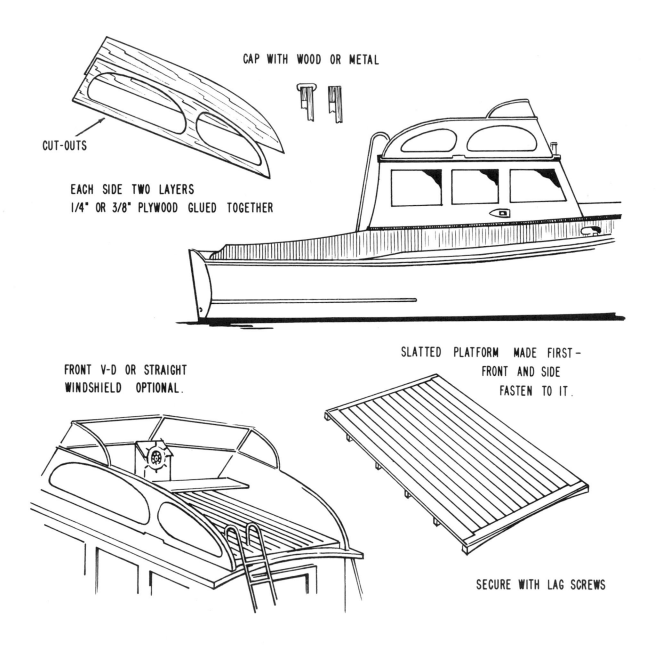

CAP WITH WOOD OR METAL

CUT-OUTS

EACH SIDE TWO LAYERS
1/4" OR 3/8" PLYWOOD GLUED TOGETHER

FRONT V-D OR STRAIGHT
WINDSHIELD OPTIONAL.

SLATTED PLATFORM MADE FIRST —
FRONT AND SIDE
FASTEN TO IT.

SECURE WITH LAG SCREWS

FLYING BRIDGE

Here is a simple but good-looking flying bridge, as seen recently on a boat whose owner told me that the slatted platform was built first to take in the length of deckhouse roof. Then, using common plywood, he experimented with the shape of the sides, finally getting what looked best. In making them up, he used the two-layer type of construction shown in order to get a cut-out effect, which relieves the otherwise-flat surface. The sides, made as a pair, were finally secured to the platform and to a plain front or cross section. If the structure is rather short, such a front looks good, but if the sides are long, a V shape or even making the front slightly round will help. The windshield is optional. Here, the owner made his own, using rectangular-shaped aluminum tubing with a slot along one face for a frame to take heavy glass which had been cut to fit.

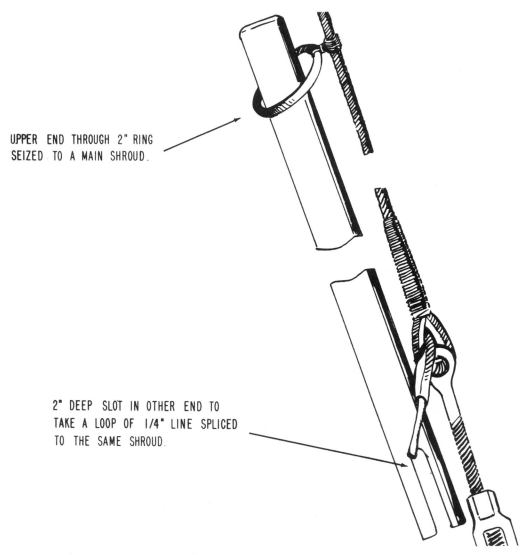

UPPER END THROUGH 2" RING
SEIZED TO A MAIN SHROUD.

2" DEEP SLOT IN OTHER END TO
TAKE A LOOP OF 1/4" LINE SPLICED
TO THE SAME SHROUD.

CARRYING THE SOUNDING POLE

Despite its advantages for shoal-water work, a long sounding pole can be difficult to carry aboard a small boat. Where one can be kept in the main rigging (it will not jump out of place there), the slotted-end method shown can solve the problem, yet leave the pole readily available. A 2-inch galvanized ring, or a proper-size loop of ¼-inch line, is seized aloft to one of the shrouds, a foot or so from the end of the pole, preferably lower than indicated in the sketch. To stow the upended pole, merely shove its tip through this loop, then drop the other slotted end into another slightly larger loop of line secured to the lower section of the same shroud. An intermediate lanyard, attached to the shroud at a point conveniently reached, could also be used to hold the pole to the shroud, but should be required only when heeled under sail in rough going.

Because such a pole is bound to have paint chafed off it, or because its different color may mark the deck, I like to have one, preferably of spruce, either left bare or merely oiled, with the depth marks painted on or marked with distinctive servings of marline. Such markings allow either end of the pole to be used. Soundings are taken by a sort of twirling or end-for-end use of the pole, rather than by merely jabbing it in and out.

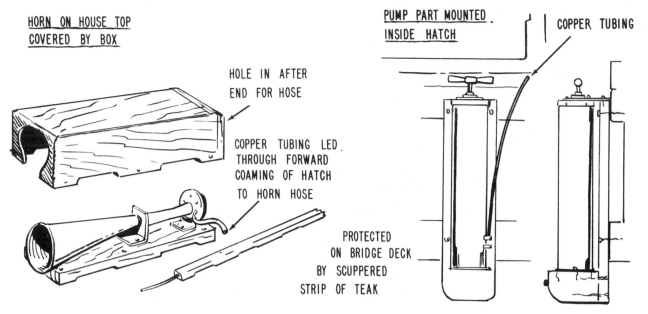

HORN ON HOUSE TOP
COVERED BY BOX

HOLE IN AFTER
END FOR HOSE

COPPER TUBING LED
THROUGH FORWARD
COAMING OF HATCH
TO HORN HOSE

PUMP PART MOUNTED.
INSIDE HATCH

COPPER TUBING

PROTECTED
ON BRIDGE DECK
BY SCUPPERED
STRIP OF TEAK

MOUNTING THE HORN

One of the best buys I have seen in war-surplus products has been an air-type foghorn, the kind which comes mounted on a base and operates tire-pump fashion. Certainly, there is no doubt about its being heard, and it seems well made, with most parts of brass.

Of course, where to carry it presents a problem, for it stands almost 2 feet high and is an unwieldly shape for handling. But this was finally solved, as shown in the illustration.

The outfit was first dismantled—the pump part unbolted from the base or foot piece and the latter discarded, leaving pump and horn as separate units connected only by a short length of rubber hose. The pump, we decided, would best go inside the hatch on the bridge deck, where it would be to one side of the engine and pretty much out of the way, yet convenient to the cockpit. This merely involved mounting it on a piece of ⅞-inch oak with a base attached to take heavy, round-headed screws through the old bolt holes in the lower flange of the pump. Such support is necessary and must be strong, for considerable down pressure is put on the pump in using it. The upper end was then held by using the original bracket or holder, sawed off to fit atop the oak support, and fastened by a couple of screws. The whole thing was then fastened to the deck and cockpit beams with the height such that the sliding screen used in

the hatch would just clear the handle.

The horn, which, of course, had been disconnected by unclamping the hose, was then secured to a piece of 1¼-inch cedar by using the original bracket about its neck and making a small brass one to hold the after end. The base is scuppered to drain and, with its underface dressed to allow for the camber of the housetop, it is made just large enough so that the edges can be used to take the few screws holding the box over the horn. The cover is made of ⅜-inch plywood for the top and sides, with heavy end pieces rabbeted out to take all edges and rounded nicely. The forward end is open, of course, except for the shaped piece added to take away the bare look. While this box may not be necessary, it does prevent lines from fouling the horn and, to my mind, looks better than an exposed horn.

The rubber hose on the horn leads through a hole on the after end of the box, down over the atfer end of the house, and is then connected by means of copper tubing to the pump, where it is again clamped to a short length of hose. Fortunately, we were able to carry the tubing out of the way inside the hatch coaming, out through the forward end and across the bridge deck to the house. Most of it is concealed by rabbeted-out teak strips, with a scuppered or drain-fitted length used on the deck.

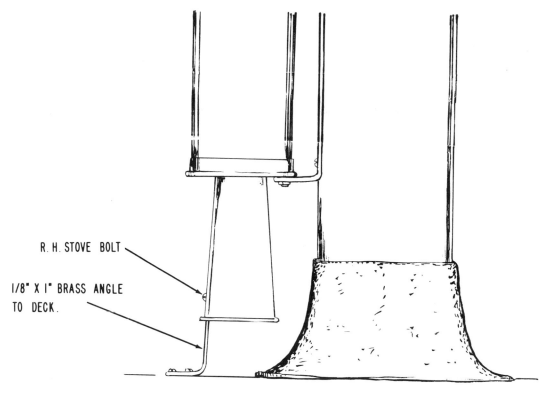

R. H. STOVE BOLT

1/8" X 1" BRASS ANGLE TO DECK.

HORN ON THE MAST

OR

ON THE DECK OR CABINTOP

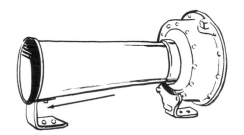

U-SHAPED STRAP WITH ONE BOLT IN HORN AND TWO SCREWS IN DECK.

NONFOULING HORN

To meet present requirements, a mechanically operated horn must be of good size. Where to mount this new piece of equipment becomes a problem. Often it must be placed where it will be sure to foul a halliard and run the risk of being uprooted, should a bight of one get caught beneath it when a sail is being lowered. So, where possible, use a simple brass angle or strap made to suit the installation and secured to the horn with a round-headed stove bolt and to the deck or housetop with a couple of screws. This will serve not only as a guard to prevent lines fouling the horn, but also to stiffen its mounting.

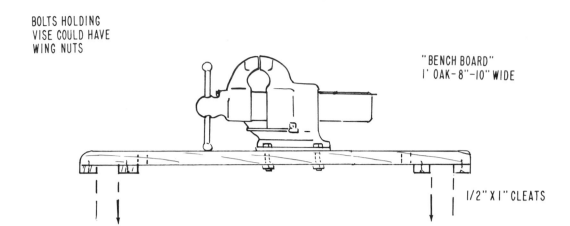

BOLTS HOLDING
VISE COULD HAVE
WING NUTS

"BENCH BOARD"
1" OAK-8"-10" WIDE

1/2" X I" CLEATS

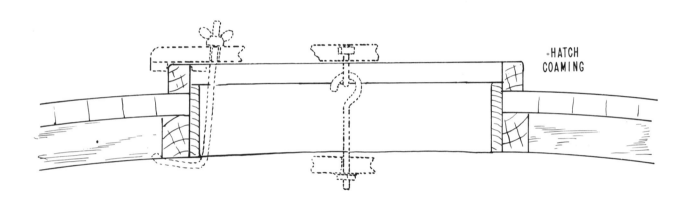

HATCH
COAMING

HOLD DOWN WITH A   OR   ONE THROUGH AN
HOOK-SHAPED BOLT   AN EYE-BOLT WITH A
ON EACH END   CROSSPIECE BELOW

VISE ON BENCHBOARD

A small machinist's vise is handy to have aboard, but on the small boat can hardly be left fastened in one permanent place. If there is a hatch in the bridge deck or the after deck within reach of the cockpit, the bench board shown above can be used. The vise can be left bolted to it, or if wing nuts are used, then board and all can easily be taken off for more convenient stowing. The small cleats beneath take

any twisting strain, and with a hooklike bolt at each end or a single one through a crosspiece beneath, lock the board in place so that one can work at the vise while kneeling in the cockpit.

A refinement not shown would prevent cuttings from dropping below. It consists of a square of stiff canvas large enough to more than cover the hatch opening, placed between the vise and board when the former is fastened down.

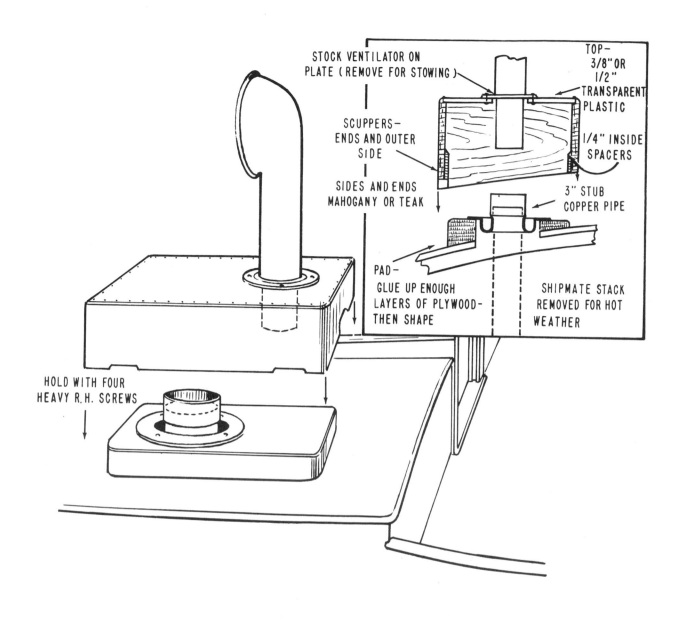

STOCK VENTILATOR ON
PLATE (REMOVE FOR STOWING)

TOP—
3/8" OR
1/2"
TRANSPARENT
PLASTIC

SCUPPERS—
ENDS AND OUTER
SIDE

1/4" INSIDE
SPACERS

SIDES AND ENDS
MAHOGANY OR TEAK

3" STUB
COPPER PIPE

PAD—
GLUE UP ENOUGH
LAYERS OF PLYWOOD-
THEN SHAPE

SHIPMATE STACK
REMOVED FOR HOT
WEATHER

HOLD WITH FOUR
HEAVY R.H. SCREWS

DECK IRON VENTILATORS II

This use made of a dorade-type ventilator on the ketch *Picaroon* is a sensible idea for any boat that· is used early and late in the season. There probably will be a Shipmate range or a coal or wood heater aboard and, naturally, there will be little need for the ventilator. For the hot months, it can be put in place after re-

moving the range's stack and cleaning out the deck iron. It solves the problem of getting air into the closed-up cabin during the week. For, when the boat is in use, it is surprising how much air and light the usual 5-inch opening will let in, right where it is appreciated most.

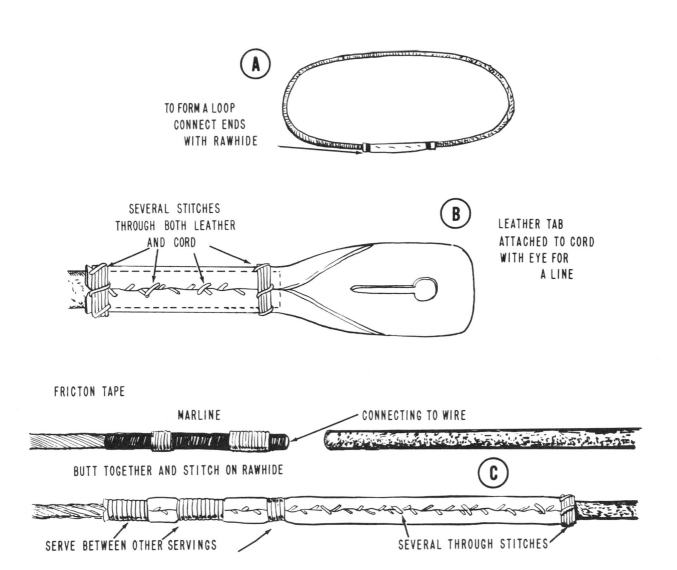

A

TO FORM A LOOP
CONNECT ENDS
WITH RAWHIDE

B

SEVERAL STITCHES
THROUGH BOTH LEATHER
AND CORD

LEATHER TAB
ATTACHED TO CORD
WITH EYE FOR
A LINE

FRICTON TAPE

MARLINE

CONNECTING TO WIRE

BUTT TOGETHER AND STITCH ON RAWHIDE

C

SERVE BETWEEN OTHER SERVINGS

SEVERAL THROUGH STITCHES

HANDLING RUBBER SHOCK CORD

Airplane rubber shock cord can be used in many ways aboard a boat, but it is difficult to join its ends or to attach it to wire or rope and have the job both neat and strong. Using rawhide or other leather seems as good a way as any. *A,* for example, shows a covering used to hold the two butted ends for forming a loop that is handy for holding a canvas hatch or skylight cover. An 8-inch covering should be long enough, if stitched on tightly with neat end whippings and several stitches. Or, on a short length of the cord, handy for keeping the whip out of halliards purposely left slack, both ends

should be fitted with leather tabs, as in *B.* Such cord can even be made to hold wire by connecting, as in *C,* initially using friction tape and a couple of tight marline servings on the wire. Start the covering by stitching it tightly about the wire part, then butt the cord in place, and complete the covering with several stitches taken completely through as you go along. Finish with a neat end whipping. The real holding power comes mostly from several tight marline servings finally applied on top of the covering between those originally put on the wire.

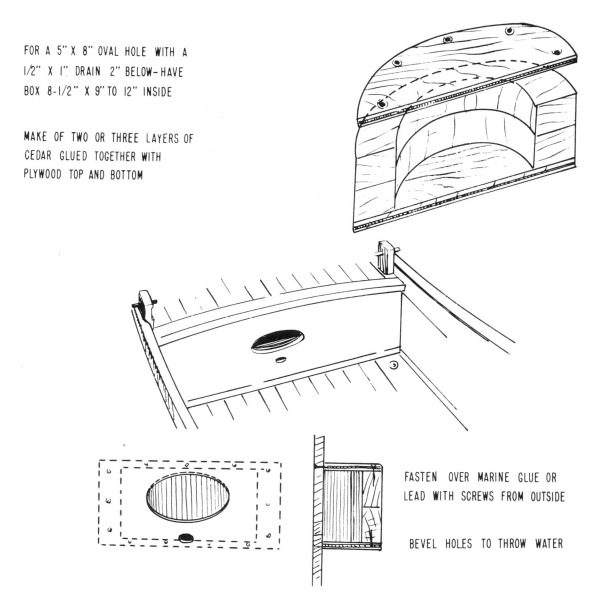

FOR A 5" X 8" OVAL HOLE WITH A
1/2" X 1" DRAIN 2" BELOW—HAVE
BOX 8-1/2" X 9" TO 12" INSIDE

MAKE OF TWO OR THREE LAYERS OF
CEDAR GLUED TOGETHER WITH
PLYWOOD TOP AND BOTTOM

FASTEN OVER MARINE GLUE OR
LEAD WITH SCREWS FROM OUTSIDE

BEVEL HOLES TO THROW WATER

COCKPIT LOCKER

Either a cockpit locker or cubbyhole is a handy place to keep spectacles, notebook and pencil, and other small things without destroying any watertight principle of the cockpit itself.

Make a box about as shown of watertight construction, with its face true for fastening it behind either the after or forward bulkhead of the cockpit, whichever you can get at from behind to get the box in and to hold it in place while it is being fastened.

An oval-shaped opening will look best, and there should be a small drain hole an inch or two below it; the latter to be located exactly at the bottom of the box. Cut these openings before fastening the box in place and bevel the top and bottom edges of the openings, so that rain will drip off and not follow inside.

Accurately mark out for screw holes and drill for them; then, bed the box in marine glue or white lead paste and hold securely in place while fastening from the outside.

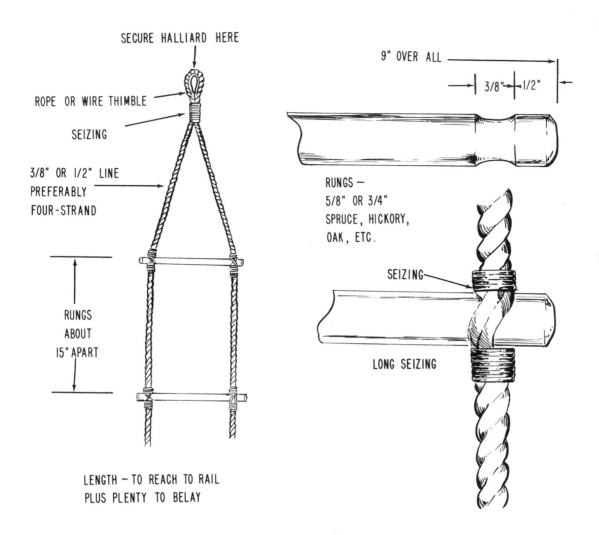

SECURE HALLIARD HERE

ROPE OR WIRE THIMBLE

SEIZING

3/8" OR 1/2" LINE
PREFERABLY
FOUR-STRAND

RUNGS
ABOUT
15" APART

LENGTH — TO REACH TO RAIL
PLUS PLENTY TO BELAY

9" OVER ALL

3/8" 1/2"

RUNGS —
5/8" OR 3/4"
SPRUCE, HICKORY,
OAK, ETC.

SEIZING

LONG SEIZING

ROPE LADDER

Despite their advantages, ratlines hardly suit a modern-type boat. A rope ladder can take their place for many jobs aloft. For certain work, a rope ladder is also much handier than a bosun's chair, particularly where you have to work alone, and it is not cumbersome to stow, if the size of the parts is kept down. Three-eighth-inch manila will usually suffice for the one-piece side lines (½ inch if the boat is large), for there is comparatively little strain on them, but use four-strand rope if obtainable.

The rungs should be of wood, ⅝ to ¾ inch in diameter, according to the size of the boat and the toughness of the wood used. They can be square or round in section, with shallow end grooves cut in with a rasp or knife. Cross grain should be avoided; this is one reason why dowel stock cannot always be used. The length of the ladder should be such that, when it is hoisted aloft, there are enough tails or ends for belaying to the rail, to a sheer pole, or about the lower shrouds to hold the ladder taut.

In making up, pass one end of the line between the strands, then bring it out through another set, and finally seize to hold the thimble in place. Slip each end of a rung between the strands to have them an even distance, around 15 inches apart. Bed them well into the groove by seizing above and below; the lower seizing, naturally, is the more important. In stowing the ladder, avoid tangling by rolling it up and passing a line around the roll.

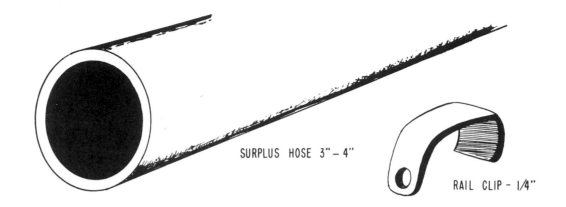

SURPLUS HOSE 3" – 4"

RAIL CLIP – 1/4"

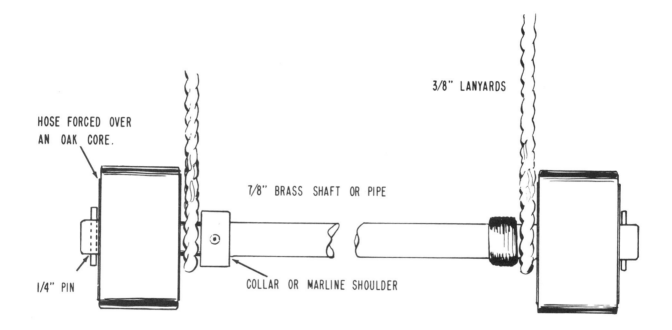

HOSE FORCED OVER
AN OAK CORE.

3/8" LANYARDS

7/8" BRASS SHAFT OR PIPE

1/4" PIN

COLLAR OR MARLINE SHOULDER

FENDER AND LADDER

This is an improvement on a friend's use of fish-net corks and several lengths of ½-inch galvanized rod to make a swimming ladder that is easy to stow. After picking up a short length of heavy 4-inch hose in a surplus store and finding that its black did not rub off, he visualized different uses for it. One was to cut several 3- or 4-inch lengths and force them over an oak core drilled with a hole to take a length of rod. But why not make it a piece of used bronze

shafting? The extra weight would be advantageous and would be strong enough so that a pair of the rollers could be used as a fender board to protect the boat's topsides against a rough pile. He made three pairs, which gives him that many fenders. When connected by their lanyards, the three provide a swimming ladder long enough for one rung to be below the water. The weight of the ladder keeps it in place.

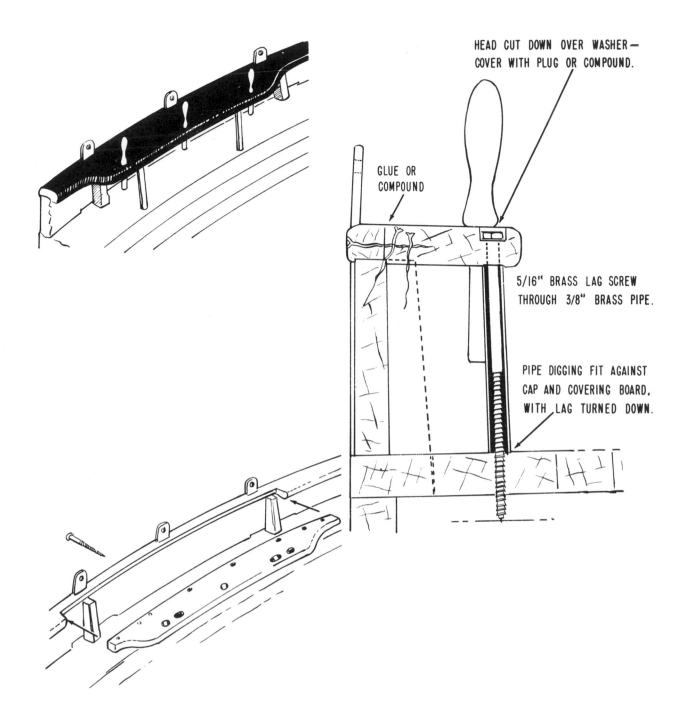

HEAD CUT DOWN OVER WASHER— COVER WITH PLUG OR COMPOUND.

GLUE OR COMPOUND

5/16" BRASS LAG SCREW THROUGH 3/8" BRASS PIPE.

PIPE DIGGING FIT AGAINST CAP AND COVERING BOARD, WITH LAG TURNED DOWN.

RAIL CAP EXTENSION

This idea was recently observed on a ketch. The rail caps in the way of the forward and after rigging were swollen out to relieve the plainness of its straight run and to allow pins to be used for the lighter halliards of the running rigging.

Installation was merely a matter of cutting out a section of the actual cap, as shown, and then making a shaped section to go in its place. On another boat, the job would have to be done to suit the particular bulwark construction.

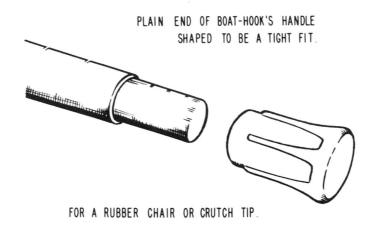

PLAIN END OF BOAT-HOOK'S HANDLE
SHAPED TO BE A TIGHT FIT.

FOR A RUBBER CHAIR OR CRUTCH TIP.

RUBBER SHOD BOATHOOK

Above is a rubber chair or crutch tip to slip on and off the inboard or plain end of the handle of the boat hook. It can be left off or used, according to the situation. The rubber-shod tip, when holding off another boat, will be much easier on the other fellow's paint. And even when shoving off from a dock or piling, the rubber is better because it is not so apt to slip.

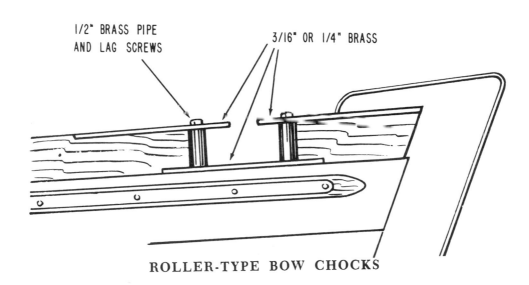

1/2" BRASS PIPE AND LAG SCREWS

3/16" OR 1/4" BRASS

ROLLER-TYPE BOW CHOCKS

This type of bow chock is both efficient and low in cost. Where observed on the raised deck sloop *Sea Way*, the lower brass plate was V-shaped and was carried right across inside the stem head to serve as the lower plate for both chocks. The pipe rollers should be a turning fit on their lags, and the outer corners of the plate should be rounded off to avoid cutting the line.

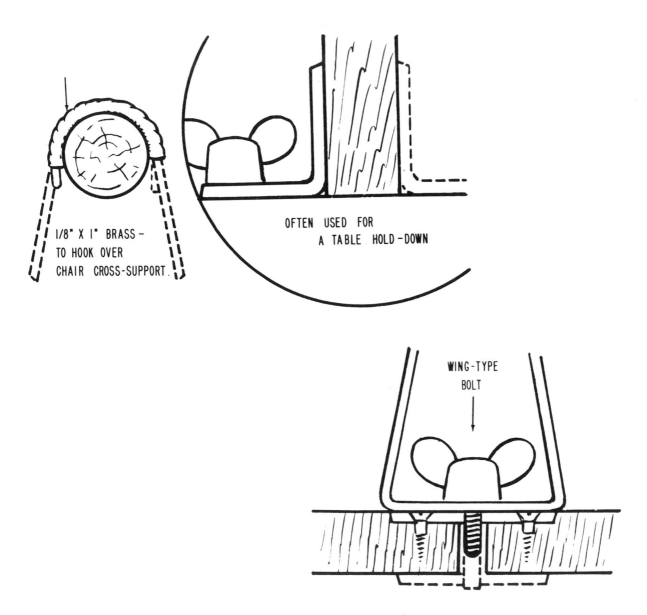

1/8" X 1" BRASS –
TO HOOK OVER
CHAIR CROSS-SUPPORT.

OFTEN USED FOR
A TABLE HOLD-DOWN

WING-TYPE
BOLT

1/8" BRASS PLATE SET FLUSH IN FLOOR,
ANOTHER BENEATH, IF POSSIBLE.

HOLD-DOWN PLATES

Brass plates let into carefully decided locations in the cabin sole are not a bad idea. Used with wing bolts they will be handy for holding down a table or other pieces of furniture. For instance, a chair of the folding type secured in whatever location seems best, and held in place this way, will behave itself in hard going. Otherwise, there is always the chance that it will take charge of the boat, unless secured with a lanyard.

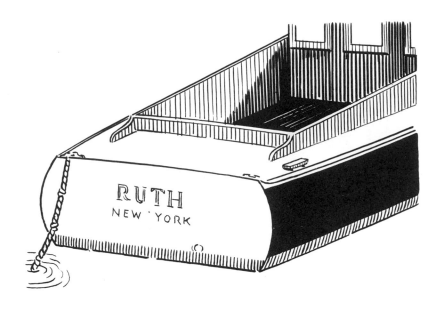

KNOTTED LINE OVER STERN

There is nothing new about this idea of the knotted line over the stern, but it bears repeating as a good safety precaution. A well-made-up line should have an eye splice that will just go over a quarter-cleat, and in addition to several knots should reach far enough below the water that a nonswimmer, or a poor one, who may be over the side can get his foot into a stirruplike loop spliced in the other end and clamber back aboard unaided.

CHAPTER 7

Below Deck

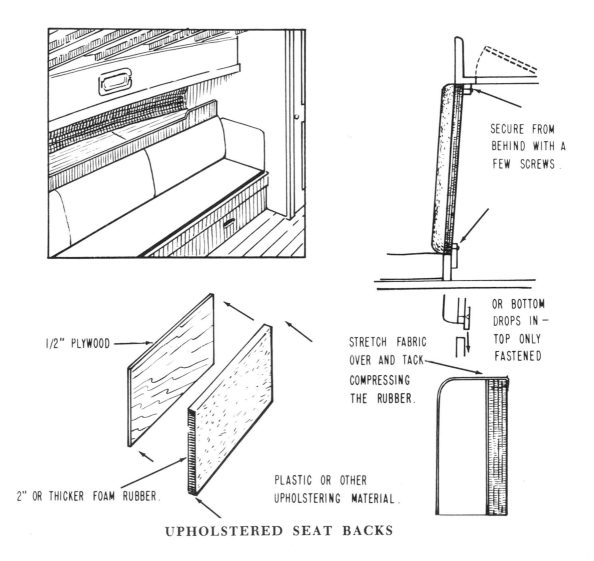

1/2" PLYWOOD

2" OR THICKER FOAM RUBBER.

SECURE FROM BEHIND WITH A FEW SCREWS.

STRETCH FABRIC OVER AND TACK COMPRESSING THE RUBBER.

OR BOTTOM DROPS IN — TOP ONLY FASTENED

PLASTIC OR OTHER UPHOLSTERING MATERIAL.

UPHOLSTERED SEAT BACKS

If your settee or bunk layout is suitable, padded or upholstered back and ends are quite comfortable and improve the appearance of a cabin or deckhouse. To install them, the main requirement is some way of supporting the units and holding them in place. A common way is to depend on the usual shelf above the berth, as shown. The shelf should be such that the back can be mounted at a slight slant. In a deckhouse, where the back can often be secured to a bulkhead, a 1- or 2-inch strip can be used to back the panel at the bottom to give the desired slant. Ends ordinarily look best if kept straight up and down.

While a one-part back *can* be used, the three-section type is more easily made and, I think, looks better. Sometimes one can hinge the cen-

ter section in order to get at the storage space behind. As shown, the sections are more or less permanently fastened, each being held by four screws driven from behind. The screws for the ends are put in from inside the adjoining locker or toilet room and those for the back through the removable sections of the shelf.

The customary way of making the padded sections is simply to cut pieces of plywood and lay foam rubber over them, usually with a few daubs of glue to keep it from working down. Then, stretch on the covering material, tacking it from the back. If a rather lightweight fabric is used, stretch on canvas first, then the actual covering. Use your own judgment as to how much to compress the rubber. The stiffer the foam rubber, the better.

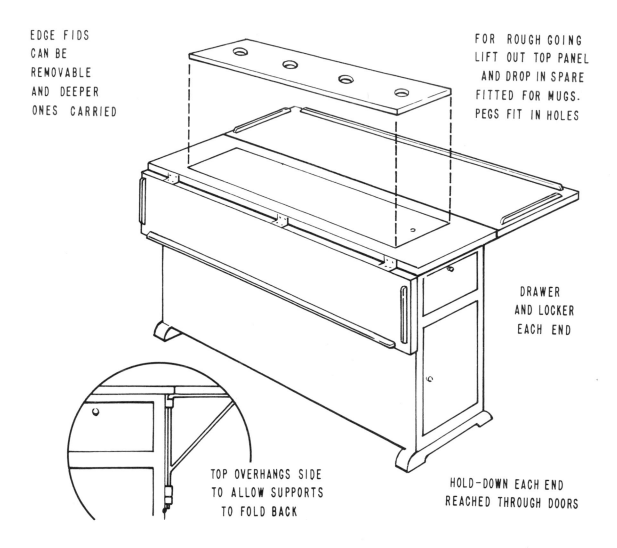

EDGE FIDS
CAN BE
REMOVABLE
AND DEEPER
ONES CARRIED

FOR ROUGH GOING
LIFT OUT TOP PANEL
AND DROP IN SPARE
FITTED FOR MUGS.
PEGS FIT IN HOLES

DRAWER
AND LOCKER
EACH END

TOP OVERHANGS SIDE
TO ALLOW SUPPORTS
TO FOLD BACK

HOLD-DOWN EACH END
REACHED THROUGH DOORS

BOX-TYPE TABLE

This box-type table, noticed aboard an old-but-lovely cruiser, has at least two worthwhile features, and, although the size has to be reduced to suit one's floor space, both could be used. The base allows space for a drawer and linen locker, with a shelf in each end so that their contents are more accessible. The rather wide top permits the spare or rough-weather panel arrangement. This removable panel is made as large as the size of the top permits. The spare one, the same size, can be fitted with holes for mugs or glasses and small holes to take pegs that can be placed as required to hold other items in place.

The drop leaves can be made to suit and may have their corners sharp or rounded. If deeper-edge fids or rails about the edges are wanted, the top of the table should be kept a good inch lower than usual to allow for the rough-weather set being 1½ or more inches high. The top and leaves should be made heavy enough to take the greater strain of brass-rod pegs dropped into brass-pipe bushed holes. A hold-down arrangement at each end, easily reached through the end doors, holds the table down to flush floor fittings. One set is below for use in spring and fall, and another set is in the deckhouse floor for setting up the table there in warm weather.

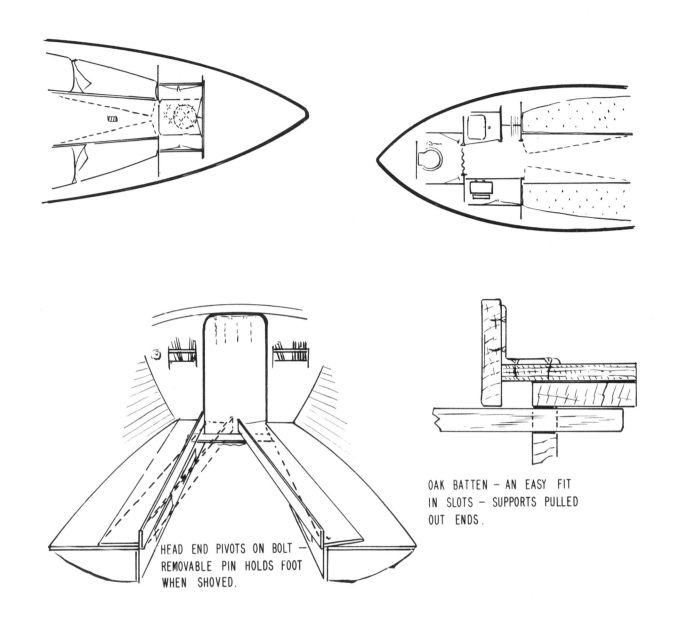

OAK BATTEN – AN EASY FIT
IN SLOTS – SUPPORTS PULLED
OUT ENDS.

HEAD END PIVOTS ON BOLT –
REMOVABLE PIN HOLDS FOOT
WHEN SHOVED.

WIDENING A BERTH

The simplest way to widen out a narrow berth, or a pair of berths, is to fit what is called a "jackknife extension." Quite often, the after end of a berth is wide enough, but the foot is too narrow for the berth to be entirely comfortable. Such an extension is merely a width of ½-inch plywood, or a slightly heavier regular board, fitted with a retainer for the cushion and having its after end pivoting on a bolt which holds it in place. By removing a pin, the other end is made free to be pulled out; the board and its mate for the other side can be supported by a batten slipped into slots cut in the seat fronts. When the berth cushion is slid forward, a long, wedge-shaped space is left behind it; but excess bedding can be laid in there or a cushion can be made to fit the space.

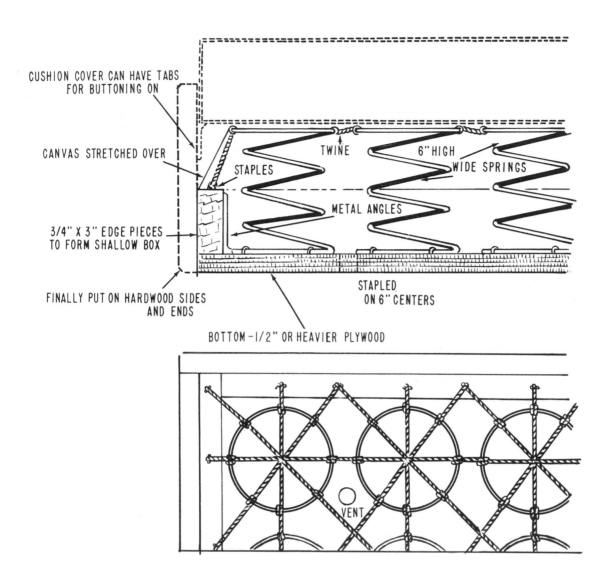

CUSHION COVER CAN HAVE TABS
FOR BUTTONING ON

CANVAS STRETCHED OVER

STAPLES

TWINE

6" HIGH
WIDE SPRINGS

METAL ANGLES

3/4" X 3" EDGE PIECES
TO FORM SHALLOW BOX

FINALLY PUT ON HARDWOOD SIDES
AND ENDS

STAPLED
ON 6" CENTERS

BOTTOM — 1/2" OR HEAVIER PLYWOOD

VENT

BOX SPRINGS

Glen Campbell says he has found that box springs, made as shown and used with a light cushion, make much more comfortable berths than his old mattresses alone. In his 35-foot cruiser he has them on both lowers and uppers, the latter the usual hinged-type that serve as back rests during the day. He says this type of construction is particularly satisfactory in such a case.

The box can be made any desired shape—rectangular or to fit an odd-shaped space. Four ½-inch holes should be bored in the bottom for ventilation and to allow impounded air to escape when the berth is sat upon. The 6-inch-high coil springs should be what are called the "soft-wide-center" type, obtainable at upholstery supply places. Fasten them to the wood bottom with staples. Then use stout twine to tie the springs, pulling the ends down to staples driven in the edges of the shallow sides and ends of the box. Next, stretch 6- or 8-ounce canvas over and tack the edges. The hardwood sides and ends can then be put on.

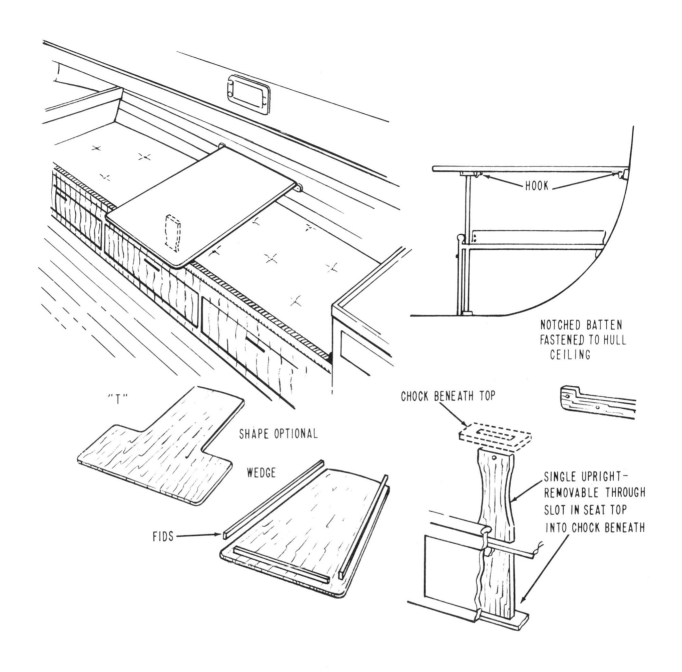

"T"

SHAPE OPTIONAL

WEDGE

FIDS

HOOK

NOTCHED BATTEN
FASTENED TO HULL
CEILING

CHOCK BENEATH TOP

SINGLE UPRIGHT—
REMOVABLE THROUGH
SLOT IN SEAT TOP
INTO CHOCK BENEATH

OVER-THE-SETTEE TABLE

This lunchroom-type table is as good as any for a small boat. It can be quickly set up or taken down, it is rigid when in use, and it can be made longer to seat a third person on a stool. The top is shown as a single piece, but to make stowing simpler it is sometimes made in two parts, hinged lengthwise. Then, two battens beneath, made to pivot to engage holders on the opposite leaf, hold the top flat for setting up, usually on a pair of uprights rather than on the single one shown.

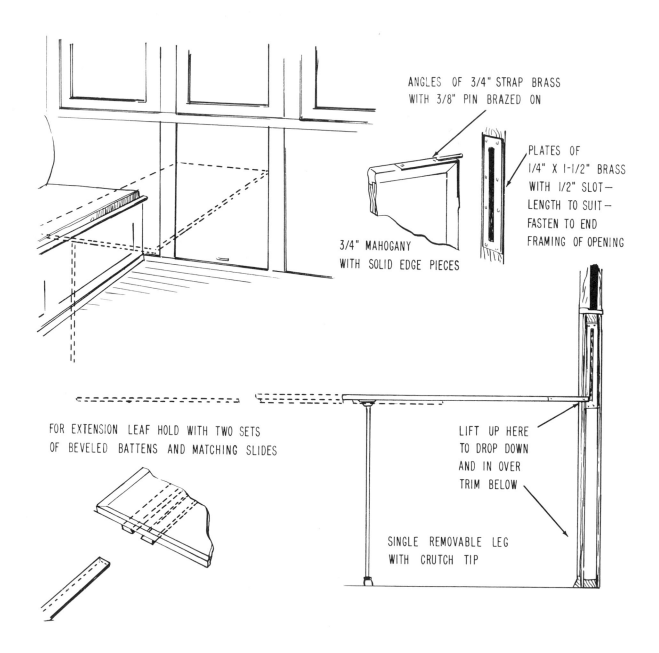

ANGLES OF 3/4" STRAP BRASS
WITH 3/8" PIN BRAZED ON

PLATES OF
1/4" X 1-1/2" BRASS
WITH 1/2" SLOT—
LENGTH TO SUIT—
FASTEN TO END
FRAMING OF OPENING

3/4" MAHOGANY
WITH SOLID EDGE PIECES

FOR EXTENSION LEAF HOLD WITH TWO SETS
OF BEVELED BATTENS AND MATCHING SLIDES

LIFT UP HERE
TO DROP DOWN
AND IN OVER
TRIM BELOW

SINGLE REMOVABLE LEG
WITH CRUTCH TIP

IN-THE-WALL TABLE

I recently came across this table arrangement on a power cruiser. The owner told me that, in framing up, the deckhouse allowance was made for the opening in which the table would be built. Notice that it is out of the way and practically unnoticeable when not in use. To set it up, the lower end is lifted just enough to free it; then, it is raised and the upper end is eased down into place. Although supported only by a pipe leg, the table is quite secure. The length of the leaf is whatever the height of the deckhouse side will allow. In this case, an extra 2-foot extension leaf has been used, attached by means of two sets of beveled battens and slides. Such a leaf should have its own leg, even though it need not always be used.

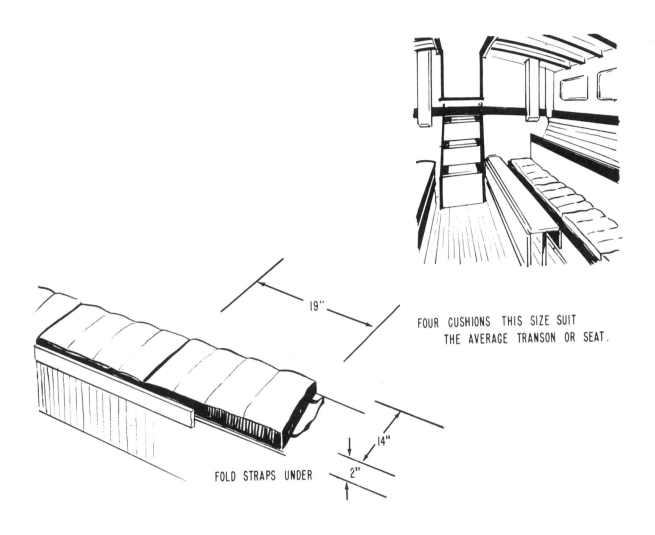

FOUR CUSHIONS THIS SIZE SUIT
THE AVERAGE TRANSON OR SEAT.

19"

14"

2"

FOLD STRAPS UNDER

DUAL-PURPOSE CUSHIONS

I was aboard a ketch recently where the life-preserver or safety-type cushions serve a double purpose. The owner likes to carry four of them, a number which would ordinarily be a nuisance to stow, he explained. What he did was to look around to find a size and shape of cushion that would suit his cabin transom settee. There may be other manufacturers of this 19-inch long size, but Tapatco's "Fisherman's Pride" style is the one used. With the kapok sealed in vinyl inserts, the cushions are quite comfortable to use and should stand up well. The width, which, when compressed, fills in a 15- or 16-inch space, is just right for the average transom. This idea should also be a good one for an outboard cruiser with narrow berths.

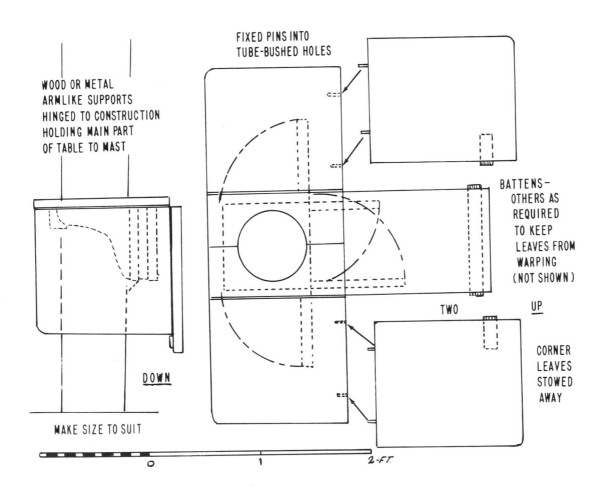

FIXED PINS INTO
TUBE-BUSHED HOLES

WOOD OR METAL
ARMLIKE SUPPORTS
HINGED TO CONSTRUCTION
HOLDING MAIN PART
OF TABLE TO MAST

BATTENS—
OTHERS AS
REQUIRED
TO KEEP
LEAVES FROM
WARPING
(NOT SHOWN)

TWO   UP

DOWN

CORNER
LEAVES
STOWED
AWAY

MAKE SIZE TO SUIT

0   1   2-FT.

MAST-HELD TABLE

The table idea shown above is used on the cutter *Vaeringer II* and works well wherever a mast is convenient for its mounting. It takes up a minimum of floor room and affords excellent top or dining space when up. The size should be to suit your boat, the floor width, and so on, but the principle is to provide a good solid base about the mast atop which the small main section can be fastened and the hinged arms to support the leaves can be secured. Three leaves are permanently hinged, while the two corner leaves are separate, being slipped into place after the main ones are raised. Their pins merely slip into holes, with the tips of the batten beneath the center leaf holding up their ends. The play of the pins in their holes and the length of battens left extending must be experimented with until the corner leaves will just slip into place. Buttons or hooks beneath do not seem necessary, although either might be used.

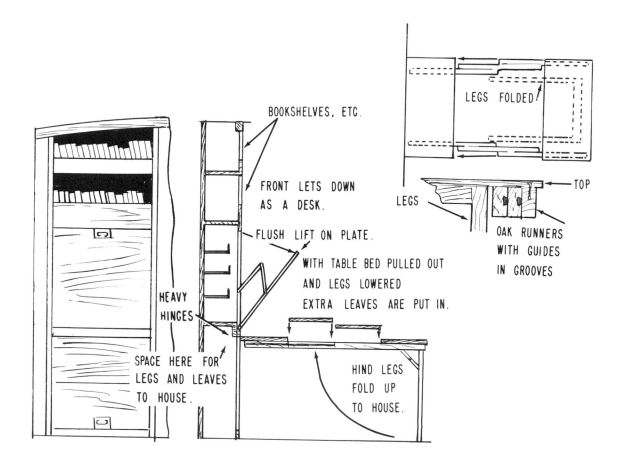

BOOKSHELVES, ETC.

FRONT LETS DOWN
AS A DESK.

FLUSH LIFT ON PLATE.

WITH TABLE BED PULLED OUT
AND LEGS LOWERED
EXTRA LEAVES ARE PUT IN.

HEAVY
HINGES

SPACE HERE FOR
LEGS AND LEAVES
TO HOUSE.

HIND LEGS
FOLD UP
TO HOUSE.

LEGS FOLDED

TOP

LEGS

OAK RUNNERS
WITH GUIDES
IN GROOVES

DESK-AND-TABLE ARRANGEMENT

The desk-and-table arrangement shown here is a good one to use, if your boat has enough beam or width of cabin sole to give 18 or more inches of bulkhead space, preferably at the foot of one of the settees or transom seats. It can then be built in flush, as it was on the motor sailer *Lady Luck,* where I saw it. Or, it can be added as a separate unit not to project more than 8 inches from the bulkhead, if space is a problem.

In any case, the width of the table should be in accordance with the size of the boat and the bulkhead space available. The height of the table top from the cabin sole should, of course, suit the seat that will come along one side of it.

The upper leaf of the table should be strongly hinged, and both the upper and lower ones should be attached to a pair of oak runners. Between these another pair is fitted with glued-on splines or guides sliding in matching grooves. The pair of legs is hinged as a U-shaped unit to the outer leaf, and both should have folding bracket fittings to hold them rigid when down. Also, there should be stops or hooks to prevent the top from being pulled out farther when the extra leaves have been put in.

If everything is right, setting up the table should be merely a matter of raising the lift and then dropping the legs down and pulling out the top, putting in any extra leaves required. The reverse of this procedure should put the table away. The extra leaves can be stowed in padded chocks in the same compartment.

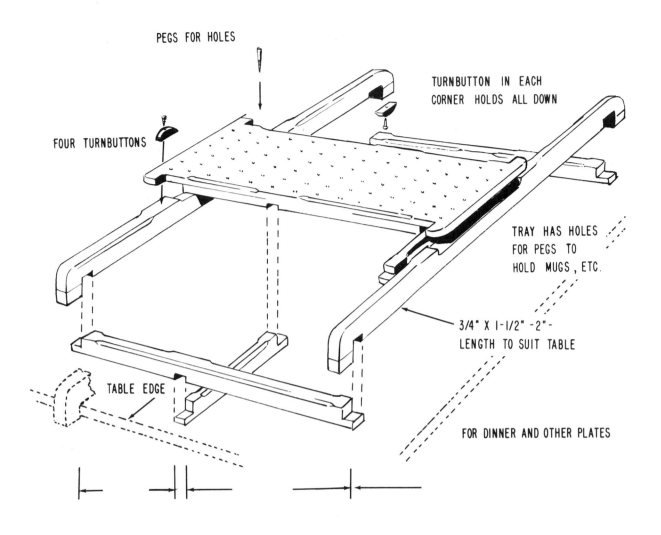

PEGS FOR HOLES

TURNBUTTON IN EACH
CORNER HOLDS ALL DOWN

FOUR TURNBUTTONS

TRAY HAS HOLES
FOR PEGS TO
HOLD MUGS, ETC.

3/4" X 1-1/2" -2"-
LENGTH TO SUIT TABLE

TABLE EDGE

FOR DINNER AND OTHER PLATES

TABLE RACK

Very intricate arrangements on the cabin table seem an affectation aboard the usual boat, because so few serious meals are eaten under way. The removable type shown does give effective holding when it is needed and can be stowed out of the way at other times. The two side pieces should be long enough so that their lug ends will drop down over the edges of the table to be held there by turnbuttons in each corner. Width should be to suit whatever dishes you'll want to use (the fewer the better). In this case, dinner and bread-and-butter plates are provided for two diners in large and small compartments on each side.

The diameter of the plates, an inch of play for each, and the thickness of the division determines the inside measurement between sides and gives length of end pieces holding sides apart. In assembling for use, ends are laid first, then sides; divisions are shoved under into their notches and the tray is dropped in place to hold other ends of divisions; four small turnbuttons hold the tray down and lock all into place. In the set we use, the tray is bored with two holes to take heavy mugs and there is still enough room between for a series of holes into which pegs can be shoved. Enough of these are used to hold whatever dish is wanted.

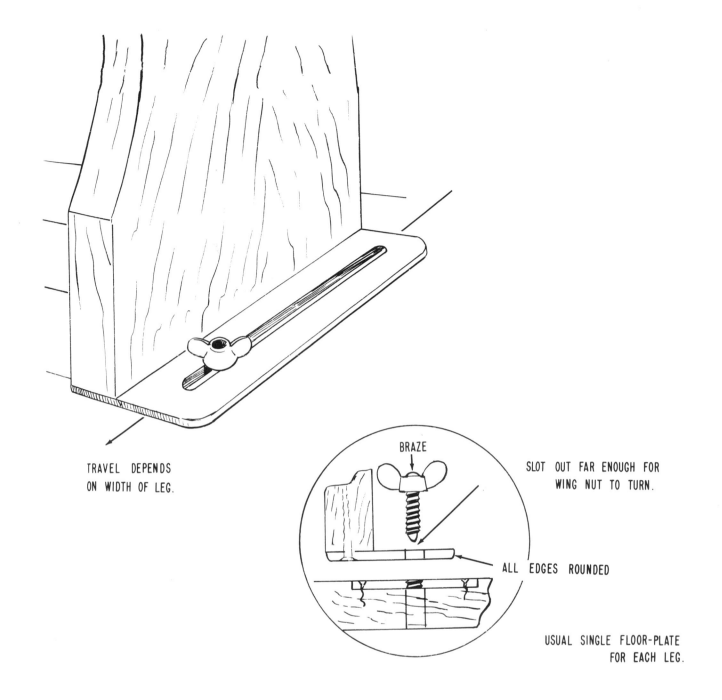

TRAVEL DEPENDS
ON WIDTH OF LEG.

BRAZE

SLOT OUT FAR ENOUGH FOR
WING NUT TO TURN.

ALL EDGES ROUNDED

USUAL SINGLE FLOOR-PLATE
FOR EACH LEG.

ADJUSTABLE TABLE BASE

The illustration shows a table-base arrangement suggested by George Haldimand, who uses it on his cutter so that the table can be shifted closer to the settee to increase floor space at other than meal times. He tried pieces of brass angle first, but the slot, which must be kept far enough out for the wing nut to turn, left little metal outside it. The brass plates used should be fastened with long screws. The threaded length of rod, or cutoff bolt, brazed in the wing nut should have its end ground "finder"-fashion, although actually it is slacked off only enough to allow the table to be slid in or out. The edges of the plates should be rounded, so that they will not mar the cabin sole.

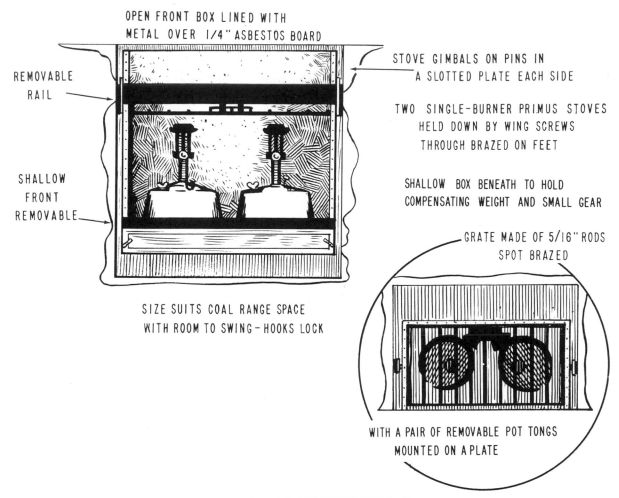

OPEN FRONT BOX LINED WITH
METAL OVER 1/4" ASBESTOS BOARD

STOVE GIMBALS ON PINS IN
A SLOTTED PLATE EACH SIDE

REMOVABLE
RAIL

TWO SINGLE-BURNER PRIMUS STOVES
HELD DOWN BY WING SCREWS
THROUGH BRAZED ON FEET

SHALLOW
FRONT
REMOVABLE

SHALLOW BOX BENEATH TO HOLD
COMPENSATING WEIGHT AND SMALL GEAR

GRATE MADE OF 5/16" RODS
SPOT BRAZED

SIZE SUITS COAL RANGE SPACE
WITH ROOM TO SWING-HOOKS LOCK

WITH A PAIR OF REMOVABLE POT TONGS
MOUNTED ON A PLATE

STOVE ARRANGEMENTS I

The stove arrangement shown above was worked out by Dick Parsons, who says it has behaved satisfactorily in quite rough going. His idea was to have a stove which would be usable under all conditions and which would adjust itself to any reasonable angle of heel. He also wanted the advantages of two wholly independent burners

Because he uses a coal range in spring and fall and takes it out in warm weather, this stove was made to fit the insulated space, which predetermined the length of the metal and asbestos-lined box; its depth from front to back and its height were kept down to permit swinging. The pair of single-burner, Primus-type stoves was fastened to the bottom of this by wing-headed screws, which went through the brazed-on feet of each stove. This permits removing the stoves,

something that is necessary only for servicing them or for cleaning the space; a special funnel allows refilling them in place. The stout grate has a pair of removable pot tongs for use when needed, but the deep-front rail and the height of the box suffice for ordinary cooking.

While a compensating weight could have been merely bolted beneath the box proper, it should be noted that there is a shallow box or locker for that purpose and for the stowage of odd stove gear. Because it was necessary to experiment to get the weight just right, it is not certain just how much lead was used. It was found that, by spreading out the lead, using several pieces held by bolts through the bottom, the stove remained steadier than when a single piece was used.

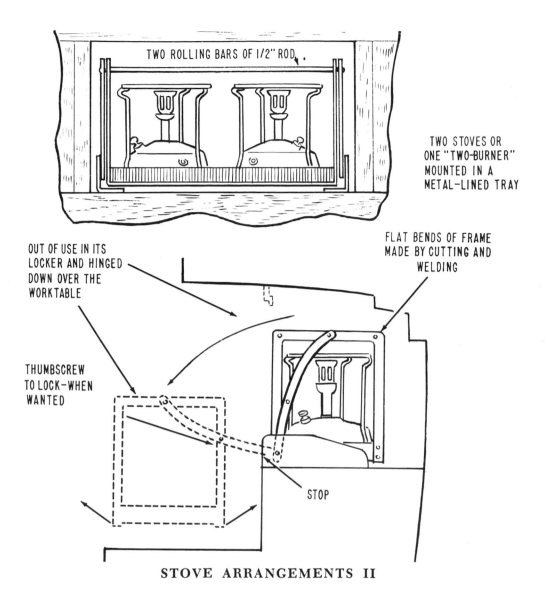

TWO ROLLING BARS OF 1/2" ROD.

TWO STOVES OR
ONE "TWO-BURNER"
MOUNTED IN A
METAL-LINED TRAY

OUT OF USE IN ITS
LOCKER AND HINGED
DOWN OVER THE
WORKTABLE

FLAT BENDS OF FRAME
MADE BY CUTTING AND
WELDING

THUMBSCREW
TO LOCK—WHEN
WANTED

STOP

STOVE ARRANGEMENTS II

This stove arrangement, which I saw recently aboard the ketch *Circe,* has several interesting features. No doubt a two-burner stove could be used instead of the pair of single Primus-type burners shown, but the owner prefers the latter because he feels that one or the other of the units will always be in working order. Tank or pump failure in the usual two-burner stove with its single tank can, as he points out, make both burners useless. Also, he prefers either the old roarer form of burner or the silent kind requiring pricking, claiming these are more reliable than the self-pricking heads which most two-burner pressure kerosene stoves require.

In any case, as shown, the two stoves are fastened in a demountable way in a shallow, metal-lined tray which is encased by a frame having U-shaped ends. These take a pair of rolling bars and, at the balancing points, pins pivoting the frame to the pair of arms. The other ends are pivoted to base plates attached to the bottom of the locker, in which the stove stows when out of use.

To be used, the stove is merely pulled out to drop down over the worktable below the locker. If there is room, space can be allowed for swinging to adjust to the boat's heel under sail; otherwise, it can be arranged to drop down solidly on the table top.

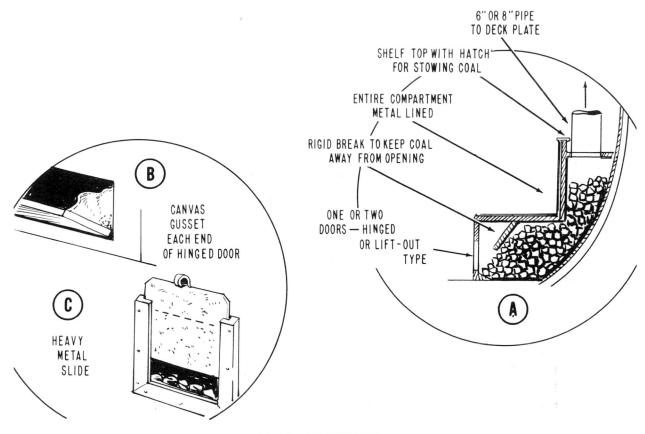

6" OR 8" PIPE
TO DECK PLATE

SHELF TOP WITH HATCH
FOR STOWING COAL

ENTIRE COMPARTMENT
METAL LINED

RIGID BREAK TO KEEP COAL
AWAY FROM OPENING

ONE OR TWO
DOORS — HINGED
OR LIFT-OUT
TYPE

CANVAS
GUSSET
EACH END
OF HINGED DOOR

B

C

HEAVY
METAL
SLIDE

A

COAL BUNKERS

A proper coal bunker can be a great convenience, but it is not easy to build. In planning the location, the effect of the weight of the coal on the trim of the boat must be considered, particularly where the bunker must be outboard with the range mounted over it. The combined weight can be compensated for in the placement of other things or by trimming ballast. Where a fill pipe can be led to the deck, refilling will not dirty up the cabin, but the pipe must be large enough to prevent the coal from clogging it. When filling must be done from inside the boat, the top of the bunker is often made as a shelf at stove-top height, or higher, with a sizable hatch.

Even when a bunker of any size has a fill pipe, there should be some way of stowing the coal from below, in order to utilize the full space. Figure *A* shows this shelf-top type, with a pipe for filling from outside and a small hatch for inside stowing. The whole thing is metal lined, with tight joints so that dust will not get out.

The bottom of the bunker is as important as its top; here, a shovel front is shown. A break made of a 1-inch board, its ends and top well-secured, is fitted across the space to keep the weight of the coal from the opening and to permit getting coal out without having it run through the door. A wedge-shaped strip should be secured to the bottom of the bunker, with its top surface just below the opening, and there should be enough space between this, or between the bottom and the edge of the break above, to draw out a good shovelful of coal.

Where the bunker is wide, two doors rather than a single one are sometimes fitted. When the coal locker is small, a gusset-type door, as shown in *B*, is sometimes used, the canvas ends tending to keep dust in. Another common type of door is the metal-slide style (*C*). This works well if the space is small or if the lower part of the bunker leading to it is tapered. However, there should be the slanted break to prevent the weight of the coal from jamming the slide.

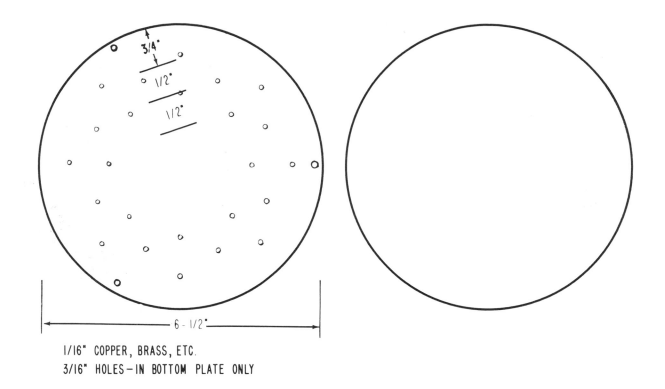

3/4"

1/2"

1/2"

6 - 1/2"

1/16" COPPER, BRASS, ETC.
3/16" HOLES—IN BOTTOM PLATE ONLY

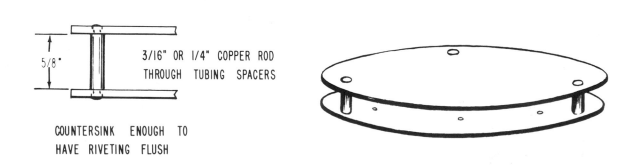

5/8"

3/16" OR 1/4" COPPER ROD
THROUGH TUBING SPACERS

COUNTERSINK ENOUGH TO
HAVE RIVETING FLUSH

PRIMUS PLATES

I have used different gadgets for cutting down the heat of my Primus stove's burner, but by far the best is one given me by a friend who made up several of them. Such a stove, as do some other types, operates best at full flame. Carbon accumulates and gives trouble if the flame is kept low for any length of time when slow cooking is necessary. Most discs sold for the purpose seem to confine the hot flame too much, a fact which does not help the burner any. This simple type does its job well and, at the same time, is easy on the stove and the pot being used. In making one, it is important to have the spacing of the plates as shown and the twenty-seven vent holes of the right size.

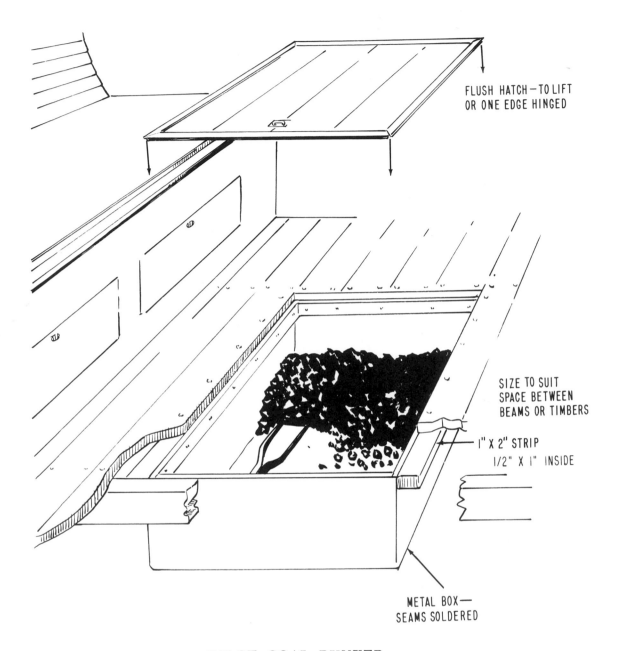

FLUSH HATCH—TO LIFT
OR ONE EDGE HINGED

SIZE TO SUIT
SPACE BETWEEN
BEAMS OR TIMBERS

1" X 2" STRIP
1/2" X 1" INSIDE

METAL BOX—
SEAMS SOLDERED

BILGE COAL BUNKER

The built-in-the-floor type coal bunker shown above works out well where a regular bunker is not built into the boat. It is easy to install and takes advantage of what is usually waste space. As installed on the ketch *Pilgrim* to hold coal for the cabin fireplace, this is simply a metal box long enough to fit between a pair of floor beams, with width and depth to suit the space beneath.

Although coal seems to burn as well wet as dry, the corner seams should be soldered. To keep coal dust out of the bilge, the inside strips which hold the box to the beams and the headers between them should be securely screw-fastened. They also act as stops to keep the hatch flush.

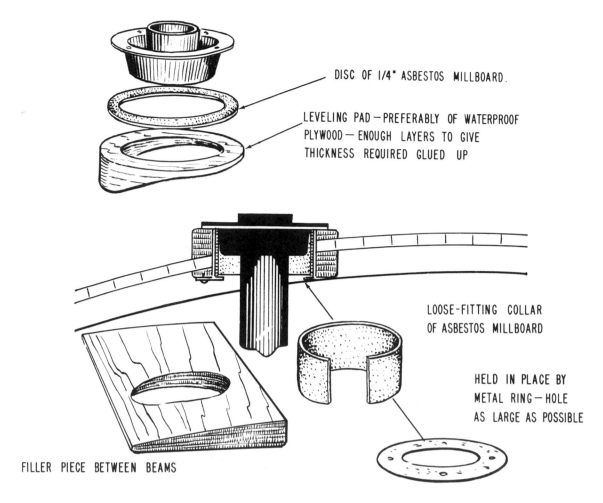

DISC OF 1/4" ASBESTOS MILLBOARD.

LEVELING PAD — PREFERABLY OF WATERPROOF PLYWOOD — ENOUGH LAYERS TO GIVE THICKNESS REQUIRED GLUED UP

LOOSE-FITTING COLLAR OF ASBESTOS MILLBOARD

HELD IN PLACE BY METAL RING — HOLE AS LARGE AS POSSIBLE

FILLER PIECE BETWEEN BEAMS

FITTING A WATER DECK IRON

On the ketch *Dulcie,* a boat where great pains have been taken to make even the little things right, the mounting of the water deck iron for the cabin-heating stove gives a safe and neat job. The iron itself is of bronze, which is being used more now, perhaps because some boat yards and supply houses have made patterns for the most-used sizes and can have them cast at low cost by a small foundry. The iron goes atop a ring of ¼-inch asbestos millboard, and both are fastened down on the usual wood pad which has been shaped to allow for the camber of the housetop. Waterproof plywood is used for this. Enough layers of whatever thickness is available are glued together with resin-type glue to give the total thickness required. The shape is then sawed out on a bandsaw.

The different parts should be well-bedded down. If Johns-Manville asbestos board is used, the trimmed edge can be satisfactorily painted. It will soak up a good deal of paint, but with several coats it can be sealed smooth and the fibers seemingly hardened.

The hole in the housetop is, as usual, kept as large as the fastening holes in the deck iron will permit. The unit is finished off below, with a filler piece between the beams. This allows space for an asbestos collar made by carefully rolling a piece of the board into such a shape that it will spring out and hold itself in place. A stainless steel ring, as shown, will lock the collar permanently in place. It is important that the inner diameter of the ring be no larger than is necessary to hold the edges of the collar; the more air that can get into the space, the better will be the protection afforded.

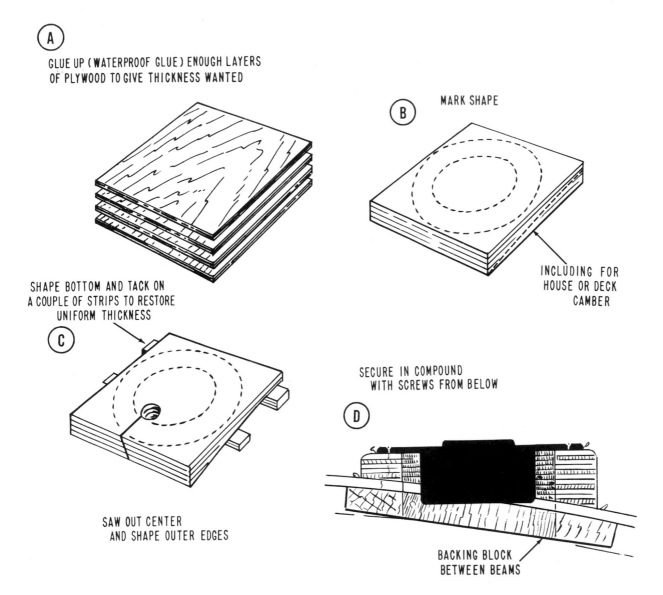

Ⓐ GLUE UP (WATERPROOF GLUE) ENOUGH LAYERS OF PLYWOOD TO GIVE THICKNESS WANTED

Ⓑ MARK SHAPE

INCLUDING FOR HOUSE OR DECK CAMBER

SHAPE BOTTOM AND TACK ON A COUPLE OF STRIPS TO RESTORE UNIFORM THICKNESS

Ⓒ

SAW OUT CENTER AND SHAPE OUTER EDGES

SECURE IN COMPOUND WITH SCREWS FROM BELOW

Ⓓ

BACKING BLOCK BETWEEN BEAMS

WATER DECK IRON PAD

A reader wrote recently to urge that I show for the benefit of beginners how to make a proper pad for a water deck iron or other through fitting that leaves little wood after the shaping has been done. Plywood is the answer, for even the best of wood in block form will check and crack, particularly where it is subjected to the heat a stove's stack gives off.

As thick-enough plywood is seldom available, the usual way is to glue up enough layers of whatever thickness of waterproof plywood you can secure, ending with a block thick enough to allow for the camber of the housetop or deck. It should be a little larger than necessary. Draw two circles, the inner one of a diameter that will allow a 1-inch clearance all around between the iron and the wood. The outer circle should give the size of the ring of wood wanted—enough to take the flange of the iron and permit rounding the edge off pleasingly. Also, mark on a pair of parallel edges the curve to allow for the camber of the deck, for the top of the pad must be perfectly horizontal. Shape this under surface first, because it is much easier to hold the piece in a vise in this square form.

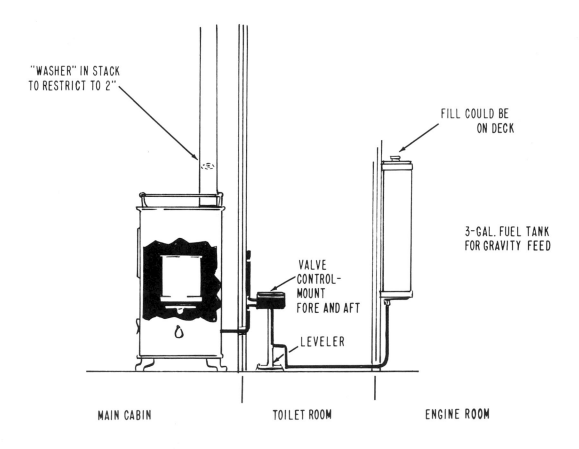

"WASHER" IN STACK
TO RESTRICT TO 2"

FILL COULD BE
ON DECK

3-GAL. FUEL TANK
FOR GRAVITY FEED

VALVE
CONTROL-
MOUNT
FORE AND AFT

LEVELER

MAIN CABIN   TOILET ROOM   ENGINE ROOM

COAL STOVE CONVERSION

The above drawing illustrates a good stove conversion where liquid fuel will be used instead of coal. As used by Capt. Baker on the power cruiser *Suriana*, a cabin heater is installed in the usual way against the after bulkhead in the main cabin. Fitted in the firebox is a regular household oil burner, the type having two asbestos wicks in round channels. The 4-inch stack of the heater is reduced to a 2-inch opening by a sort of washer fitted inside it. Immediately behind the bulkhead, in an out-of-the-way place in the toilet room, the oil-control valve is located, fed by means of a line. The 3-gallon fuel tank is mounted in the engine room, to give gravity flow, with a line leading from the valve to the burner.

It is important, Capt. Baker pointed out, to have this control device not only correct as to height and level but in good fore-and-aft alignment as well. The one used seemed to be the ordinary type, but I have learned since that valves can be had that are designed to meter and control the oil flow on heaters which are not normally always in a level position. Some of them are supposed to deliver a continuous supply of oil with safety even when tipped as much as 25 degrees. As it is, though, the heater behaves perfectly when used with the boat under way. There is no fan, so operation is noiseless. When I was aboard, at Pompano Beach with a cold Norther blowing, the heater was doing its job of keeping the cabin and the deckhouse above snug.

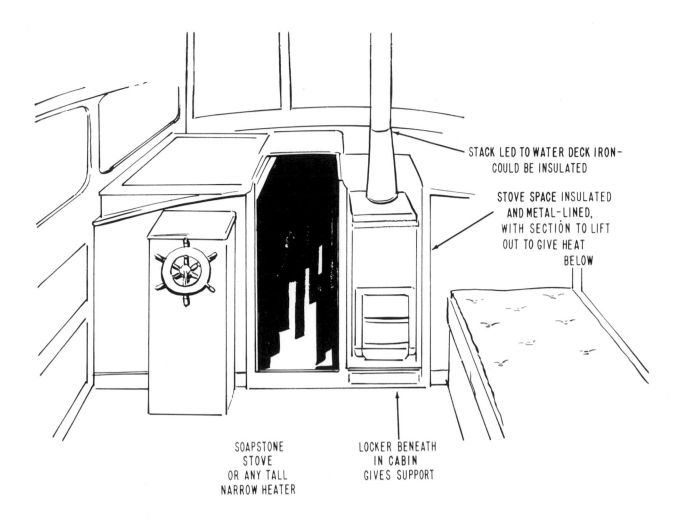

STACK LED TO WATER DECK IRON—
COULD BE INSULATED

STOVE SPACE INSULATED
AND METAL-LINED,
WITH SECTION TO LIFT
OUT TO GIVE HEAT
BELOW

SOAPSTONE
STOVE
OR ANY TALL
NARROW HEATER

LOCKER BENEATH
IN CABIN
GIVES SUPPORT

DECKHOUSE HEATER

Many owners of power cruisers realize that a stove burning coal or charcoal briquettes is a better heating arrangement for cool spring and fall weather than one using liquid fuel. The dryness of the heat given off by solid fuels defeats condensation rather than encouraging it. However, it is seldom an easy matter to figure out a proper place for such a stove aboard, especially on a stock-built boat. If the heater is installed below in the cabin, the sleeping quarters are apt to be too hot, while the deckhouse will not be warm enough. The deckhouse is the best location for it, and a novel way of placing a stove there is found aboard the yacht *Thetis*. A soapstone-type heater used in this installation, not only because its open front offers much of the charm of a fireplace but also because it is tall and narrow, a shape well suited to the installation shown.

A 15-inch-square compartment is built into the cabin top on one side of the companionway; beneath it is a locker which continues down to the cabin sole to make the construction strong. The galley in this case loses that much room, although the locker itself is used for storage. The bottom and three walls of the stove compartment are insulated and metal covered. The forward insulated wall and the one next to the companionway have removable sections which can be lifted out to permit heat to filter below. The stack is carried up to the usual water deck iron in the deckhouse top, and can be insulated or even jacketed, if one desires. In addition to giving heat where it is most wanted, the stove adds to the attractiveness of the deckhouse and is entirely out of the way.

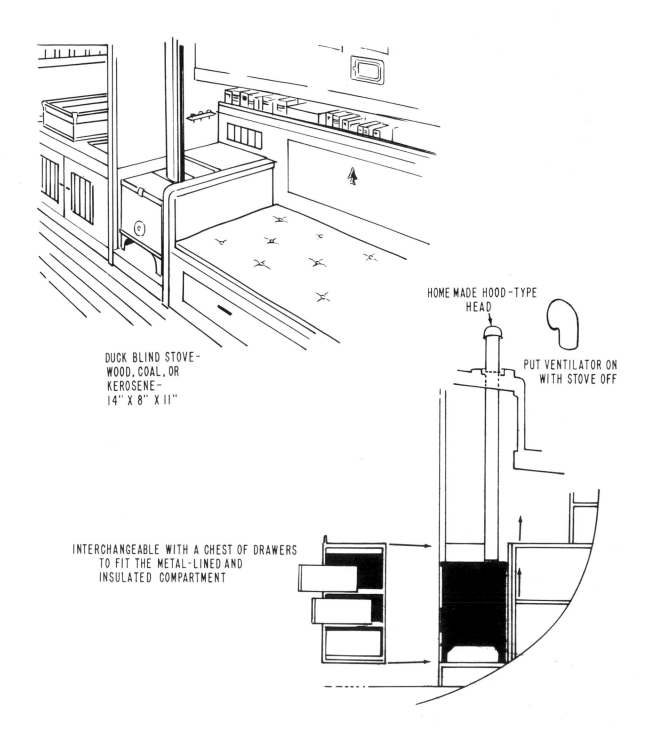

DUCK BLIND STOVE-
WOOD, COAL, OR
KEROSENE-
14" X 8" X 11"

HOME MADE HOOD-TYPE
HEAD

PUT VENTILATOR ON
WITH STOVE OFF

INTERCHANGEABLE WITH A CHEST OF DRAWERS
TO FIT THE METAL-LINED AND
INSULATED COMPARTMENT

INTERCHANGEABLE STOVE

The neatest heating arrangement for a small boat is the temporary or cool-weather set-up I noticed recently on the ketch *Andros*. This is what is called a duck-blind stove and is sold by those concerns which handle duck hunters' accessories. The wood or coal stove costs around $4, the kerosene-burning model about $8. Both are made of 18-gauge steel, the wood-burning model weighing but 8 pounds and the kerosene model a few pounds more. Either takes up a minimum amount of space and gives off more than enough heat for the average boat.

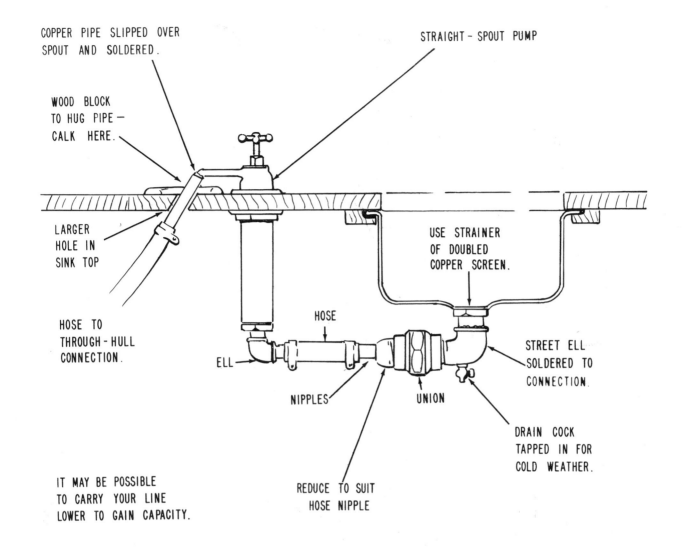

COPPER PIPE SLIPPED OVER
SPOUT AND SOLDERED.

STRAIGHT - SPOUT PUMP

WOOD BLOCK
TO HUG PIPE —
CALK HERE.

LARGER
HOLE IN
SINK TOP

USE STRAINER
OF DOUBLED
COPPER SCREEN.

HOSE TO
THROUGH - HULL
CONNECTION.

HOSE

ELL

STREET ELL
SOLDERED TO
CONNECTION.

NIPPLES

UNION

DRAIN COCK
TAPPED IN FOR
COLD WEATHER.

IT MAY BE POSSIBLE
TO CARRY YOUR LINE
LOWER TO GAIN CAPACITY.

REDUCE TO SUIT
HOSE NIPPLE

SINK SUMP

On boats where the sink is installed close to the waterline, it is advisable to provide a way of emptying it. The arrangement shown above is compact enough to fit in the usually small space beneath the sink; it is also easy and cheap to install and gives little trouble. The pump can, of course, be to either side or at the back of the sink, with the line made up of fittings to suit. If there is room, the line can be dropped to gain capacity, but as shown it will hold about half the contents of the sink. When its capacity has been reached, the water will back up and then must be pumped out. A strainer made of a double thickness of copper window screening, preferably with edges soldered, is necessary to avoid clogging the line or pump.

If anyone is living aboard, the line will probably need cleaning out about every third month. This is easily done by reaching through the door of the locker beneath and, using a bucket, either unscrewing the union or slipping off the hose and pouring boiling water into the sink. Should the pump need attention, the barrel can be unscrewed and removed.

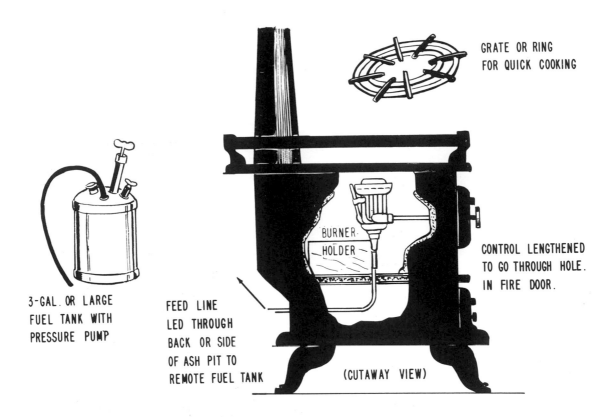

GRATE OR RING
FOR QUICK COOKING

3-GAL. OR LARGE
FUEL TANK WITH
PRESSURE PUMP

FEED LINE
LED THROUGH
BACK OR SIDE
OF ASH PIT TO
REMOTE FUEL TANK

BURNER·
HOLDER

CONTROL LENGTHENED
TO GO THROUGH HOLE.
IN FIRE DOOR.

(CUTAWAY VIEW)

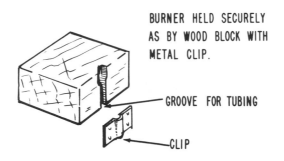

BURNER HELD SECURELY
AS BY WOOD BLOCK WITH
METAL CLIP.

GROOVE FOR TUBING

CLIP

PRIMUS-TYPE BURNER

I have often been asked why some manu-facturer did not make a hot-weather unit for a Shipmate stove, something using one or two Primus-type burners that could be installed in the firebox and supplied with fuel from a re-mote tank fitted with a pump to give the neces-sary pressure. The complete unit could be made so that it would not be too hard to put in or take out, with no major changes in the stove neces-sary.

The best arrangement I have seen along these lines was aboard the *Uncatena*, where the owner uses a single burner, as illustrated. I am not sure how the burner is held in place, so the block of wood shown is merely a suggestion. The control handle is lengthened to extend through a hole drilled in the fire door, and the fuel line is led to a remote tank fitted with a pump to give the required pressure. A similar burner is used beneath a coil for heating water in a well-insulated hot-water tank. About half an hour's heating will give enough hot water for a day's use.

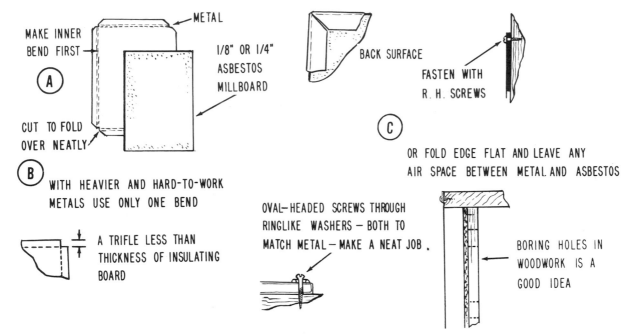

ASBESTOS-METAL INSTALLATION

When using metal along with the usual ⅛- or ¼-inch asbestos millboard for insulating woodwork against heat, the metal being used often governs how the work must be done. Stainless steel, which will probably be desirable if cost is not too much of a consideration, can be hard to bend and, without proper facilities, there is a definite limit as to what an individual should attempt. Copper, on the other hand, is easily bent but also easily distorted. Zinc sheeting often will work nicely, but because it is sometimes rather brittle, it may crack in making a flat bend. And galvanized sheet metal can be considered easy or difficult, not so much according to its weight but as to whether it matters that its coating is affected by hard bending.

A simple method of insulation is shown in A. Here, the metal is clamped on the insulating board to form a stiff, removable panel. But while copper is easy to bend in this way, other harder metals may give trouble. B shows a better method for use with harder metals. C can be used with any metal, although the flat bend is pretty sure to chip the coating off galvanized steel sheeting.

If there is much of this work to be done, it will pay to have the bending done by a metal-working shop. Otherwise, pieces of oak used

with a bench vise, clamps, and a mallet or hammer will have to be relied upon.

If at all possible, air space should be used for extra insulation. Some keep the asbestos flush with the metal; others tack it to the woodwork being protected and leave air space between the asbestos and the metal, as in C. Where there is much heat involved, such a space must get hot; with this as a consideration, the latter probably gives the best protection. In any case, and even without the air space, it is well to bore a number of holes in the wood to let heat escape.

Improper fastenings often can distort an otherwise-well-made panel or spoil a smoothly bent edge. Punching for these, rather than drilling—even where it is possible—is bad, for the surface is pretty sure to show hollow about the fastening. Fastening the metal too tightly is also to be avoided, because a wavy surface will result from too much heat. Both faults can be avoided by drilling for fastenings and by having holes large enough to allow a little come and go. Naturally, the fastenings must be of a type which does not have to be driven tightly to hold, preferably round-head brass screws with or without copper or brass washers, or oval-head screws with ring-type washers.

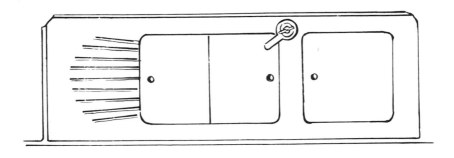

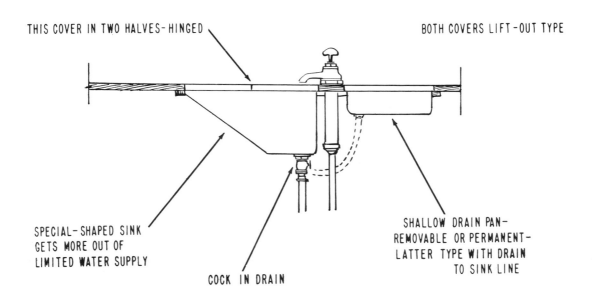

THIS COVER IN TWO HALVES-HINGED

BOTH COVERS LIFT-OUT TYPE

SPECIAL-SHAPED SINK
GETS MORE OUT OF
LIMITED WATER SUPPLY

COCK IN DRAIN

SHALLOW DRAIN PAN-
REMOVABLE OR PERMANENT-
LATTER TYPE WITH DRAIN
TO SINK LINE

DOUBLE-SINK ARRANGEMENT

Not so long ago you had to be satisfied with a shallow galley sink or have one made to order. Now, however, stock sizes and shapes and even depths are available, and you can have one large enough and sufficiently deep to be practical. Along this line I recently came across the sink-and-drainpan arrangement shown above, which seems to be a good one to keep in mind if you are planning a galley arrangement for the new boat or changing the work space of your present one.

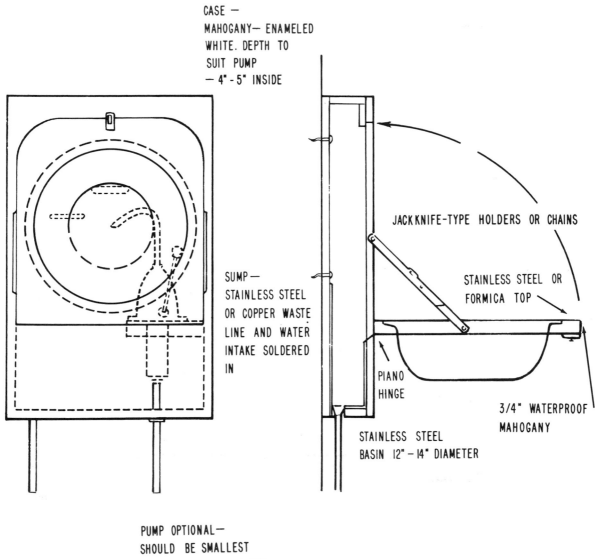

CASE —
MAHOGANY— ENAMELED
WHITE. DEPTH TO
SUIT PUMP
— 4" - 5" INSIDE

JACKKNIFE-TYPE HOLDERS OR CHAINS

STAINLESS STEEL OR
FORMICA TOP

SUMP —
STAINLESS STEEL
OR COPPER WASTE
LINE AND WATER
INTAKE SOLDERED
IN

PIANO
HINGE

3/4" WATERPROOF
MAHOGANY

STAINLESS STEEL
BASIN 12" – 14" DIAMETER

PUMP OPTIONAL—
SHOULD BE SMALLEST
SIZE WITH SWING SPOUT

FOLDING BASINS I

If you have been wondering what you could make of one of those stainless steel bowls or basins frequently offered as surplus at bargain prices, here is a suggestion from Dave Phelps.

As Mr. Phelps points out, this folding head may be old fashioned, but it is still best where toilet-room space is at a premium. I think

enough is shown in the sketch to explain the making. But the main point is to get the pump first, if you are going to use one. Then, make your sump to suit the depth of case that it will require. Finally, work out the size of the front, taking the basin and then the height and width of the case or box.

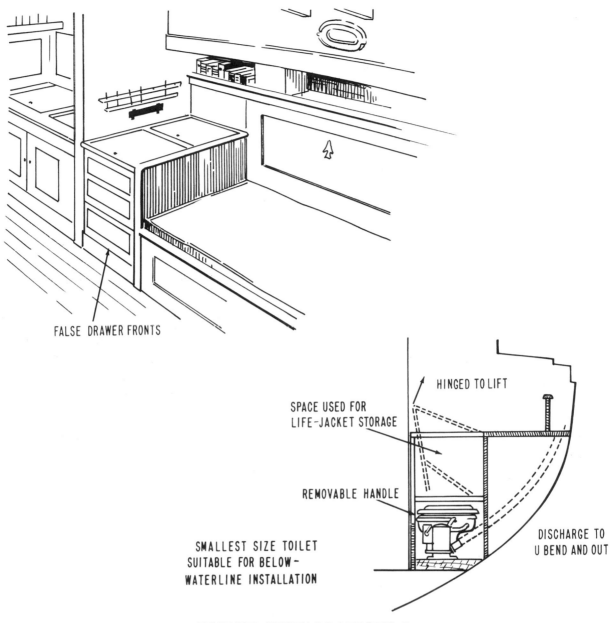

FALSE DRAWER FRONTS

HINGED TO LIFT

SPACE USED FOR
LIFE-JACKET STORAGE

REMOVABLE HANDLE

SMALLEST SIZE TOILET
SUITABLE FOR BELOW-
WATERLINE INSTALLATION

DISCHARGE TO
U BEND AND OUT

TOILET INSTALLATIONS I

It used to be that one considered himself lucky if he had a toilet aboard his sailboat. Yet, only recently, I was aboard a 36-foot ketch where a second toilet had been installed.

The owner explained that he and his wife frequently had landlubber guests aboard—sometimes friends, but occasionally another couple as a charter party. As the cabin is laid out, with a forward stateroom which can be closed with the toilet room door, common use of the toilet is inconvenient. What he and his wife wanted was a toilet in the main cabin.

The sketch shows how they solved the problem. What made the solution practical was the availability of very compact and lightweight toilets which require a minimum of space to install. What was originally a narrow chest of drawers between the main cabin and the doghouse galley was rebuilt as shown to accommodate the fixture. The top forms a small chart table, and the stowage locker utilizes the otherwise wasted space.

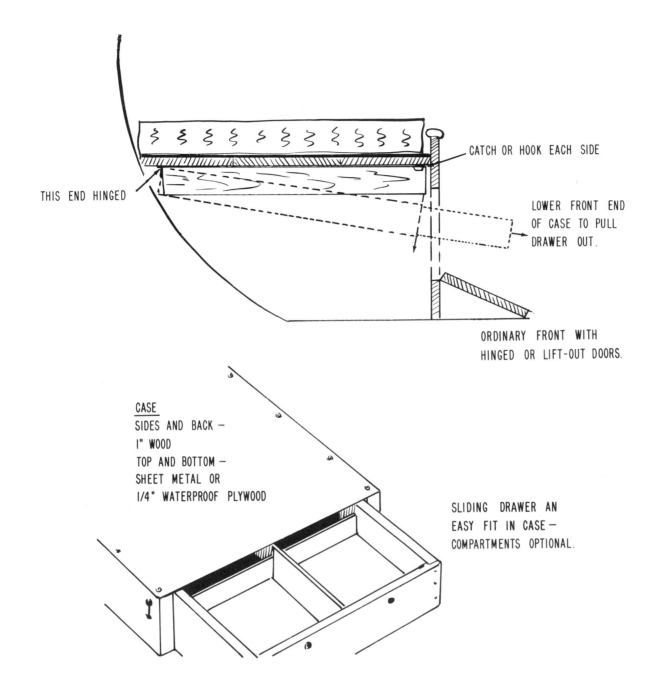

CATCH OR HOOK EACH SIDE

THIS END HINGED

LOWER FRONT END
OF CASE TO PULL
DRAWER OUT.

ORDINARY FRONT WITH
HINGED OR LIFT-OUT DOORS.

CASE
SIDES AND BACK —
1" WOOD
TOP AND BOTTOM —
SHEET METAL OR
1/4" WATERPROOF PLYWOOD

SLIDING DRAWER AN
EASY FIT IN CASE —
COMPARTMENTS OPTIONAL.

UNDER-BERTH DRAWER

I like this idea because it provides a way of using the otherwise-wasted space beneath a berth or settee. Here, things can be stowed neatly and yet be accessible. As this is worked out on Harold Mossler's ketch *Holiday,* there is a case-held drawer in each of the three compartments under the main cabin settees. Each case is around 18 inches wide, and because they are only 4 inches deep they do not interfere with ordinary stowage lower down. A hook or suitable catch on each side of the case at the front end holds the unit up; of course, with these released, the end drops down so that the drawer can be slid out.

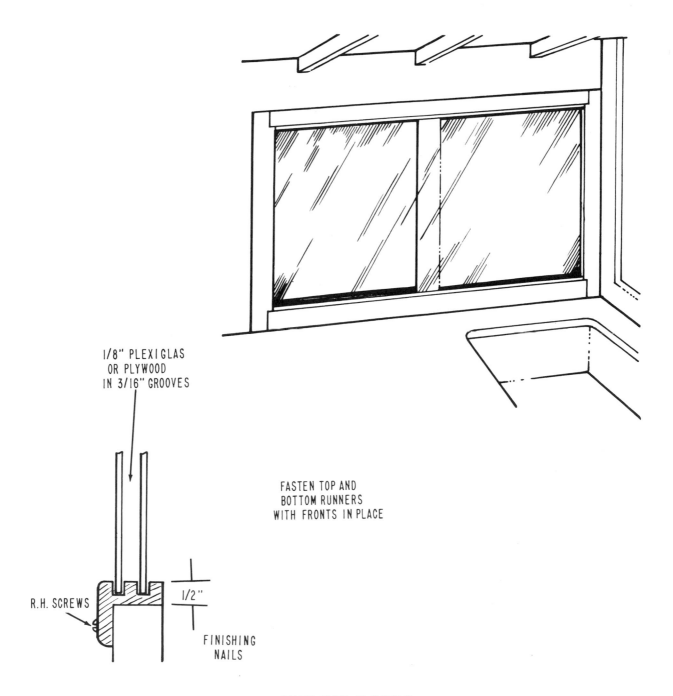

1/8" PLEXIGLAS
OR PLYWOOD
IN 3/16" GROOVES

FASTEN TOP AND
BOTTOM RUNNERS
WITH FRONTS IN PLACE

R.H. SCREWS

1/2"

FINISHING
NAILS

SLIDING DOORS

Sliding doors are such space savers aboard a boat that one wonders why they are not more often fitted. Here is shown how one owner put them in to replace the original hinged type, which interfered too much with the sink and worktable arrangement. Plexiglas was used, with the two panels overlapping 2 inches or so.

The top and bottom runners were made to fit flush in the opening, with the grooves extending inside the locker. A finger hole in each panel is the simplest way of sliding them. Other ventilation holes should not be necessary, since a good bit of air can get into the locker through the space between the panels.

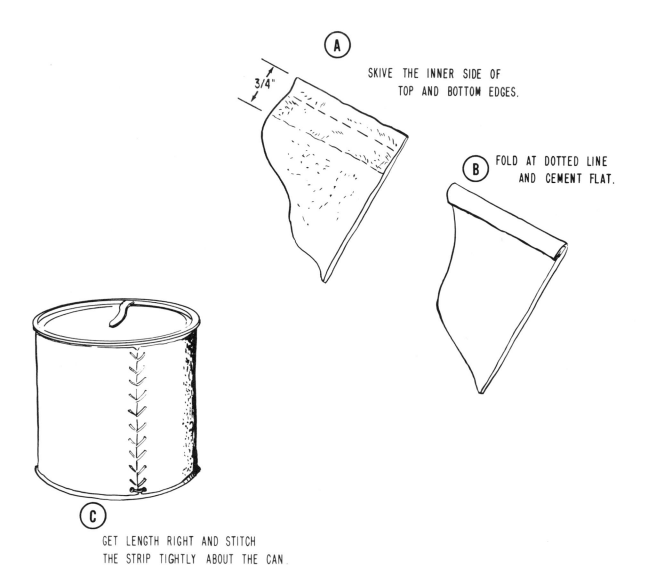

(A) SKIVE THE INNER SIDE OF TOP AND BOTTOM EDGES.

3/4"

(B) FOLD AT DOTTED LINE AND CEMENT FLAT.

(C) GET LENGTH RIGHT AND STITCH THE STRIP TIGHTLY ABOUT THE CAN.

LEATHER-COVERED CANS

Good-looking containers for tobacco, cigarettes, match folders, boxes, etc., can be made up by covering cans of suitable size and shape with leather. A plastic material can also be used, but, regardless of material, the top and bottom edges should be turned under and cemented.

Personally, I prefer leather, and to prevent this fold from being bulky it is necessary to skive or taper the turned edges with a good sharp knife. The width of the material should

be sufficient to fit between the top and bottom ridges or seams about the can, so that these, along with a bit of cement applied to the inside surface, will hold it in place. For a neat job, obtain the length first, so that holes for the stitching can be pricked beforehand in two straight rows, all uniformly spaced. Then pull the leather tightly about the can by using any fancy stitch you wish; conceal the final knotting by tucking it under.

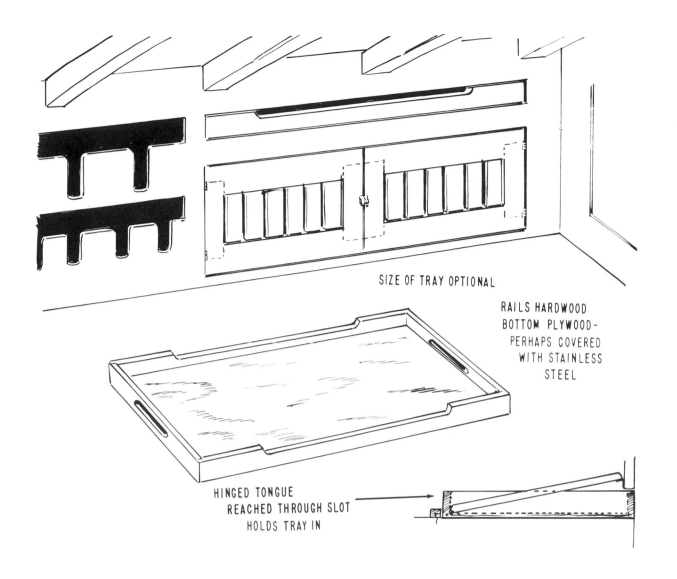

SIZE OF TRAY OPTIONAL

RAILS HARDWOOD
BOTTOM PLYWOOD—
PERHAPS COVERED
WITH STAINLESS
STEEL

HINGED TONGUE
REACHED THROUGH SLOT
HOLDS TRAY IN

SERVING TRAY

One of the handiest gadgets for the cook, particularly where meals are often eaten in the cockpit, is some sort of serving tray. It is not difficult to make your own and get the size and shape you want as well as a tray that will be in harmony with your boat's interior. That is the most interesting feature about the one shown here, for the owner made the tray to suit a shallow compartment above the galley worktable, where it stows easily.

Two feet long and 1 foot wide, with 2-inch depth at the ends, makes a good size. The ends and sides should be made of some wood that will finish bright, and the ¼-inch plywood bottom should be rabbeted into these to conceal its edges. If possible, secure matching plywood; or, if it is necessary to use fir (waterproof grade, of course), paint the bottom some bright color. Or, stainless steel can be laid over the plywood to give a good-looking and serviceable surface.

You will notice that the tray is kept from sliding out of its compartment by a simple hinged tongue. This lifts and drops of its own accord when the tray is being put away, but, to get the tray out, the tongue must be raised to clear, usually by reaching through the slotlike opening with a slat kept for that purpose.

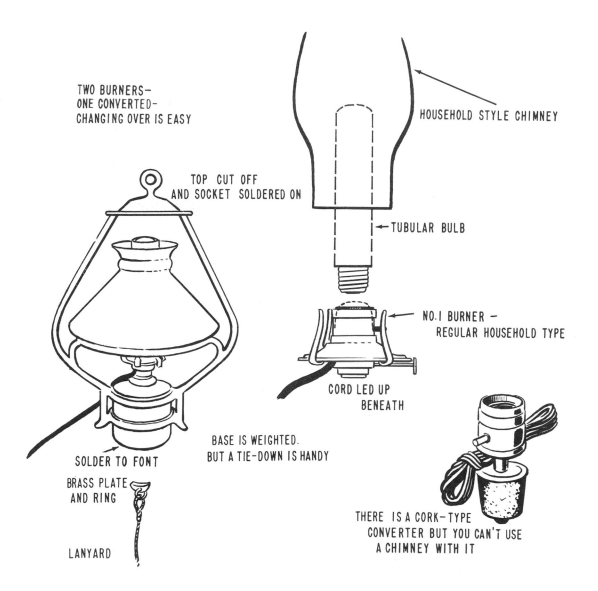

TWO BURNERS—
ONE CONVERTED—
CHANGING OVER IS EASY

HOUSEHOLD STYLE CHIMNEY

TOP CUT OFF
AND SOCKET SOLDERED ON

← TUBULAR BULB

NO.1 BURNER —
REGULAR HOUSEHOLD TYPE

CORD LED UP
BENEATH

SOLDER TO FONT

BASE IS WEIGHTED.
BUT A TIE-DOWN IS HANDY

BRASS PLATE
AND RING

LANYARD

THERE IS A CORK-TYPE
CONVERTER BUT YOU CAN'T USE
A CHIMNEY WITH IT

OIL-ELECTRIC LAMP

This is a simple way of converting a kerosene-burning cabin lamp and still be able to use it when current is not available. Notice that household-type burners are used. The No. 1 size will fit most all marine lamps, but if not, try the No. 2 size. In any case, they give double the light of the marine-type and the chimneys cost around 15 cents as against the usual $1.

The simplest way to convert them is to cut off the top part so that an electric socket can be soldered on, with its cord going through a hole cut in the base of the burner. To fit into the chimney, a tubular-shaped bulb should be used. Changing over is then merely a matter of

switching burners. The kerosene can safely be left in the lamp. There is a cork-type converter which avoids all this, but you cannot use a chimney with it, and the lamp does not look right with the bare bulb.

While the lamp shown is an imported, swinging type, any of our marine types can be converted in this way; or, for use with kerosene only, this type of burner and chimney will give better light. The bottom fitting, for taking a lanyard, is simply something that we find handy on our swinging lamp. When not tied down in some way, it swings too freely under sail or in a rough anchorage.

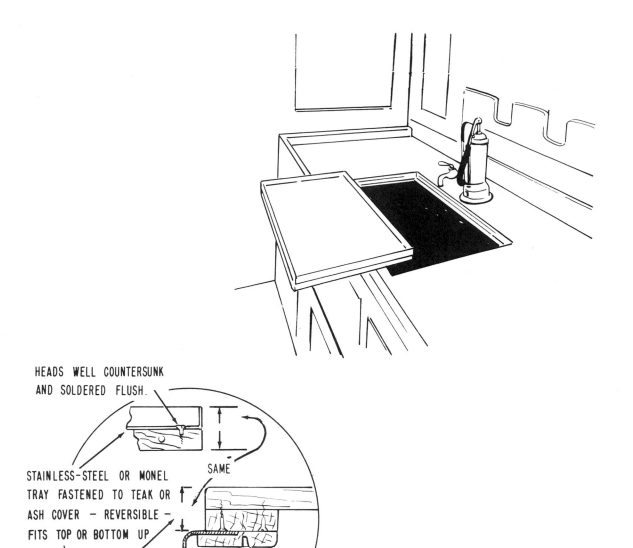

HEADS WELL COUNTERSUNK
AND SOLDERED FLUSH.

STAINLESS-STEEL OR MONEL
TRAY FASTENED TO TEAK OR
ASH COVER — REVERSIBLE —
FITS TOP OR BOTTOM UP

SAME

SINK IS LOWERED AN
EXTRA INCH OR SO.

SINK-COVER TRAY

Here is a sink-cover arrangement used on the ketch *Cairn.* In the building of the galley work-table, the large sink was lowered a good inch, with the idea of having its cover serve as a drain tray or as a serving tray when meals are eaten on deck. Of course, the cover should fit with either side up, with a flush-type lifting handle or ring in the wood or solid part. On the *Cairn,* the latter is of teak to match the worktable, and the shallow tray of rather heavyweight Monel is fastened to it with flat-headed screws well countersunk and heads neatly soldered over. However, with a metal-covered worktable, the same idea could be used by making of the cover an even deeper tray, which would fit the open-ing either way.

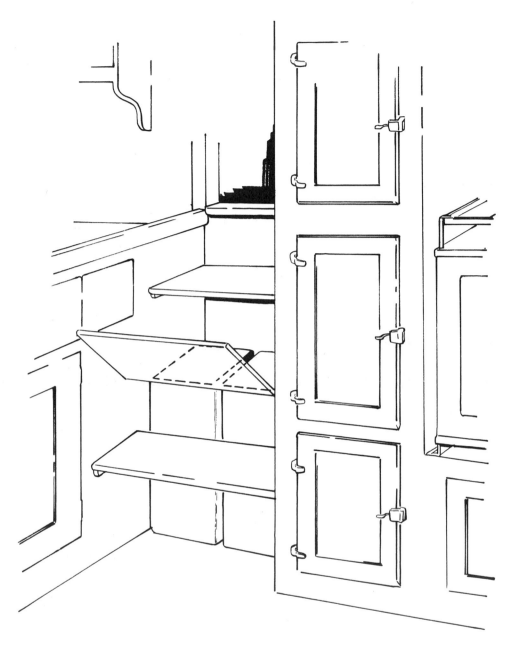

GALLEY ARRANGEMENT

This is a galley arrangement noticed recently on a lovely old power cruiser of the raised-deck type. Notice that the center companionway step has been hinged to permit easier access to the space there, which houses two metal containers used for vegetables and extra food supplies. Another feature is the rebuilt refrigerator, which is carried right up to the deck, where a hatch permits outside access to the ice compartment. In the lower compartment, a small refrigerator unit, utilizing dockside current, is installed. Although there are various ways of attempting to solve the ice problem, this one of being able to use electricity when tied up and regular ice when away from the dock seems as satisfactory as any.

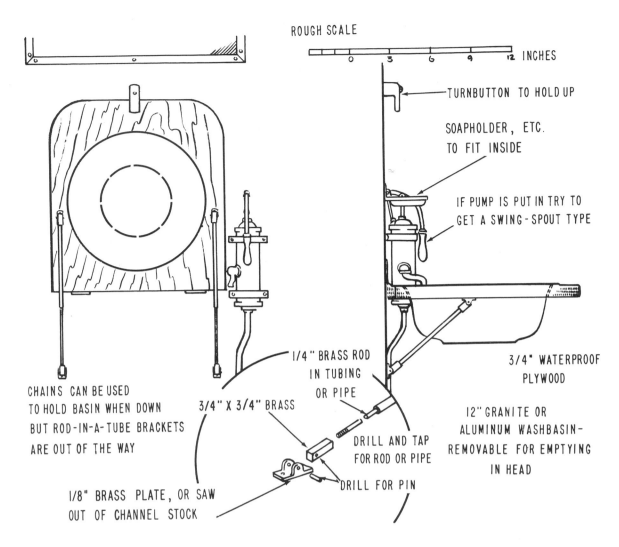

ROUGH SCALE

INCHES

TURNBUTTON TO HOLD UP

SOAPHOLDER, ETC.
TO FIT INSIDE

IF PUMP IS PUT IN TRY TO
GET A SWING-SPOUT TYPE

CHAINS CAN BE USED
TO HOLD BASIN WHEN DOWN
BUT ROD-IN-A-TUBE BRACKETS
ARE OUT OF THE WAY

3/4" X 3/4" BRASS

1/4" BRASS ROD
IN TUBING
OR PIPE

3/4" WATERPROOF
PLYWOOD

12" GRANITE OR
ALUMINUM WASHBASIN-
REMOVABLE FOR EMPTYING
IN HEAD

DRILL AND TAP
FOR ROD OR PIPE

DRILL FOR PIN

1/8" BRASS PLATE, OR SAW
OUT OF CHANNEL STOCK

FOLDING BASINS II

This toilet-room basin arrangement has several advantages over a standard folding lavatory, the low cost being among the most important. Certainly, it works in well where space is a consideration and, if you like to keep things aboard as simple as possible, you'll prefer lifting the basin out to empty it in the head as against an extra hull connection or a connection to the toilet outlet. Although a pump is shown to service this, it is not properly a part of the idea and there is no reason why a small metal water pitcher kept on a lipped shelf would not be satisfactory.

The holder for the granite or aluminum washbasin is best made of ¾-inch waterproof plywood, with the cutout shaped to suit. The lip or edges of the basin should rest flat on the plywood, with the fit in the opening such that it can be easily lifted out, yet snug enough to hold it when up. Although a pair of chains, or a couple of folding brackets, could be used to hold the basin level when lowered, the rod-in-a-tube type of brackets shown are less in the way because they are fitted below rather than above the basin holder. As these brackets might be hard to obtain, the inset shows how they can be made. The brass rod must be filed down or rubbed with emery cloth to produce a sliding fit in the pipe. Holders and mounting flanges must then be made for the four ends.

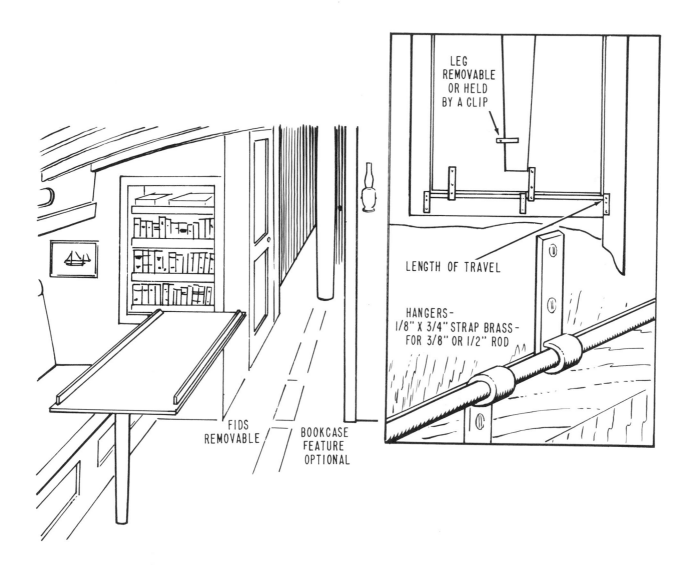

LEG
REMOVABLE
OR HELD
BY A CLIP

LENGTH OF TRAVEL

HANGERS-
1/8" X 3/4" STRAP BRASS-
FOR 3/8" OR 1/2" ROD

FIDS
REMOVABLE

BOOKCASE
FEATURE
OPTIONAL

TABLE ON A TRAVELER

The ketch *Tahiti* has a clever table arrangement that could be used to advantage on many boats. As is so often the case, the bulkhead projection at the foot of one of the main cabin settees is not sufficient to permit the permanent mounting of a table there without interfering with floor space. Instead, the single leaf is mounted to swing from the bulkhead, about as shown in this drawing.

Although the one shown folds flush into the bookcase opening, that feature is optional. The main point is to have the hangers spaced on the rod or traveler so that, in lowering the table, it can be pulled out to clear the settee and permit comfortable seating. If the single leg is permanently attached, it should be hinged in a way that will keep it rigid when down. A removable pipe leg could be used instead, with a pipe flange fastened beneath the leaf into which it can be screwed.

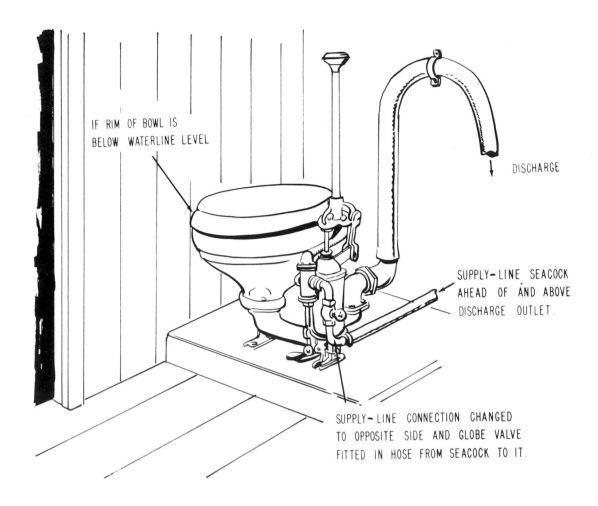

IF RIM OF BOWL IS
BELOW WATERLINE LEVEL

DISCHARGE

SUPPLY-LINE SEACOCK
AHEAD OF AND ABOVE
DISCHARGE OUTLET.

SUPPLY-LINE CONNECTION CHANGED
TO OPPOSITE SIDE AND GLOBE VALVE
FITTED IN HOSE FROM SEACOCK TO IT.

TOILET INSTALLATIONS II

I have come across several cases where toilets of the foot-operated, supply-valve type have been fitted with a globe valve in the supply line when the supply seacock could not be conveniently reached. This seems a wise precaution when the rim of the bowl is below the waterline level, and particularly on the types which permit changing the supply line over to the opposite side. The supply valve does seem to give trouble as a toilet gets older (not always enough

to warrant an overhaul and new parts, the proper way of ending any such trouble), causing the bowl to flood or overflow. Very often, a toilet is located with the rim of its bowl so little below the waterline level that it could easily have been raised the required few inches. Either this or fitting some sort of dependable shutoff seems wiser than depending on the seacock, particularly if it is placed in a hard-to-reach location.

STAINLESS STEEL COVER—
TURN OVER AS A DRAINING
TRAY FOR DISHES

WATERTIGHT
COAMING

BIN

GALLEY COUNTER

This figure shows the galley range set athwartships in the best position for working, yet a location which did not complicate the layout of the storage space beneath the end of the worktable. Naturally, this space had to be reached from the top, and so it turned out to be merely the usual deep bin for pans and larger cooking utensils. Still, even here the tendency of water to leak past the flush-type cover was a nuisance. To avoid this, the bin opening was enlarged and a shallow, watertight coaming fastened about it to take a lipped cover. This was made of stainless steel to form a slightly raised section of the worktable top upon which hot pans could be placed.

As he progressed with the job, the owner decided to make the cover so that, when turned over, it sat atop the coaming as a tray for draining washed dishes. Also, because water could hardly get below, he improved the space beneath by fitting two shelves on each side for stowing can containers.

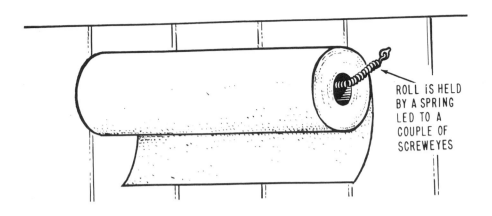

ROLL IS HELD
BY A SPRING
LED TO A
COUPLE OF
SCREWEYES

PAPER-TOWEL HOLDER

The coil-spring arrangement for holding a roll of paper towels is used aboard the sloop owned by Jack and Anne Koman. This may be a simple idea, but it has the advantage over the ordinary holder that if the spring is hooked up so that there will always be some tension on it, towels can be torn off with one hand.

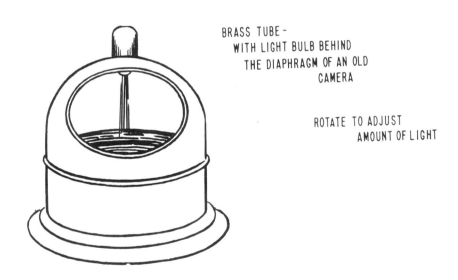

BRASS TUBE –
WITH LIGHT BULB BEHIND
THE DIAPHRAGM OF AN OLD
CAMERA

ROTATE TO ADJUST
AMOUNT OF LIGHT

BINNACLE LIGHT

While this compass light idea is not shown too clearly (I was unable to take apart the one I saw to find exactly how it was made), I think it will be understood by anyone at all familiar with the innards of a camera. Anyhow, the diaphragm of an old camera is fitted in the brass tube secured to the head of the binnacle, with the light bulb back of it and the whole thing made so that rotating the tube opens or closes the diaphragm to control the amount of light thrown on the compass card.

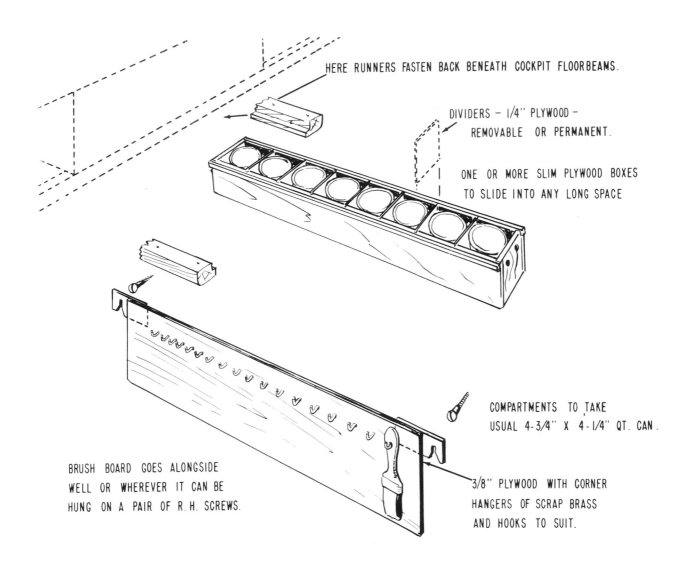

HERE RUNNERS FASTEN BACK BENEATH COCKPIT FLOOR BEAMS.

DIVIDERS – 1/4" PLYWOOD –
REMOVABLE OR PERMANENT.

ONE OR MORE SLIM PLYWOOD BOXES
TO SLIDE INTO ANY LONG SPACE

COMPARTMENTS TO TAKE
USUAL 4-3/4" X 4-1/4" QT. CAN.

BRUSH BOARD GOES ALONGSIDE
WELL OR WHEREVER IT CAN BE
HUNG ON A PAIR OF R.H. SCREWS.

3/8" PLYWOOD WITH CORNER
HANGERS OF SCRAP BRASS
AND HOOKS TO SUIT.

PAINT LOCKER

Joe Brent on his ketch *Lucinda* has worked out a good way of carrying paints and brushes aboard. The idea is to utilize odd space that otherwise would be at least partly wasted; of course, the space depends on the boat. On the 30-foot *Lucinda*, there was space beneath and alongside the hanging cockpit well. A slim box in a space about 4 feet long was made to slide on top runners fastened to the beams. It was fitted with compartments to take quart-size cans with the tops labeled. With one divider removed, the combined space accommodates three pint cans, but a shallower box for small cans can be made.

The brush board, which is simply a long piece of plywood with end hangers and hooks, permits keeping cleaned brushes in good condition. Mr. Brent says he drops his brushes in fuel oil after cleaning and before stowing, and then removes them and wipes off the excess. The board of brushes is hung out of the way, alongside the cockpit well, with the end hangers slipping over the protruding heads of heavy round-headed screws. In getting them ready for painting, both the box and board are moved to the job.

The same idea is used to advantage on the ketch *Freedom* in a deep galley locker. The box has individual compartments for quart bottles and slides on bottom runners.

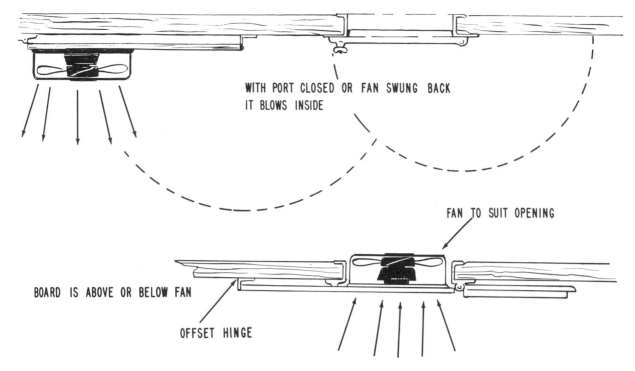

WITH PORT CLOSED OR FAN SWUNG BACK
IT BLOWS INSIDE

FAN TO SUIT OPENING

BOARD IS ABOVE OR BELOW FAN

OFFSET HINGE

TO EXHAUST AIR BOARD IS SWUNG TO PUT FAN IN OPENING

GALLEY FAN

The clever ventilating-fan arrangement which is shown above is an idea from Lyman Hewins' *Maid of Kent.* This is simply a fan mounted on a board in such a way that it can be swung either to blow inside the galley or to exhaust air from it. Of course, the size of the fan must suit the port opening, and it must be mounted to come either above or below the board, not be backed by it.

CHAPTER 8

Chart Work

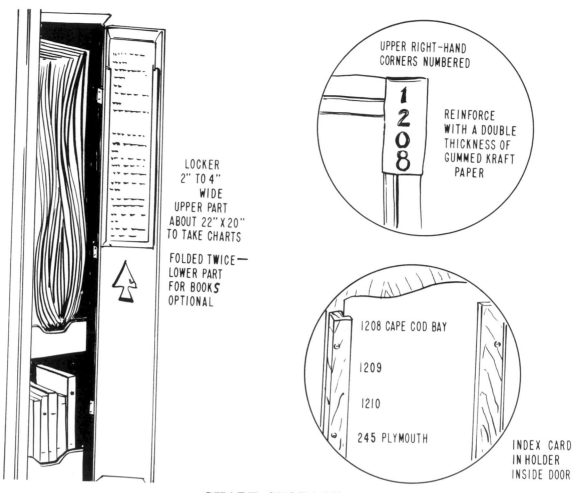

LOCKER
2" TO 4"
WIDE
UPPER PART
ABOUT 22" X 20"
TO TAKE CHARTS

FOLDED TWICE—
LOWER PART
FOR BOOKS
OPTIONAL

UPPER RIGHT-HAND
CORNERS NUMBERED

1208

REINFORCE
WITH A DOUBLE
THICKNESS OF
GUMMED KRAFT
PAPER

1208 CAPE COD BAY

1209

1210

245 PLYMOUTH

INDEX CARD
IN HOLDER
INSIDE DOOR

CHART STORAGE

Fold charts twice, to be about 18 by 22½ inches, and you have a size that seems to suit the small cruiser—not too difficult a shape to work over and one that can be conveniently stowed. Thumbtacked to a panel of plywood with the part being referred to uppermost, a chart can be kept on deck for better following in shoal-water work, and, in such a folded form, any reasonable number can be kept in good shape stowed in a remarkably small locker or bin.

The type shown above can be built in as part of the cabin work on a new boat; otherwise, a few inches of the side of an existing locker large enough to give a space about 22 inches deep and 20 inches high can be utilized. As shown, the locker was built in athwartships; the part below was used for a shelf to take the Coast Pilot and other books. The indexing method makes it easy to locate any chart quickly. A piece of 2-inch gummed kraft tape is folded and fastened to the upper righthand corner of the chart to stiffen it and take the number in large figures, using waterproof ink; all charts are stowed on edge in the locker in numerical order, with these tabs uppermost. An index card, made by pasting ruled paper on both sides of a piece of fairly stiff cardboard, is kept in holders on the inside of the door, loose enough to permit removal. A good way to list charts is to fill in from a chart catalog all the numbers of charts available for the waters where you are apt to be cruising; but opposite the numbers, fill in only the titles (you will likely have to use abbreviations) of the charts you actually have on board, adding the titles of others as they are bought.

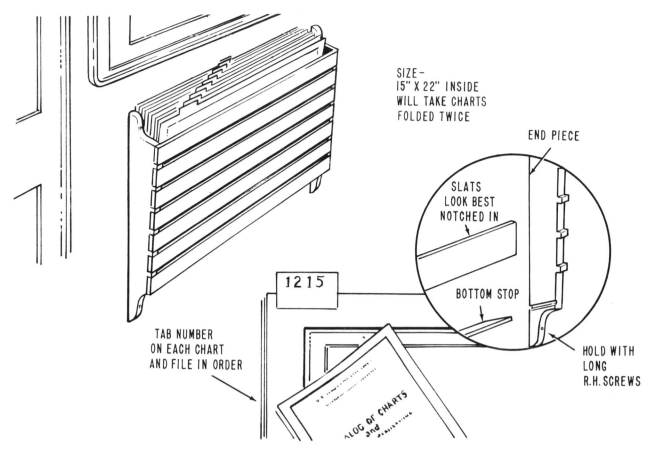

SIZE –
15" X 22" INSIDE
WILL TAKE CHARTS
FOLDED TWICE

END PIECE

SLATS
LOOK BEST
NOTCHED IN

BOTTOM STOP

HOLD WITH
LONG
R.H. SCREWS

12 15

TAB NUMBER
ON EACH CHART
AND FILE IN ORDER

DECKHOUSE CHART CASE

Owners of both power cruisers and auxiliaries generally find that the most practical way of handling charts is to fold them twice, since they can then be stowed easily and be fairly handy for use. Some stow charts in a canvas envelope or two, with the idea of keeping the envelopes beneath a seat cushion or mattress. Another idea is to have a narrow, upright chart locker built in alongside a larger locker, with the folded charts kept on edge where they can be reached through a front opening or door. I have also seen the locker built as a deep slot or well, with the charts accessible through the top opening.

The rack method often works out best, particularly for a powerboat with a deckhouse or for the doghouse of an auxiliary. As shown, the arrangement and details are similar to those worked out on the *Belle II*, where the whole thing is well-planned and in keeping with the boat. The case itself is of mahogany, with the workmanship and finish matching that of the deckhouse interior, and is fastened permanently to a wall or side of the house convenient to the wheel. The ends can be shaped as shown, or might be squared at the top and bottom, so long as the case can be properly fastened. Of course, the front can be either solid, or slatted as shown. The bottom stop should really have a dust scupper or long slot to facilitate cleaning.

A good width is 22 inches inside, and a height of 15 inches will allow the folded charts to protrude so that the index-tabbed top edges can be leafed through to locate a particular chart. The depth from the wall should suit the number of charts usually carried. A regular *Catalogue of Charts and Related Publications* as issued by the U. S. Coast and Geodetic Survey makes the ideal index. This may be marked with a ring around the number of each chart that is in the case.

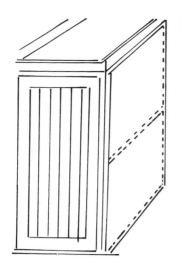

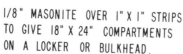

1/8" MASONITE OVER 1"X 1" STRIPS
TO GIVE 18" X 24" COMPARTMENTS
ON A LOCKER OR BULKHEAD.

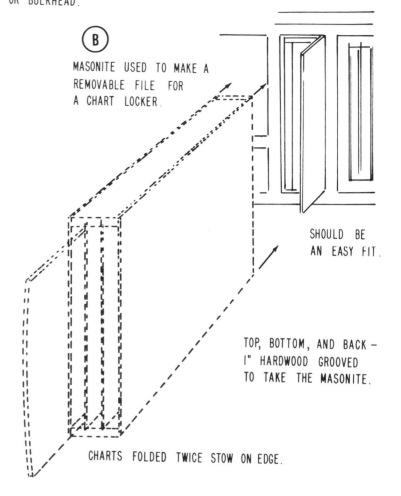

MASONITE USED TO MAKE A
REMOVABLE FILE FOR
A CHART LOCKER.

SHOULD BE
AN EASY FIT.

TOP, BOTTOM, AND BACK —
1" HARDWOOD GROOVED
TO TAKE THE MASONITE.

CHARTS FOLDED TWICE STOW ON EDGE.

CHART LOCKER

The idea shown in Figure *A* is used in stowing charts aboard the *Haligonian*. This is just a matter of fastening a piece of tempered Masonite over 1-by-1-inch strips to provide deep, narrow spaces into which charts can be shoved on edge. The available area will govern how large these compartments (or a single one) should be, but if the charts are folded twice, they stand on edge nicely and are of a good size to work with.

This brings to mind another use of Masonite for a chart locker, as noticed aboard the chunky power cruiser *Inlander*. Here, the owner used the material along with grooved-out top, bot-

tom, and back pieces for a removable case (*B*) which slid into an 8-inch-wide regular chart locker. I think the original idea was to stow charts (here again, folded twice) on edge in the locker itself, but it was found that they slumped down and were difficult to get in and out and to keep in order. Possibly the locker could have been subdivided by partitions to avoid this, but the removable case to my mind is a better idea since, as the owner pointed out, it can be removed for cleaning the inside of the locker. Also, at the end of the season, it is a simple matter to carry the charts home in it to have them available for winter planning.

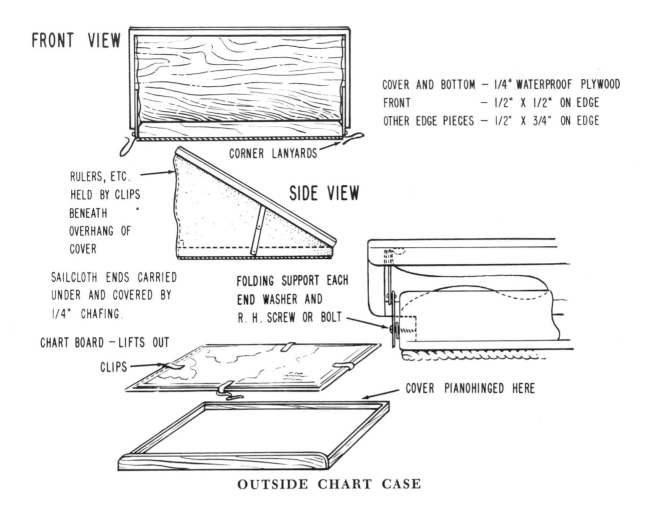

FRONT VIEW

COVER AND BOTTOM – 1/4" WATERPROOF PLYWOOD
FRONT   – 1/2" X 1/2" ON EDGE
OTHER EDGE PIECES – 1/2" X 3/4" ON EDGE

CORNER LANYARDS

RULERS, ETC.
HELD BY CLIPS
BENEATH
OVERHANG OF
COVER

SIDE VIEW

SAILCLOTH ENDS CARRIED
UNDER AND COVERED BY
1/4" CHAFING.

FOLDING SUPPORT EACH
END WASHER AND
R. H. SCREW OR BOLT

CHART BOARD – LIFTS OUT

CLIPS

COVER PIANOHINGED HERE

OUTSIDE CHART CASE

A chart holder made as illustrated above has solved the problem of carrying charts aboard the 26-foot sloop owned by Hugh MacAlpine. It is particularly convenient when under way in wet weather. The idea was to have a case in which the supply of charts could be kept and which could be taken out on deck. Below, it fits in a narrow compartment built alongside the clothes locker.

The size can be changed or the design modified, as the owner may desire. As shown, the length and width are worked out to take the average chart folded twice, perhaps with some excess trimmed off the edges. This gives an 18-by-24-inch chart board of 1/4-inch plywood on which a chart may be thumbtacked or held by four spring brass clips, as shown. The traylike bottom is then made to take this as an easy fit. Notice that the front edge piece is double the depth of the others. All edge pieces are glued

to 1/4-inch plywood, but Mr. MacAlpine says that, in making another, he would have them rabbeted so that no plywood edges would show. The cover is made with an inside length about 1/2 inch greater than the length of the bottom, in order to allow for the folding support at each end. The width of the cover should be a good 4 inches more than that of the bottom, so that, with the case opened, its outer edge will be above, or even overhang, the bottom one.

After attaching the top edge of each sailcloth gusset, the cover and bottom are hinged together along their after edges. The gussets are held up beneath the top by strips of small half-round and, after the piano hinge has been put on, the lower edges are carried under the bottom to give the desired height of opening. Finally, the folding supports are put on in a way that will allow the gussets to fall clear inside when the case is closed.

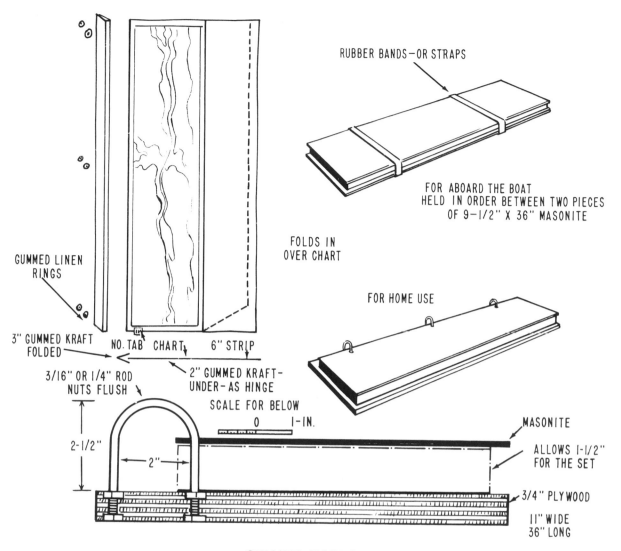

RUBBER BANDS—OR STRAPS

FOR ABOARD THE BOAT
HELD IN ORDER BETWEEN TWO PIECES
OF 9-1/2" X 36" MASONITE

FOLDS IN
OVER CHART

GUMMED LINEN
RINGS

FOR HOME USE

3" GUMMED KRAFT
FOLDED

NO. TAB   CHART   6" STRIP

3/16" OR 1/4" ROD
NUTS FLUSH

2" GUMMED KRAFT-
UNDER - AS HINGE

SCALE FOR BELOW

0   1-IN.

2-1/2"

2"

MASONITE

ALLOWS 1-1/2"
FOR THE SET

3/4" PLYWOOD

11" WIDE
36" LONG

CHART FOLIO

This idea, which is used by a friend who plans to take his boat south during the winter when retirement time comes, is a novel way of having chart information in handy form.

He has used two sets of Intracoastal Waterway strip charts, Norfolk to Key West, the extra one because they are printed on two sides. He cuts the sheets into strips and keeps them in numerical order. To each he has attached a strip of heavy kraft paper on which he makes his own notes right opposite the place in question ("good anchorage in the mouth of such and such a creek,"—"a bad side current here," "an easy place to get your markers confused," and so on). He has secured some of this information

from friends who have made the trip and who have helped him mark his charts, but a lot of it has come from reading magazine accounts of cruises. The plywood-and-Masonite file holds the made-up strips so that they are easy to refer to.

When the time comes to go, he will need up-to-date charts, but it will be easy to cut them into strips, remove the side strips from the old ones, and, paste them to the new. A pair of Masonite boards could be used instead of the file. The charts are used a strip at a time; a strip is placed on the bottom when you are through with it and the next one is taken from the top of the stack.

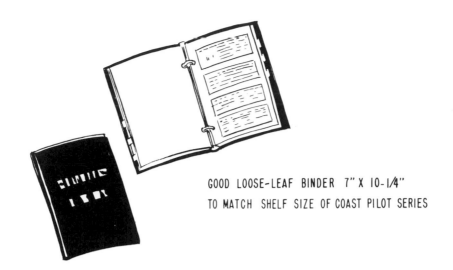

GOOD LOOSE-LEAF BINDER 7" X 10-1/4"
TO MATCH SHELF SIZE OF COAST PILOT SERIES

YOUR OWN PILOT BOOK

The idea shown above is merely the building up of scrapbooks of information that will be helpful in the operation of your boat and in your cruising. The idea is to have pertinent data all under one cover; the loose-leaf style is best because everything can be properly arranged and indexed under subjects.

There is no need to confine oneself to a single binder. It is a good idea to have them for (1) the power plant, with clipped articles or excerpts on engine operation, (2) trouble-shooting, (3) manufacturer's literature applying to your model, (4) data concerning your propeller, and (5) even literature on fittings you would like to install eventually. Another binder could hold information on piloting or navigation, with typed information on buoyage, harbors and their facilities, tidal conditions, mileages, and so on. Or, for that lengthy cruise you propose to take some day, a wealth of worthwhile information for the waters you have in mind can be culled from government publications and back numbers of boating magazines, oil companies' literature, and so on.

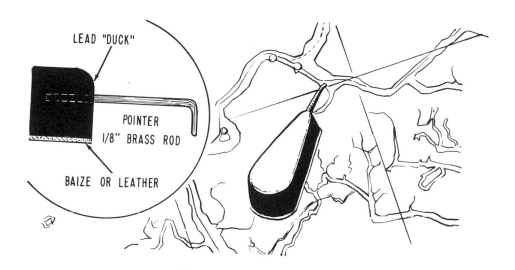

LEAD "DUCK"

POINTER
1/8" BRASS ROD

BAIZE OR LEATHER

CHART FINGER

This gadget is handy for chart work in narrow waters, such as those in the Inland Waterways South, where the multiplicity of markers and buoys along certain stretches requires constant reference to the chart. What is required is a holder, preferably weighted, with a small finger or pointer embedded in it. It can be moved along the chart from marker to marker as they are passed on such stretches, so that a glance will suffice to locate yourself on the chart. One does not have to be a slave to this, but it is handy for certain places.

CHAPTER 9

Tenders

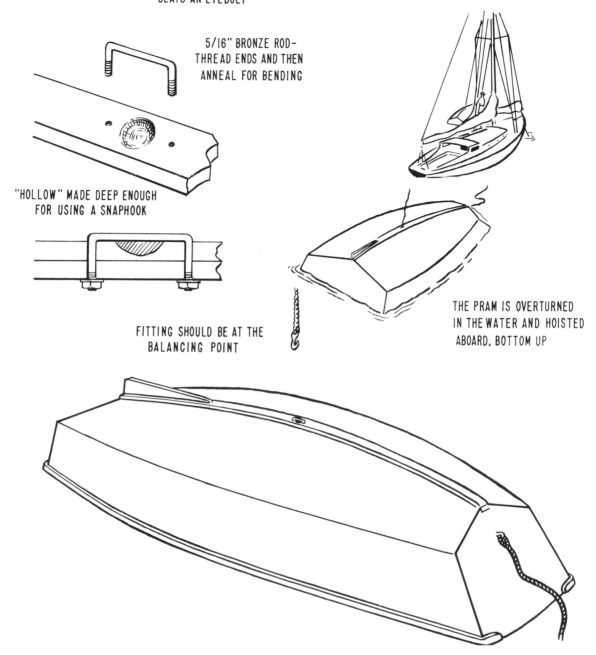

A NEARLY FLUSH FITTING LIKE THIS
BEATS AN EYEBOLT

5/16" BRONZE ROD—
THREAD ENDS AND THEN
ANNEAL FOR BENDING

"HOLLOW" MADE DEEP ENOUGH
FOR USING A SNAPHOOK

FITTING SHOULD BE AT THE
BALANCING POINT

THE PRAM IS OVERTURNED
IN THE WATER AND HOISTED
ABOARD, BOTTOM UP

GETTING A PRAM ABOARD

This is the easiest way I have seen of getting a pram aboard and into position for carrying. It is especially useful when the pram is heavy. It is just a matter of flipping the pram over in the water, reaching out to hook a line to a fitting in her bottom, and then using a halliard for hoisting her out and lowering to the desired position. Naturally, the fitting should be located at or near the balancing point, and the less it protrudes the better. The type shown, which I saw on a pram having an outside keel or shoe, is not too difficult to make and install and does not interfere with normal use of the boat.

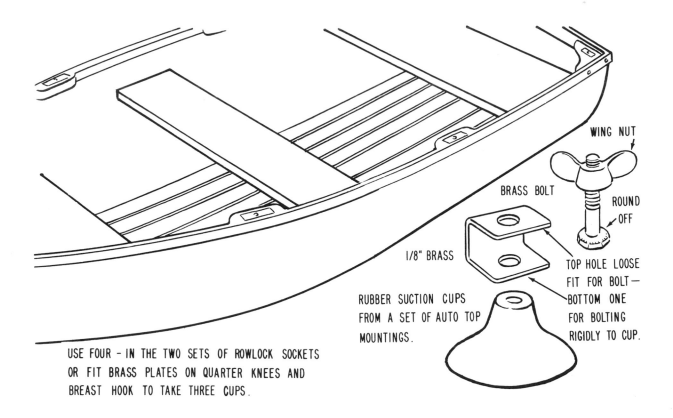

WING NUT

BRASS BOLT

ROUND OFF

1/8" BRASS

TOP HOLE LOOSE FIT FOR BOLT — BOTTOM ONE FOR BOLTING RIGIDLY TO CUP.

RUBBER SUCTION CUPS FROM A SET OF AUTO TOP MOUNTINGS.

USE FOUR - IN THE TWO SETS OF ROWLOCK SOCKETS OR FIT BRASS PLATES ON QUARTER KNEES AND BREAST HOOK TO TAKE THREE CUPS.

SUCTION CUPS TO HOLD TENDER

Rubber suction cups can be used to hold a tender on the cabin top, thus eliminating the necessity of having permanent chocks. Some use a regular auto-top mounting set as sold for carrying a small boat atop a car. The two crossbars are placed athwartships, with the tender secured to them or, better still, mounted in chocks attached to the bars.

Others use the cups only, as shown, but what must be done will depend on how the cups are held to the mounting frames you've bought in order to secure them. It is usually possible to unbolt the cups or to remove them by cutting the rivet. Then each can be rebolted to a U-shaped piece of brass. The top hole should be a loose fit for a brass machine bolt and should be long enough to go through the rowlock sockets. The underside of the head of the bolt should be rounded off, the idea being to allow the cup to set at whatever angle the camber of the cabin top requires.

Again, the tender may be rather flat and with-

out much sheer, as many modern ones are. In this case brass plates (each drilled with a hole, which will be a loose fit for the bolts being used) are secured—one to each quarter knee aft and another to the breasthook forward, with the holes continued through the wood of these members. Three suction cup fittings instead of the four for the two sets of rowlocks are then used. In either case, washerlike pieces of rubber or leather between the brass U's and the rowlock fittings or plates will help to prevent chafe.

Personally, I would want to check the holding of such suction cups on my particular cabin top before going ahead with making them up, although they do seem to hold well on any perfectly smooth surface such as a canvas-covered one. Mounting the tender is merely a matter of securing the cups with the boat right-side up, then in positioning her upside down, and finally pressing the cups down so that they will hold.

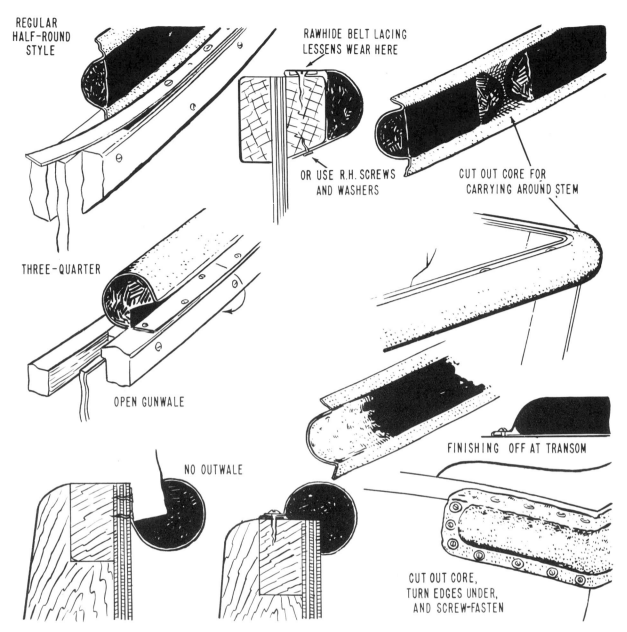

REGULAR HALF-ROUND STYLE

RAWHIDE BELT LACING LESSENS WEAR HERE

OR USE R.H. SCREWS AND WASHERS

CUT OUT CORE FOR CARRYING AROUND STEM

THREE-QUARTER

OPEN GUNWALE

NO OUTWALE

FINISHING OFF AT TRANSOM

CUT OUT CORE, TURN EDGES UNDER, AND SCREW-FASTEN

RUBBER GUNWALE GUARDS I

Getting rubber gunwale guards on neatly is largely a matter of securing properly whichever flap is fastened first. When the guard is positioned neatly along the gunwale, it should be held firmly in place by the final fastening of its other flap. However, this can throw considerable strain on that first row of fastenings. Large copper tacks are generally used and in time the webbing tends to chafe through over their heads. One way of avoiding that is to use a length of rawhide belt lacing, fastening it with flat-head brass screws and tacks in securing this edge. Ordinarily, the other flap is simply tacked as shown. Particularly where the dinghy will be pulled on and off the deck, many small round-head screws through washers will give far better holding.

If the dinghy has the usual full bow, it will not be difficult to carry the fender neatly around there. Otherwise, a good idea is to cut out a V-shaped section of the rubber core where the sharp bend will come.

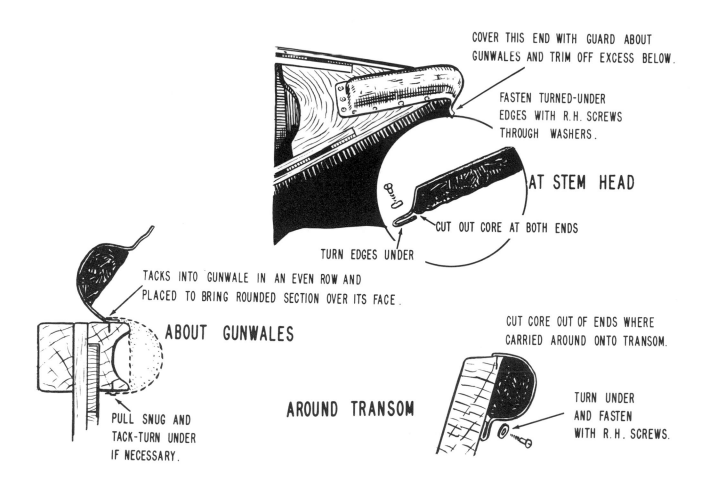

COVER THIS END WITH GUARD ABOUT GUNWALES AND TRIM OFF EXCESS BELOW.

FASTEN TURNED-UNDER EDGES WITH R.H. SCREWS THROUGH WASHERS.

AT STEM HEAD

CUT OUT CORE AT BOTH ENDS

TURN EDGES UNDER

TACKS INTO GUNWALE IN AN EVEN ROW AND PLACED TO BRING ROUNDED SECTION OVER ITS FACE.

ABOUT GUNWALES

PULL SNUG AND TACK-TURN UNDER IF NECESSARY.

CUT CORE OUT OF ENDS WHERE CARRIED AROUND ONTO TRANSOM.

AROUND TRANSOM

TURN UNDER AND FASTEN WITH R.H. SCREWS.

RUBBER GUNWALE GUARDS II

There may be as many methods of attaching the popular half-round rubber guard stock as there are ordinary kinds of rope, but the way shown here looks good, affords good protection, and stays put. A piece 12 inches long, with a couple of inches of its core cut out from the fabric at each end, should be fastened over the head of the stem first, especially if your boat has an overhanging counter.

Turn the edges in at the sides and inboard end and fasten with ½- or ¾-inch round-head screws through brass washers, carrying the forward end down onto the stem to conceal it later with the guard about the gunwales. This latter is fastened in the usual way, tacked so that when turned down the heads will be concealed, and placed so that the rounded section falls over the face of the gunwale. This may be the original grooved type, because the core of the

guard is stiff enough to bridge the gap. The top fastening, with the line of tacks, not over an inch apart and in a very even row, should be such that, with the guard pulled snugly down, the lower edge of the fabric can be tacked beneath the gunwale either as is or with its edge turned under.

Carry the guard well-around at the stern, leaving a gap wide enough to allow for the bracket of an outboard. The upper edge should be tacked to the top of the transom and the guard turned down, as in fastening about gunwales, with the fabric of the lower edge being turned under and secured with screws through washers. But before doing so, cut a couple of inches of the core away from the fabric at the ends, so that the raw edges can be turned under and screw-fastened.

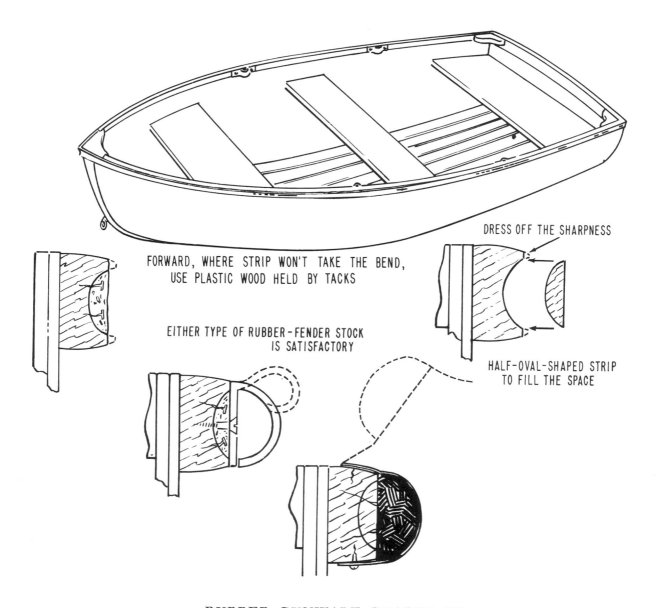

FORWARD, WHERE STRIP WON'T TAKE THE BEND,
USE PLASTIC WOOD HELD BY TACKS

DRESS OFF THE SHARPNESS

EITHER TYPE OF RUBBER-FENDER STOCK
IS SATISFACTORY

HALF-OVAL-SHAPED STRIP
TO FILL THE SPACE

RUBBER GUNWALE GUARDS III

In replacing a dinghy's rope gunwale guard with the rubber type, it is not necessary to remove the usual hollowed-out outwale strips, Jack Klien writes. He points out that if you do, and if the tender has the usual full bow, you will probably have to steam the new flat-faced strips to get them on.

Two years ago he did the job as shown here, and it is still satisfactory. First, he dressed off the sharpness of the edges alongside the groove, removed the chewed-up wood, and made the groove that much shallower. Shaped strips of spruce, held with small finishing nails, were then used to fill the major part of the length on each side. Forward, where the strips would not take the bend, a few tacks were partially driven and the hollow filled flush with plastic wood. Finally, the rubber-cored fender stock was put on. So far, there is no indication that the plastic wood is not holding as it should. If a shaped rubber guard is used, holes for its screws should be drilled carefully through the filling as well as through the filler strips.

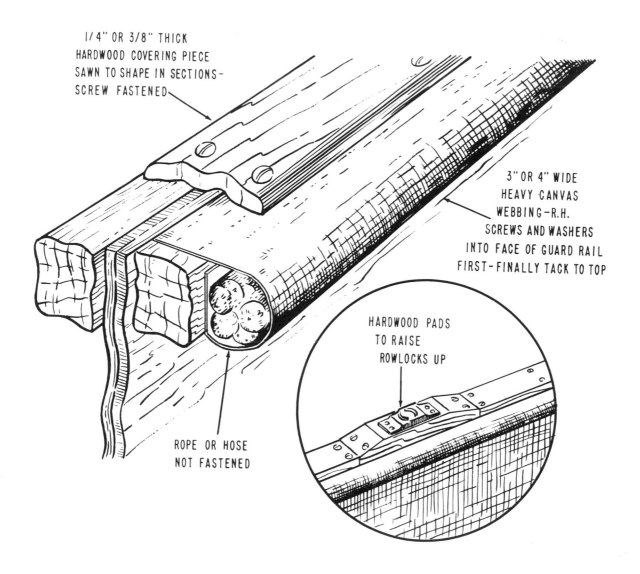

1/4" OR 3/8" THICK
HARDWOOD COVERING PIECE
SAWN TO SHAPE IN SECTIONS-
SCREW FASTENED

3" OR 4" WIDE
HEAVY CANVAS
WEBBING-R.H.
SCREWS AND WASHERS
INTO FACE OF GUARD RAIL
FIRST-FINALLY TACK TO TOP

ROPE OR HOSE
NOT FASTENED

HARDWOOD PADS
TO RAISE
ROWLOCKS UP

DINGHY FENDER

The dinghy fender illustrated works out well if your dinghy's gunwale construction is the closed type. The heavy canvas webbing used is a stock marine item and should be of a sufficient width to permit fastening, first to the face of the boat's outer guard or rail and then stretched up over a ⅞- or 1-inch-diameter rope or rubber hose. The canvas should then be tacked along the top and covered by a piece of hardwood. You cannot edge-bend a strip in place here; it must be sawed to shape in sections.

Whether used this way or as a covering for the rubber core of the manufactured fender stock, I like the heavy-webbing idea because it will not mar paint, stands up well, and can be easily scrubbed clean. Also, the covering-piece idea is a good one, whether as used here or to conceal the upper edge of the manufactured type, which otherwise will chafe through or pull away from its top fastenings in time. I would hesitate to use this fender on a dinghy with open-type gunwale construction, for I would not want to close off the spaces between the heads of the ribs with the wide covering piece.

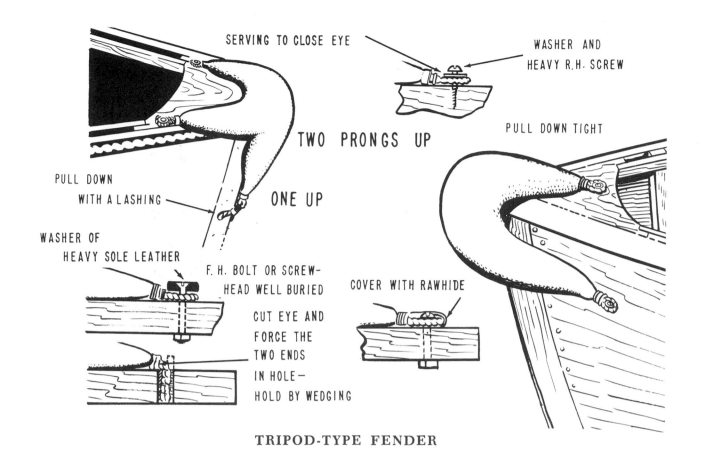

SERVING TO CLOSE EYE

WASHER AND
HEAVY R.H. SCREW

TWO PRONGS UP

PULL DOWN
WITH A LASHING

ONE UP

PULL DOWN TIGHT

WASHER OF
HEAVY SOLE LEATHER

F. H. BOLT OR SCREW-
HEAD WELL BURIED

COVER WITH RAWHIDE

CUT EYE AND
FORCE THE
TWO ENDS
IN HOLE—
HOLD BY WEDGING

TRIPOD-TYPE FENDER

The above drawing shows an effort to settle a point about which several readers have written in—whether it is proper to fasten a bow pudding or tripod-type fender on a dinghy with its two "prongs" (I guess you can call them that) up. Or, should one prong be up and two down? To my mind, it all depends on which will give the best protection and keep the fender properly in place. With two prongs up, the eyes on top should be fastened first, the fender coaxed over the stem, and the lower prong lashed through a neat hole bored far enough down through the stem to provide the necessary purchase. However, if the fender seems to fit better with one prong up, or if there is any personal preference, by all means put it on that way. But because the lower prongs must be firmly held, whatever is used to fasten them must get a good hold in something solid. Consequently, this method may not be so good with a lightly built hull. If it is the usual canvas-covered one, you may be able to strike a rib or use a neat block inside, but not with a molded-plastic or ply-wood hull.

The smaller sketches show different ways I have seen for fastening the usual rope loops or eyes of the prongs. Perhaps A is the simplest method, merely a heavy round-headed screw used with a washer, with serving on the eye to close it so the washer gets a proper bearing. I have not shown this pulled down. However, even then it has the fault that, if the dinghy is carried upside-down, the bare head of the screw may mar the paint or wood of the housetop. This can be avoided by using a sole-leather washer (as in B) heavy enough so that the flat head of the fastening can be well buried.

C shows an even neater way, a matter of cutting the rope eye at its outer end to twist or braid the strands of the two ends for forcing them through a hole bored to take them, then wedging them fast with tiny wood wedges set in glue and cut off neatly flush. D is a neat method I saw recently, a rawhide cover stitched over the whole thing, but how it was pulled down tight I did not find out.

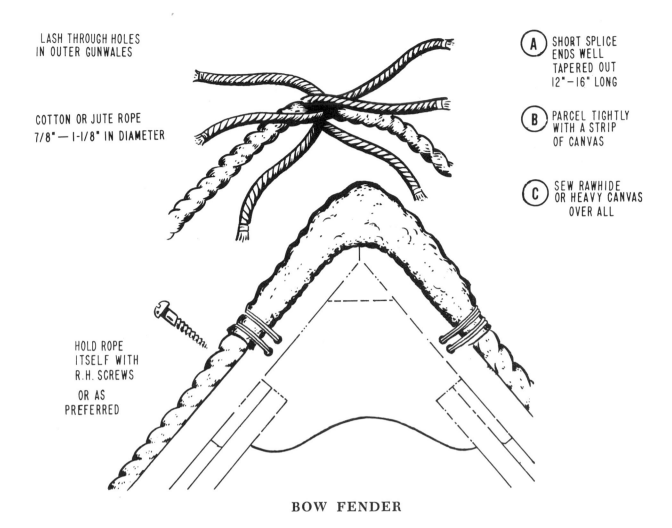

LASH THROUGH HOLES
IN OUTER GUNWALES

COTTON OR JUTE ROPE
7/8" — 1-1/8" IN DIAMETER

HOLD ROPE
ITSELF WITH
R.H. SCREWS

OR AS
PREFERRED

A SHORT SPLICE
ENDS WELL
TAPERED OUT
12"—16" LONG

B PARCEL TIGHTLY
WITH A STRIP
OF CANVAS

C SEW RAWHIDE
OR HEAVY CANVAS
OVER ALL

BOW FENDER

A bow fender or bumper that is neat, yet still gives good protection, can be worked on a tender's fender rope as shown here. The rope should be bought a couple of feet longer than otherwise required, cut into two equal lengths, and short-spliced together with the ends of the splice well-tapered out. Roll this smooth and then parcel tightly with a strip of canvas, making an effort to gain a shape that will hug the bow of the boat. Stitch on a cover of rawhide or heavy canvas (the stitching inside the angle), position it on the bow, and stretch the rope itself aft and fasten in whatever way is preferred, holding the ends of the bumper itself with a couple of lashings through holes in the outer gunwale. Where this is grooved out in the usual way, I've found that the best method of attaching rope is perhaps the easiest one: heavy, round-headed brass screws, driven about 8 inches apart, going between the two outer strands of the rope and likely through the inner one, but with their heads well buried so as not to mar anything.

Where additional protection is wanted, as when the tender is used for a boat with a long stern overhang, carry a 1-inch strap of leather from the breasthook or stemhead under and around the bumper, back onto itself, for fastening with a couple of flat-head screws. This spliced-in type bumper can also be made tripod-fashion by working into the splice a third short, tapered tail of rope to form the third leg of the bumper or fender. A loop of light line should have first been sewn into its tapered end, to permit securing either atop the breasthook or for carrying this third leg down the stem beneath, whichever way is preferred.

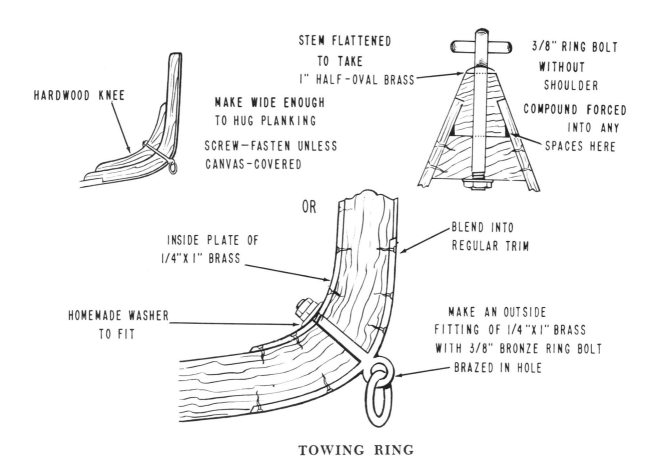

HARDWOOD KNEE

STEM FLATTENED
TO TAKE
1" HALF-OVAL BRASS

MAKE WIDE ENOUGH
TO HUG PLANKING

SCREW-FASTEN UNLESS
CANVAS-COVERED

3/8" RING BOLT
WITHOUT
SHOULDER

COMPOUND FORCED
INTO ANY
SPACES HERE

OR

INSIDE PLATE OF
1/4" X 1" BRASS

BLEND INTO
REGULAR TRIM

HOMEMADE WASHER
TO FIT

MAKE AN OUTSIDE
FITTING OF 1/4" X 1" BRASS
WITH 3/8" BRONZE RING BOLT
BRAZED IN HOLE

TOWING RING

If a tender must be towed, it is sensible to install a strong towing ring low down on the stem. However, as most lightly built boats are rather weak at this point, reinforcing is usually required to make for a proper job and to avoid having the towing painter literally tear the stem out in heavy going. The figure shows two suitable methods. The one in the upper sketch I observed in a lightly built, clinker-planked tender which had begun to show signs of the forefoot's being strained by the towing. Preferably, the inside knee should be cut from a natural-growth crook and made wide enough to fit neatly against the planking, so that screws can be driven into it and thereby distribute the strain over a greater area of the forefoot. This usually leaves on either side of the stem a space which must be filled with compound, as indicated on the drawing.

The installation shown in the lower sketch was in a larger boat with a fairly heavy stem. But it can be used with any boat, if the fitting is done in sequence. That is, the inside brass plate or strip should be made up first and fastened in place, with the hole through it located as wanted. The hole through the stem is then continued through this from within, and finally the outside fitting is made by bending and letting in the strip itself, marking the location of the hole from inside, and drilling. But be sure to make proper allowance for the angle of the hole in relation to the shape of the ring bolt.

While we are on this subject, it might be well to mention that a tightly fitted, and usually wide, stern seat is an objectionable feature in any dinghy that must be towed. This seat should be fitted in a way that will tie in the stern, but it should be done with the framework and not the actual seat. Leave a space open at the after end or along the sides, or have 1-inch spaces between the several boards of the seat, so that water draining to beneath the seat can, if enough collects, slop through as the boat is towed with its bow high and stern low.

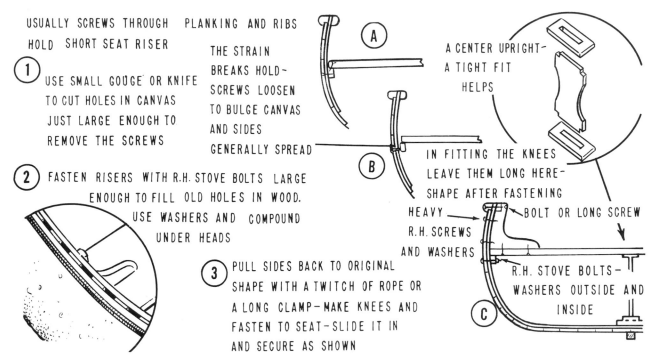

USUALLY SCREWS THROUGH PLANKING AND RIBS HOLD SHORT SEAT RISER

1 USE SMALL GOUGE OR KNIFE TO CUT HOLES IN CANVAS JUST LARGE ENOUGH TO REMOVE THE SCREWS

THE STRAIN BREAKS HOLD-SCREWS LOOSEN TO BULGE CANVAS AND SIDES GENERALLY SPREAD

2 FASTEN RISERS WITH R.H. STOVE BOLTS LARGE ENOUGH TO FILL OLD HOLES IN WOOD. USE WASHERS AND COMPOUND UNDER HEADS

3 PULL SIDES BACK TO ORIGINAL SHAPE WITH A TWITCH OF ROPE OR A LONG CLAMP-MAKE KNEES AND FASTEN TO SEAT-SLIDE IT IN AND SECURE AS SHOWN

A

B

C

A CENTER UPRIGHT-A TIGHT FIT HELPS

IN FITTING THE KNEES LEAVE THEM LONG HERE-SHAPE AFTER FASTENING

HEAVY R.H. SCREWS AND WASHERS

BOLT OR LONG SCREW

R.H. STOVE BOLTS-WASHERS OUTSIDE AND INSIDE

REINFORCING A CANVAS-COVERED BOAT

The drawing shows a way of correcting a fault that is rather common with canvas-covered boats and canoes. The center seat throws considerable strain on its end risers or strips. If these are short and not bolted, but fastened with screws through the planking and ribs as shown in *A*, you are almost sure to develop the condition shown in *B*. The screws loosen or break off and work in their holes, making bulges in the canvas, eventually causing the fabric to fail at such places.

C shows how this condition can be corrected, although the method has the fault that the round heads of the bolts and screws show outside the canvas. There seems no alternative, however, for the light ribs and thin planking with their soft wood will not hold screw fastenings driven from inside. It is absolutely necessary to remove the old screws to end the harm being done to the covering. Locate each from its bulge; then, do not slit the canvas, but cut out a tiny disc of it, using a small gouge or sharp knife an removing only enough to permit removal of the screw. The washer to be used with the new fastening will more than take in the hole.

With the seat and its risers removed, renew the latter, if it is in doubtful condiion, and refasten in place, using brass or Everdur round-head stove bolts, 3/16 inch or whatever is a tight fit for the old holes. Insert one through each rib, heads outside over washers, using some plastic compound. Pull the nuts down over the washers and then inside to bed well over the canvas; do not cut into it. As the sides will have spread, use a long cabinet clamp or a rope and stick to pull them together until the ends of the seat, slipped back in temporarily, are gripped. Then, cut cardboard patterns for the knees. If proper crooks are not available, make these heavier in the throat than shown and shape the outer edge to notch under the inner gunwale and hug the rib. Use a bolt or long screw to secure each knee at the gunwale and a couple of heavy round-head brass screws with washers from the outside. There should also be screws through the ends of the seat into risers, preferably in fresh locations. An upright support beneath the center of the seat will ease the strain on the ends by acting as a strut, if it is made a crowding fit and its top and bottom are properly held as in chocks.

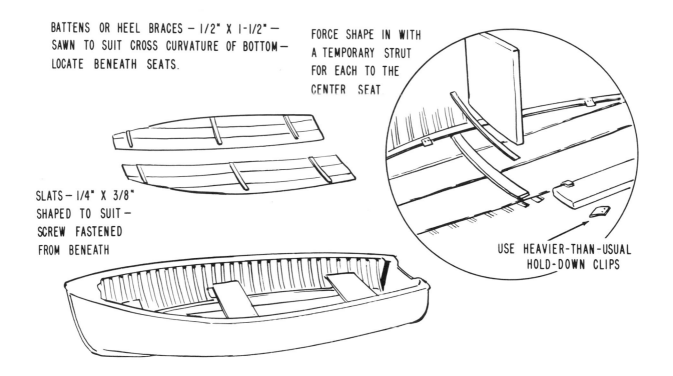

BATTENS OR HEEL BRACES — 1/2" X 1-1/2" — SAWN TO SUIT CROSS CURVATURE OF BOTTOM — LOCATE BENEATH SEATS.

FORCE SHAPE IN WITH A TEMPORARY STRUT FOR EACH TO THE CENTER SEAT.

SLATS — 1/4" X 3/8" SHAPED TO SUIT — SCREW FASTENED FROM BENEATH

USE HEAVIER-THAN-USUAL HOLD-DOWN CLIPS

TEAK FLOORBOARDS

To my mind, teak makes not only the best-looking but also the most-practical floorboards for a tender or any other boat. It is expensive wood, but for such thin slats and the few crosspieces the cost is not excessive and is offset by the fact that no painting or varnishing is necessary and that such wood never becomes slippery.

Although it is no great problem to make the slats for a flat bottom or even a semi-V-bottom tender, it is not as easy for a round-bottom boat. With this wood, you cannot rely on springing the floor boards to shape, but you must do what you can to build the shape into them. The best way is to have the battens holding the several slats of each rack on top, rather than beneath. The weight on the slats is then better distributed over the bottom, and the battens can act as heel braces for rowing, a feature that most boats lack. Also, and this is important if the boat is canvas-covered, the weight is carried by the ribs and not thrown on the thin planking, as when the battens are underneath.

The top ones can be made on the heavy side, with the curvature sawed into them rather than attempting later to force the rack to shape. Fastenings should be bronze or brass screws driven from beneath, so that any points which break through the battens can be filed flush.

Another trick in installing such floorboards is not to rely entirely at first on the hold-down clips to keep them in place. It may be well to make extra heavy clips, but it is usually difficult to fasten them securely. If there is much fore-and-aft curvature and twist which the racks must take, place a slat of ¼-inch plywood on top of the center batten of each and then cut two struts or braces from wide common stock, with the bottom ends shaped to suit. Their length should be such that they will crowd in beneath the center seat when the racks are forced down against the bottom. They are only temporary and will not look too bad, if left in place for a week or so until the racks set to shape. Then the regular hold-down clips can be used.

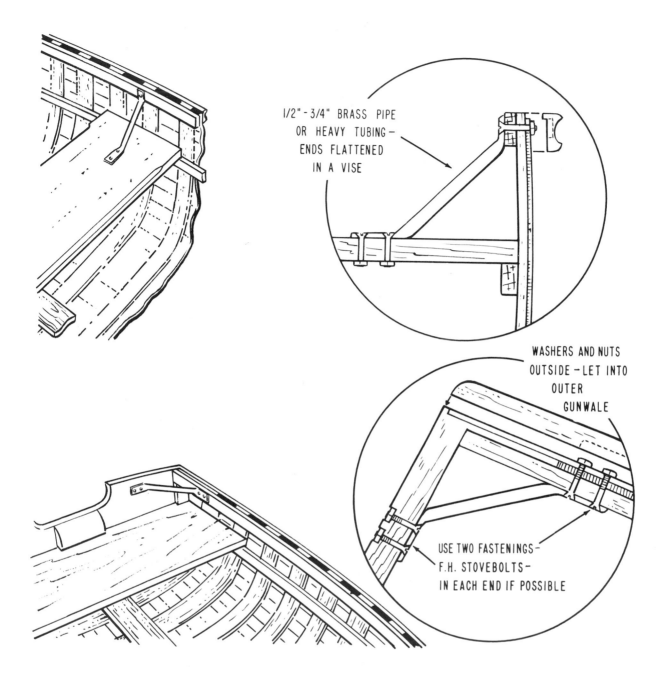

1/2" - 3/4" BRASS PIPE
OR HEAVY TUBING—
ENDS FLATTENED
IN A VISE

WASHERS AND NUTS
OUTSIDE—LET INTO
OUTER
GUNWALE

USE TWO FASTENINGS—
F.H. STOVEBOLTS—
IN EACH END IF POSSIBLE

STIFFENING KNEES

A lightly built boat particularly deserves quarter knees and seat knees, the former to strengthen the stern construction (especially if an outboard motor is used) and the seat knees to prevent the gunwales from being racked in turning the boat up on her side. The type shown above serve well when natural crooks for making proper wood knees cannot be had. They are simply lengths of brass pipe or heavy tubing of a size in keeping with that of the boat, with their ends flattened and bent to the correct angles in a vise.

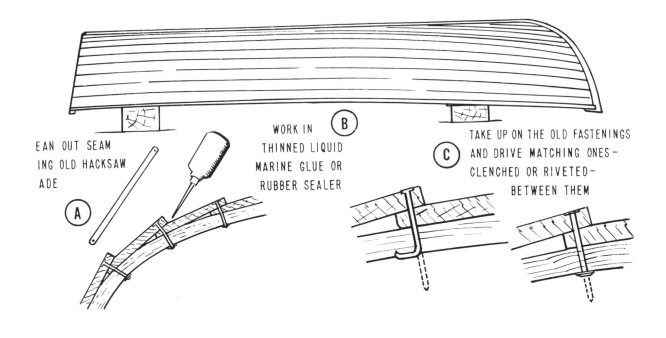

EAN OUT SEAM
ING OLD HACKSAW
ADE

(A)

(B) WORK IN
THINNED LIQUID
MARINE GLUE OR
RUBBER SEALER

(C) TAKE UP ON THE OLD FASTENINGS
AND DRIVE MATCHING ONES—
CLENCHED OR RIVETED—
BETWEEN THEM

OR
BARE THE PLANKING AND FIBERGLASS

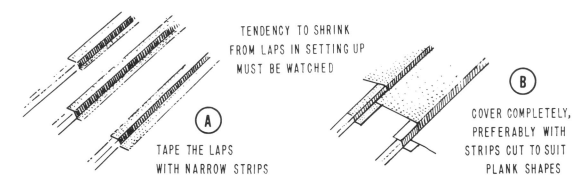

TENDENCY TO SHRINK
FROM LAPS IN SETTING UP
MUST BE WATCHED

(A) TAPE THE LAPS
WITH NARROW STRIPS

(B) COVER COMPLETELY,
PREFERABLY WITH
STRIPS CUT TO SUIT
PLANK SHAPES

FIXING A LEAKING LAPSTRAKE BOAT

I can remember my dad telling me that any lapstrake boat was worth working on because it almost always could be put back into usable condition. And this has proven true. For one thing, such boats are invariably well built, made originally of good materials by good men, so that one is not apt to be up against actual structural defects. What can give trouble, though, is the tendency of the lap seams to leak.

First, determine whether the leak is caused by the way the boat is being used. A lapstrake boat really should be kept in the water; so, if you use one with a trailer, give her a chance. One way is to keep the loaded boat in the shade as much as possible. Another way is to paint her, preferably inside as well as out, white or some light shade—not a dark, hot color.

In an extreme case, particularly where the wood along the rows of fastenings is badly checked, resort to fiber glass.

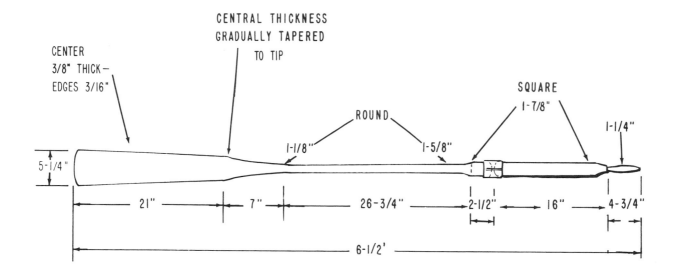

CENTRAL THICKNESS
GRADUALLY TAPERED
TO TIP

CENTER
3/8" THICK —
EDGES 3/16"

ROUND

SQUARE
1-7/8"

1-1/4"

1-1/8"   1-5/8"

5-1/4"

21"   7"   26-3/4"   2-1/2"   16"   4-3/4"

6-1/2'

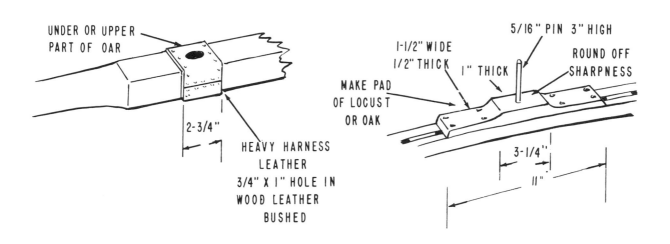

UNDER OR UPPER
PART OF OAR

2-3/4"

HEAVY HARNESS
LEATHER
3/4" X 1" HOLE IN
WOOD LEATHER
BUSHED

5/16" PIN 3" HIGH

1-1/2" WIDE
1/2" THICK   1" THICK

ROUND OFF
SHARPNESS

MAKE PAD
OF LOCUST
OR OAK

3-1/4"

11"

SQUARE-SHANKED OARS

I have always been partial to oars shaped as illustrated, and if the proportions are right, they seem perfect as to balance and are a pleasure to row with. It is a good shape to follow if you want to make a pair as a spare-time project, for the square shank, or section of the loom next to the handle, makes it easier to get the lower part of the loom and the blade true than where the loom is, as usual, round for its entire tapered length. Clear and straight-grained spruce, ash, and sassafras are all suitable woods, as well as some local woods with a good reputation for lightness, resilient strength, and retention of shape.

Starting with a 6-inch-wide plank dressed to the required 1⅞-inch thickness, the rough shaping can be done on a bandsaw; then a draw-knife can be used to round and taper the lower loom and thin down the blade to the point where a small plane, spokeshave, and a coarse file are best—until the oar is ready for sanding.

The dimensions given were taken off a pair used with a lovely old St. Lawrence skiff. The rowlock pads are also shown because, with the leather about the oar and the hole for the pin bushed with it, rowing is noiseless and each stroke is cushioned.

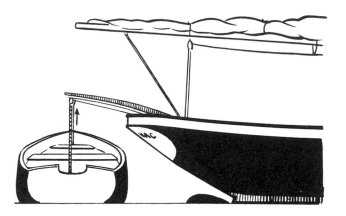

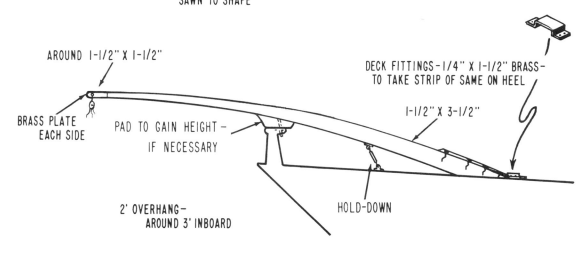

THE PAIR ARE MADE OF OAK-
SAWN TO SHAPE

AROUND 1-1/2" X 1-1/2"

BRASS PLATE
EACH SIDE

PAD TO GAIN HEIGHT —
IF NECESSARY

2' OVERHANG —
AROUND 3' INBOARD

DECK FITTINGS-1/4" X 1-1/2" BRASS-
TO TAKE STRIP OF SAME ON HEEL

1-1/2" X 3-1/2"

HOLD-DOWN

DEMOUNTABLE DAVITS

John Mains writes to say how handy he has found a pair of removable davits on his 36-foot schooner.

He explains that he did not want a permanent pair, since for open water use he much prefers to carry his small boat on deck. However, he has a rather heavy dinghy and he uses it a lot for side trips and fishing, when he wants to have it convenient to use. Still, he didn't want to have to tow it, particularly when running under power from Miami to the Keys or to Florida's West Coast.

This pair of davits was finally made and has given perfect satisfaction.

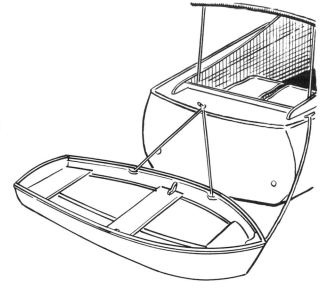

TWO STRUTS — BRASS-ROD OR WOOD —
FROM A SOCKET IN STERN RAIL
TO ROWLOCK SOCKETS. KEEP TENDER
CLEAR OF STERN AT ANCHOR.

DINGHY STRUTS

The idea shown above may or may not work out, depending largely on the freeboard of the cruiser's stern in comparison with that of the tender. Some boats use a single strut from a fitting in the rail aft to a socket located centrally inside the gunwale of the tender, also depending on bow and stern painters to the mother boat. With the struts rigged V-shaped to the rowlock sockets, the tender's painter is carried aboard merely as a precaution. There should be plenty of play in the rig to allow for the wash of waves and the surge from passing boats.

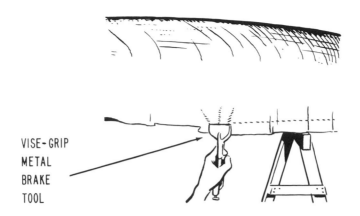

VISE-GRIP
METAL
BRAKE
TOOL

STRETCHING CANVAS

The best tool I have seen for stretching canvas when re-covering a boat, or laying it on a deck, is called a vise-grip metal brake, and carries on it the name Peterson Manufacturing Company, De Witt, Nebraska.

CHAPTER **10**

Outboard
Boats

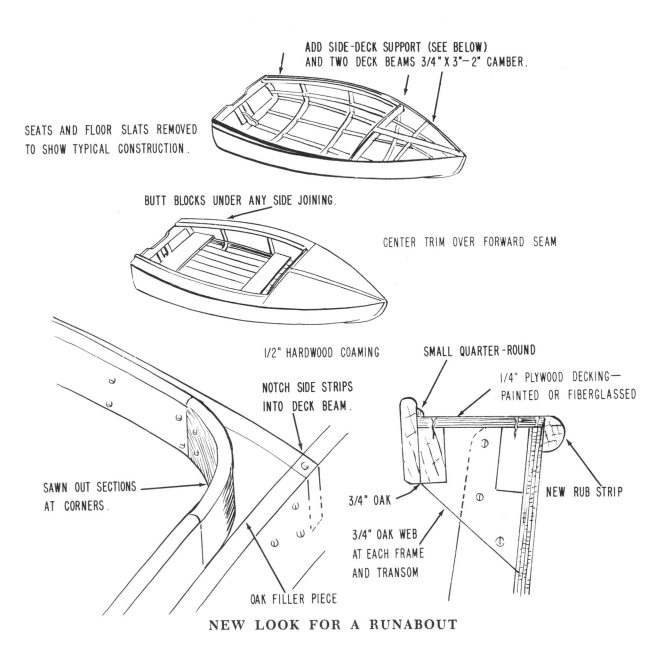

ADD SIDE-DECK SUPPORT (SEE BELOW)
AND TWO DECK BEAMS 3/4" X 3"—2" CAMBER.

SEATS AND FLOOR SLATS REMOVED
TO SHOW TYPICAL CONSTRUCTION.

BUTT BLOCKS UNDER ANY SIDE JOINING.

CENTER TRIM OVER FORWARD SEAM

1/2" HARDWOOD COAMING

SMALL QUARTER-ROUND

1/4" PLYWOOD DECKING—
PAINTED OR FIBERGLASSED

NOTCH SIDE STRIPS
INTO DECK BEAM.

SAWN OUT SECTIONS
AT CORNERS.

3/4" OAK

3/4" OAK WEB
AT EACH FRAME
AND TRANSOM

NEW RUB STRIP

OAK FILLER PIECE

NEW LOOK FOR A RUNABOUT

Most outboards of the open runabout sort can be improved, if one goes about it intelligently. The basic requirement is a suitable boat, one that is big enough (14 feet or longer) and in good-enough condition to warrant the time and money to be spent. Obviously, it would be foolish to weight down a racing-type boat with what is shown here, just as it would be unwise to try to improve a boat of flimsy build.

Nowadays, any number of boats will qualify for such improvements. Indeed, quite often the main difference between that outboard you

bought as a standard model and the deluxe variation of it that you would like to have is a forward deck and narrow side decks. The boat's construction, principally about the gunwales, will determine what can be done, but with plywood and wooden boats of the usual kind, a couple of forward beams can be fitted and several sets of side deck supports constructed, as shown; then plywood can be laid. Do not omit the coaming and try for rounded corners. From there on it is a matter of adding the fittings and accessories wanted.

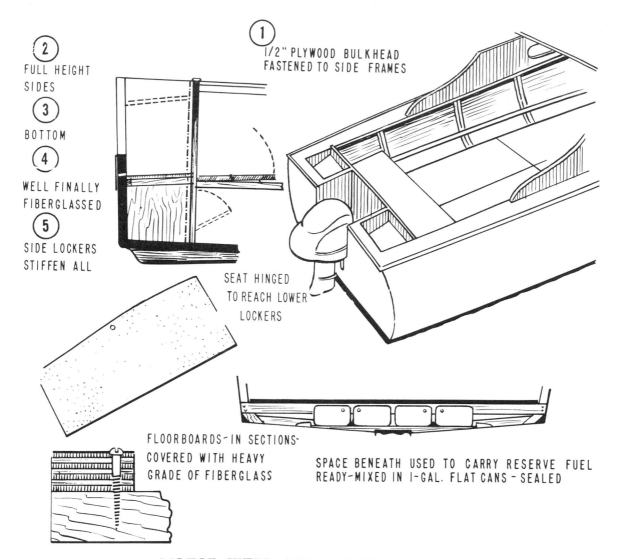

② FULL HEIGHT SIDES

③ BOTTOM

④ WELL FINALLY FIBERGLASSED

⑤ SIDE LOCKERS STIFFEN ALL

① 1/2" PLYWOOD BULKHEAD FASTENED TO SIDE FRAMES

SEAT HINGED TO REACH LOWER LOCKERS

FLOORBOARDS-IN SECTIONS-COVERED WITH HEAVY GRADE OF FIBERGLASS

SPACE BENEATH USED TO CARRY RESERVE FUEL READY-MIXED IN I-GAL. FLAT CANS - SEALED

MOTOR WELL AND FLOORBOARDS

John Hanson wrote to say how helpful he had found fiber glass in making improvements to his outboard cruiser, mentioning that he and several friends had found it particularly satisfactory for covering plywood floor boards. It is best to have the boards in sections, he says, rounding off the sharpness of the edges and carrying the fiber glass over. Use the color additive in the glue mix and a little no-skid compound in the final coat. Two of these jobs show no signs of wear after two years.

Any space in the bilge may be put to good use. By using suitably shaped, flat 1-gallon cans, Mr. Hanson is able to carry aboard a reserve supply of ready-mixed fuel. Although the storage place may be cool, the cans should not be filled completely. After turning the cap down tightly it should be temporarily sealed in some way, he says.

Mr. Hanson sent a sketch showing how motor compartments had been put into two boats. As the interpretation of it here shows, the job is largely a matter of fitting a bulkhead to the after set of side frames and having holes cut to give access to the lower lockers. The lockers result from fastening the side pieces and the bottom to form the motor compartment or well. By using fiber glass it is an easy matter to have a tight job. Both boats have been stiffened appreciably by the addition.

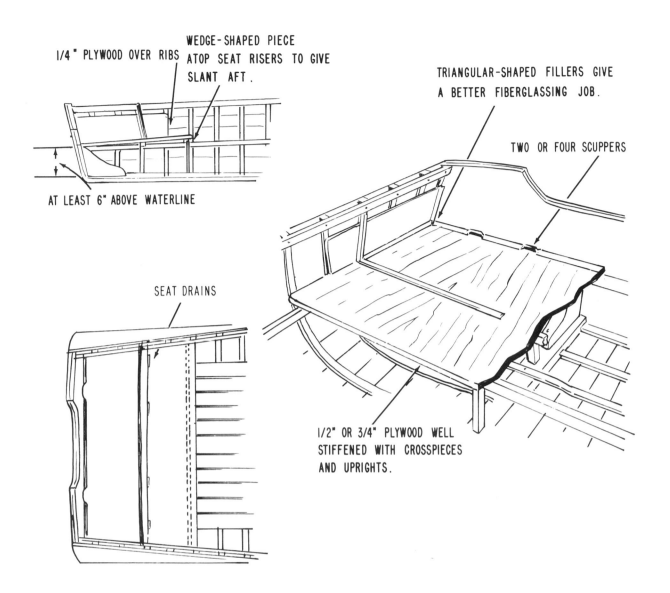

1/4" PLYWOOD OVER RIBS

WEDGE-SHAPED PIECE ATOP SEAT RISERS TO GIVE SLANT AFT.

AT LEAST 6" ABOVE WATERLINE

TRIANGULAR-SHAPED FILLERS GIVE A BETTER FIBERGLASSING JOB.

TWO OR FOUR SCUPPERS

SEAT DRAINS

1/2" OR 3/4" PLYWOOD WELL STIFFENED WITH CROSSPIECES AND UPRIGHTS.

SELF-DRAINING MOTOR WELL

As Asa Wilcox mentioned when sending in this idea, any outboard boat that is used where the water can become rough should have a "safe" stern. His way of providing for this not only gives a self-draining well or compartment for the motor, but also improves the boat's seating arrangement. The seat part could be omitted, although the space beneath it can be used for fuel tanks and reserve containers.

This is a lapstrake boat, something that ordinarily complicates making such a compartment watertight. His trick is to fasten plywood to each side over the ribs first. Then it is easy to line the finished compartment with fiber glass. Before this is done, small, triangular filler strips should be put in as shown and 4-inch-wide strips of fiber glass glued over them. Then, the bottom and sides can be covered by separate pieces to lap over. This method helps to avoid the tendency of fiber glass to pull away from such angles or corners and the risk of its being cracked by the vibration from the motor.

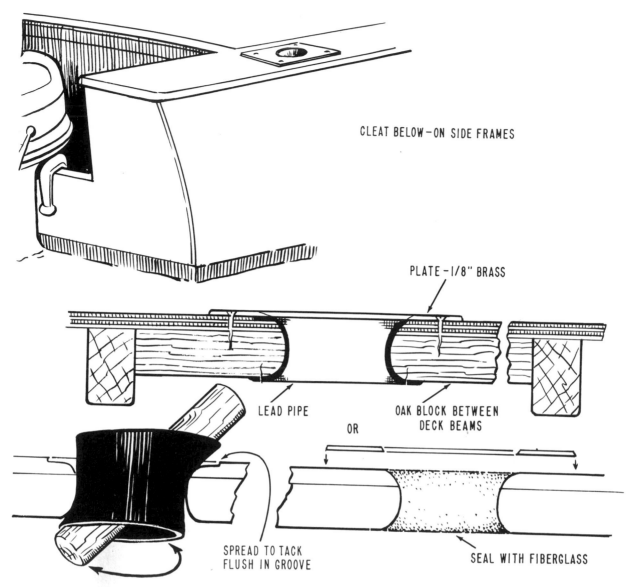

CLEAT BELOW—ON SIDE FRAMES

PLATE—1/8" BRASS

LEAD PIPE

OAK BLOCK BETWEEN
DECK BEAMS

OR

SPREAD TO TACK
FLUSH IN GROOVE

SEAL WITH FIBERGLASS

HAWSE HOLES

Cleats on the deck of any small boat are usually in the way of someone's toes. On the after deck of a boat used seriously for fishing, they are a nuisance when some one aboard is trolling or playing a fish from the stern.

More and more large outboards designed for open-water fishing are getting around this difficulty by installing deck hawse holes.

The sketch shows two types commonly installed by owners of such craft. In both cases, the deck in the way of the hole is reinforced by an oak block let in between the deck beams. The oval hole should be cut and its edges rounded. It should be amply large for the heaviest lines used. You will notice that in one example the edges are sealed by lead pipe, in the other with fiber glass. Lead pipe in a size to match the hole can be stretched or spread by rotating a short length of broomstick inside it, then carefully tapping down the ends to tack as shown. When using fiber glass it is merely a matter of building up a thick covering over the rounded edges. The plate, which gives a finished effect, is usually made of ⅛-inch brass; it may be chrome-plated to match the boat's hardware.

If nylon dock lines are used, the lead lining tends to blacken them at points of contact.

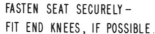
FASTEN SEAT SECURELY -
FIT END KNEES, IF POSSIBLE.

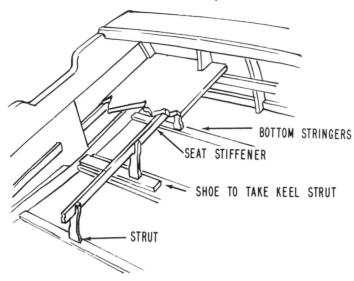

BOTTOM STRINGERS

SEAT STIFFENER

SHOE TO TAKE KEEL STRUT

STRUT

HOOK (EXAGGERATED)

STRAIGHTENING THE HOOK

George Ball points out that a hook is liable to develop in the bottom of a fast outboard which will cut down its speed more than you might think. To check for this defect, turn the boat upside-down and use a straight stick laid in line with the keel, first in the center and then on either side. The bottom should be flat, slightly rounded, or full. If it is not, the speed of the boat will suffer. When there is a hollow it shows just ahead of the transom edge. The usual cause is the weight of the motor. The bottom of Mr. Ball's boat, which was off almost an inch, was forced back into shape by fitting struts or braces, as shown. Much depends on the boat's construction, but the idea is to use the after seat as a brace.

First, you must strengthen the seat and perhaps stiffen its forward edge. Notice that the seat is tied to a batten secured to the transom and stiffened by a strip fastened on edge, which is used to take the struts. After making sure that the seat risers themselves are well-secured, the ends should be fastened tight. If the boat has a stern seat out from the transom, it might be wise to move the seat back. A transom seat that is tied in strengthens the entire stern of a boat. The struts that bear against the bottom should not throw the strain on isolated spots. The side struts can be notched into strips fastened in some way to the bottom and then carried far enough forward so that they more than take in the distorted area. The center strut can bear against the keelson or notch into a shoe. Cut tiny limbers to drain such notched places. In finally fitting the struts, make them long enough so that, when they are forced home, the bottom will be flat outside.

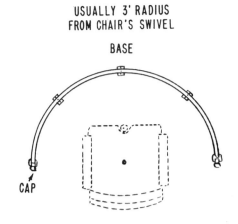

USUALLY 3' RADIUS
FROM CHAIR'S SWIVEL

BASE

CAP

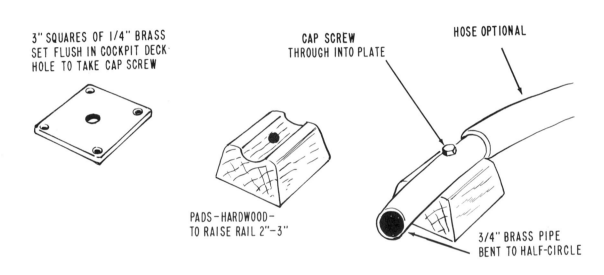

3" SQUARES OF 1/4" BRASS
SET FLUSH IN COCKPIT DECK·
HOLE TO TAKE CAP SCREW

CAP SCREW
THROUGH INTO PLATE

HOSE OPTIONAL

PADS—HARDWOOD—
TO RAISE RAIL 2"–3"

3/4" BRASS PIPE
BENT TO HALF-CIRCLE

FISHING-CHAIR FOOTREST

Now that big and husky boats can be had for outboards, they are being used more and more to fish open waters, including even those well offshore in settled weather. Some of these boats are veritable "fishing machines," with fishing chairs, outriggers, depth indicators which double as fish finders, and so on. Their owners display great ingenuity in improving their boats to make them easier to use or more efficient.

The footrest shown is a good example. Instead of using bronze fittings to secure it permanently, the owner set brass plates flush into the cockpit floor. These take cap screws which pull the shaped piece of pipe down over the hardwood pads, holding all securely against whatever strains are put on it. Removing the footrest is also an easy operation. The holes in the pipe should be an easy fit for the screws. Taper the ends of the screws so they will "find" their holes or threads.

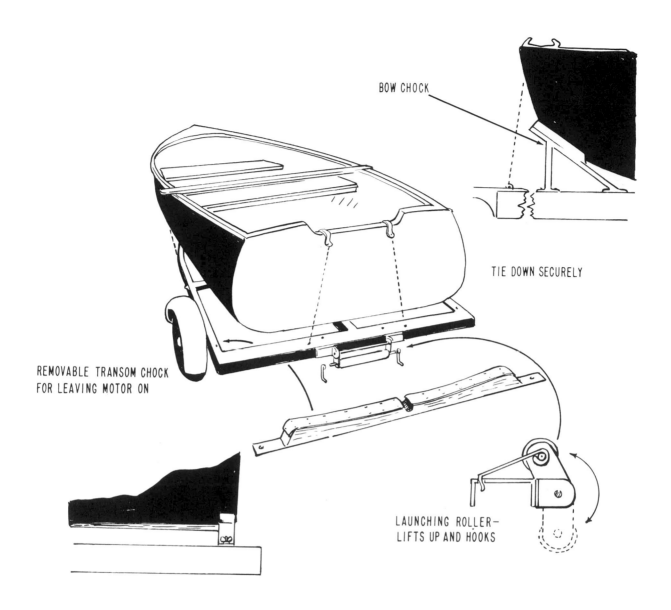

BOW CHOCK

TIE DOWN SECURELY

REMOVABLE TRANSOM CHOCK
FOR LEAVING MOTOR ON

LAUNCHING ROLLER—
LIFTS UP AND HOOKS

IMPROVING A BOAT TRAILER

As Jack Jenkins mentioned when sending me rough sketches for those reproduced here, most low-priced boat trailers lack the modern conveniences of (1) a transom support for leaving the motor in place and (2) provision for rolling the boat on and off. If you try to add these, the difficulty often is that one will interfere with the other. Jenkins solved the problem by having the transom support removable and the roller hinged. The former, which is shaped properly for the boat's bottom, is held to the frame by end bolts with wing nuts. Naturally, the chocks must be right for the hull. Proper tie-downs

should also be used. Those shown are made of heavy shock cord—a pair to lock the transom to its chock, and one to hold the bow in its chock. The latter, which is also an addition, was made of wood, cut out to take the stem, and riveted to pipe uprights bolted to the trailer frame.

The launching roller is made of a partial length of an old roller from a washing machine or a wringer. With the transom chock withdrawn for launching or loading, it is lifted up and held by a pair of hooks which slip over the end extensions.

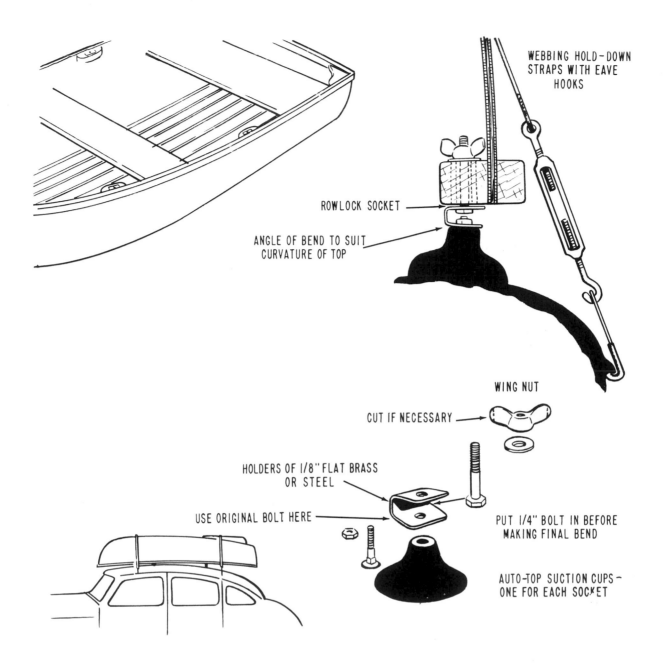

WEBBING HOLD-DOWN STRAPS WITH EAVE HOOKS

ROWLOCK SOCKET

ANGLE OF BEND TO SUIT CURVATURE OF TOP

WING NUT

CUT IF NECESSARY

HOLDERS OF 1/8" FLAT BRASS OR STEEL

USE ORIGINAL BOLT HERE

PUT 1/4" BOLT IN BEFORE MAKING FINAL BEND

AUTO-TOP SUCTION CUPS — ONE FOR EACH SOCKET

CAR-TOP MOUNTING

John Clarke, who sent me this idea, explains that he started out carrying his 10-foot, molded-plywood outboard on a standard set of car-top mountings, but found this way of attaching the rubber suction cups directly to the rowlock sockets equally satisfactory. As he points out, some boats have their rowlock sockets let in the inwales, while others have them carried by pads, as are his. In any case, the boat is not likely to be heavy enough to throw much strain on its gunwale edges. The tie-down straps are a sensible precaution whether you are mounting the boat this way or using a regular carrier. Some suction cups will leave the car's finish stained; others will not. The difference is in the sort of rubber used. The nonstaining cups are harder to locate, but are worth the trouble.

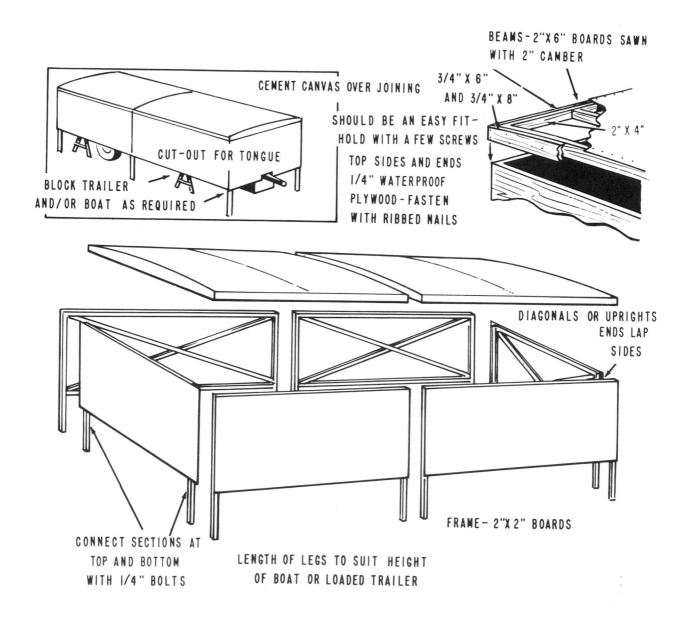

CEMENT CANVAS OVER JOINING

SHOULD BE AN EASY FIT-
HOLD WITH A FEW SCREWS

TOP SIDES AND ENDS
1/4" WATERPROOF
PLYWOOD-FASTEN
WITH RIBBED NAILS

CUT-OUT FOR TONGUE

BLOCK TRAILER
AND/OR BOAT AS REQUIRED

BEAMS-2"X6" BOARDS SAWN
WITH 2" CAMBER

3/4" X 6"
AND 3/4" X 8"

2" X 4"

DIAGONALS OR UPRIGHTS
ENDS LAP
SIDES

FRAME- 2"X 2" BOARDS

CONNECT SECTIONS AT
TOP AND BOTTOM
WITH 1/4" BOLTS

LENGTH OF LEGS TO SUIT HEIGHT
OF BOAT OR LOADED TRAILER

TAKE-DOWN BOATHOUSE

This is a good idea for the man who must leave his outboard boat outside for the winter. Actually, it is a removable boathouse that is made big enough to cover the boat and trailer. A boat is supposed to be perfectly supported by a modern trailer, so why not leave her on the trailer for winter storage?

The size of the house must suit the loaded boat, but generally stock-size plywood panels can be used to advantage. The legs help to save material and it seems a good idea to have the bottom open. The sections should be bolted together and the roof sections made to drop down, so that the whole thing can be disassembled easily and the parts stacked neatly.

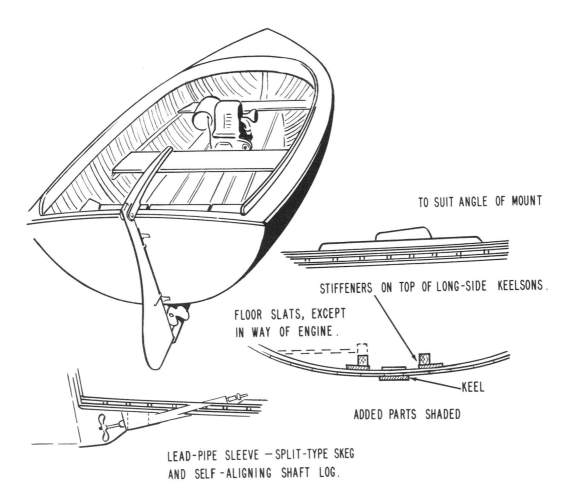

TO SUIT ANGLE OF MOUNT

STIFFENERS ON TOP OF LONG-SIDE KEELSONS.

FLOOR SLATS, EXCEPT
IN WAY OF ENGINE.

KEEL

ADDED PARTS SHADED

LEAD-PIPE SLEEVE — SPLIT-TYPE SKEG
AND SELF-ALIGNING SHAFT LOG.

AN INBOARD VARIATION

Harry Prentiss, in telling about installing a 10-horse-power, air-cooled inboard engine in a 12-foot, round-bottom boat, brought up the point that old boats of this type can often be bought at a very low cost. Such boats will not drive fast with an outboard, but they are good for inboard power. Usually you are up against two problems: (1) invariably, the hull is lightly built or, because of age, requires strengthening and stiffening and (2) the shaft must be carried through the bottom in such a way that it will remain watertight.

As the sketch shows, Harry first put in a pair of side keelsons, secured stiffeners on top of them, and substituted a heavier keel. No dimensions are given for these because the members must suit the particular boat and must be such that they can be bent into place and se-

curely fastened. Because of her construction each boat presents particular problems when it comes to the latter. In this case Mr. Prentiss steamed both the keelsons and the keel and used heavy screws for fastenings.

A lead pipe, with its ends flanged over and screw-fastened in compound, was used to provide an alley which, when sealed by screwing the self-aligning shaft log in place in compound, resulted in a rig that has remained perfectly tight. Outside, a heavy two-piece skeg was bolted in place, with long ¼-inch bolts in pairs straddling the alley. Holes for these went through the frames, and the skeg was pulled tight over a canvas gasket in compound. From there on, the installation was as usual for such a job.

CHAPTER 11

Open Sail

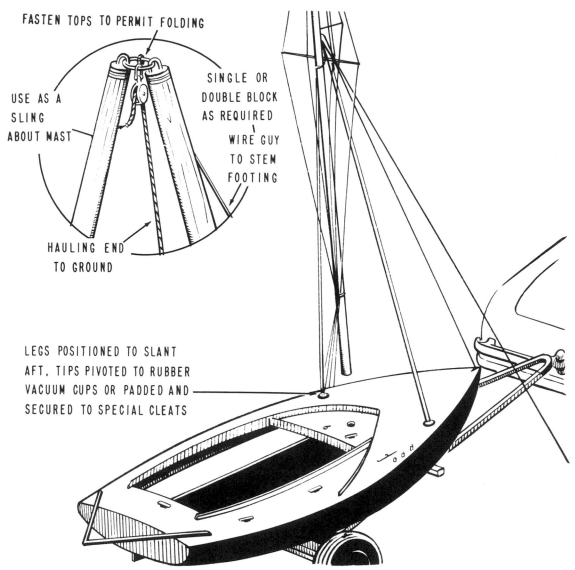

FASTEN TOPS TO PERMIT FOLDING

USE AS A SLING ABOUT MAST

SINGLE OR DOUBLE BLOCK AS REQUIRED

WIRE GUY TO STEM FOOTING

HAULING END TO GROUND

LEGS POSITIONED TO SLANT AFT, TIPS PIVOTED TO RUBBER VACUUM CUPS OR PADDED AND SECURED TO SPECIAL CLEATS

PORTABLE SHEAR LEGS FOR TRAILER CARRYING

A couple I know used two portable shear legs effectively to step the mast of their 20-foot boat. The legs, about 2 inches in diameter, were long enough to reach just above the balancing point on the mast. Each had a heavy-duty vacuum cup attached in such a way that the leg was free to pivot slightly. The tops of the pair were joined by an arrangement of staples made from brass rod and an oval connecting link. A single block was shackled into the latter; opposite, there was fastened a wire guy to lead to the boat's stem-head fitting. The legs could be folded for stowing when on a trailer.

In use, the legs were set up over predeter-mined spots on deck and steadied by the guy, which was made fast in such a manner as to allow the legs to slant well aft. The block aloft was directly above the mast partners or hole in the deck. One end of the line was then made fast about the mast with a bowline; the captain hauled away on the other, while the mate steadied the heel of the mast as it was hoisted aloft and finally lowered into place. No down-haul was necessary to get the line off the mast because the loop slid down as the legs were taken away. Now, the pulling on the line in hoisting and lowering must be from a point that will keep the guy to the stem head taut.

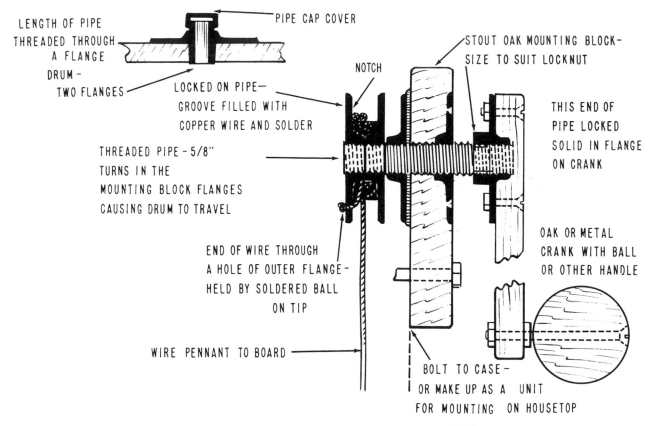

IF LOW HEADROOM MAKES IT NECESSARY
TO RAM SIUCK BOARD DOWN FROM OUTSIDE-

PIPE CAP COVER

LENGTH OF PIPE
THREADED THROUGH
A FLANGE
DRUM -
TWO FLANGES

STOUT OAK MOUNTING BLOCK-
SIZE TO SUIT LOCKNUT

NOTCH

LOCKED ON PIPE-
GROOVE FILLED WITH
COPPER WIRE AND SOLDER

THIS END OF
PIPE LOCKED
SOLID IN FLANGE
ON CRANK

THREADED PIPE - 5/8"
TURNS IN THE
MOUNTING BLOCK FLANGES
CAUSING DRUM TO TRAVEL

OAK OR METAL
CRANK WITH BALL
OR OTHER HANDLE

END OF WIRE THROUGH
A HOLE OF OUTER FLANGE-
HELD BY SOLDERED BALL
ON TIP

WIRE PENNANT TO BOARD

BOLT TO CASE-
OR MAKE UP AS A UNIT
FOR MOUNTING ON HOUSETOP

PIPE-FLANGE CENTERBOARD WINCH

The figure shows a little centerboard winch which has been used for several years on Eugene Townsend's small centerboard cabin sloop.

It will be noted that five pipe flanges and a length of threaded pipe are the main parts. Mr. Townsend used ⅝-inch pipe, but except for that in the sketch I have not given any dimensions because the size of the oak block will have to suit the installation. The strain comes on the single-side upright, but to handle a heavier board, or for an installation on top of a cabin house, it would be wise to provide a support for the opposite end.

It will be seen that the two flanges used for the drum are locked on the threaded pipe and that the groove is filled out by wrapping with copper wire and soldering. The opposite end of the pipe is locked into the flange attached to the crank, which can be made to suit (of oak, as shown, or of metal) and can be removable.

This leaves the other two flanges, one on each side of the oak support, the inside one shimmed out, as necessary, to locate the drum properly. In both flanges, the pipe is free to turn. The wire pennant of the board is held by a ball soldered to its end and passed through one of the fastening holes in the flange.

It will now be apparent that the pipe turning in the central flanges causes the drum to travel and that, once everything is right, the wire will feed on and off the drum evenly, without the usual tendency to pile up or jam. Of course, if the winch is mounted high above the centerboard case, as on a housetop, the pennant should go down through a pipe.

I have shown in the sketch a simple fitting Mr. Townsend made for use in the event the board jams in its case. It is used from outside, with the pipe cap cover removed.

TWIN WELLS ARE SOMETIMES
FITTED

RAISED DECK KEEL "AUXILIARY"
25'5" X 8'6" X 3'9"
7-1/2 H.P. MOTOR – 5 KNOTS

RUBBER-OLD TRUCK INNER TUBE-
OVER OPENING PREVENTS BACKWASH
UNDER POWER AND SEALS WELL-PLUG
UNDER SAIL

STORAGE LOCKER
IS METAL-LINED
AND CAN BE DRAINED

SLIT IS JUST LONG ENOUGH
TO TAKE PROPELLER, ETC.

QUADRANT-CLASS MOTOR WELL

The Quadrant Class, built as a stock auxiliary by the Hartge Yacht Yard, Galesville, Maryland, is chock-full of worthwhile ideas, but the best feature, to my mind, is the provision made for outboard power. The motor well itself is strongly built and should stay tight because a stout bulkhead forms its face, giving a large locker on one side and a small one on the other. There is also a storage compartment, metal-lined and watertight, for stowing the motor when not in use. Another clever idea is the simple precaution used against backwash—disturbed water finding its way out of the well and into the cockpit. A piece of sheet rubber from an old truck inner tube, secured outside the well opening and with a slit cut in it just large enough so that the motor's propeller and lower unit can be worked through, serves to good advantage. This also effectively seals the plug used to close the well while under sail with the motor removed.

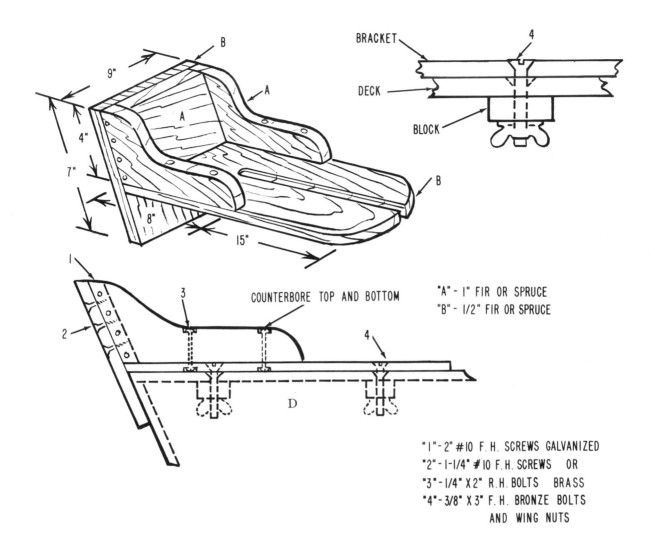

BRACKET

4

DECK

BLOCK

9"

B

A

A

4"

7"

B

8"

15"

1

3

COUNTERBORE TOP AND BOTTOM

2

4

D

"A" - 1" FIR OR SPRUCE
"B" - 1/2" FIR OR SPRUCE

"1" - 2" #10 F.H. SCREWS GALVANIZED
"2" - 1-1/4" #10 F.H. SCREWS   OR
"3" - 1/4" X 2" R.H. BOLTS   BRASS
"4" - 3/8" X 3" F.H. BRONZE BOLTS
                    AND WING NUTS

OUTBOARD BRACKET

An outboard bracket should work out satisfactorily for a small sailboat with an after deck (as long as the transom height is such as to give the motor's wheel the proper bury) or for a larger boat with one of the longer shaft models now available. Certainly, the method of attachment is simple, and with the bracket stowed there is nothing to foul anything or to mar the appearance of either the deck or transom, as is too often the case with a homemade bracket or mounting. Martin Schroder, who sent in this idea, reports it serves well on his *Snipe.*

"This bracket can be installed or removed by turning the two wing nuts (at *D*) under the deck. Two ⅜-inch-diameter holes are bored in the deck, about a foot apart, and countersunk to make the heads set flush in the deck with the bracket off. The blocks beneath are used to reinforce their hold with the bracket in use. To install it, these nuts are simply slacked off, the bolts shoved up, and then the bracket slid on and the nuts tightened again. The long slot to take them should have its edges beveled to give the heads a better hold. A layer of heavy canvas could be glued to the touching surfaces of the bracket to protect the paint."

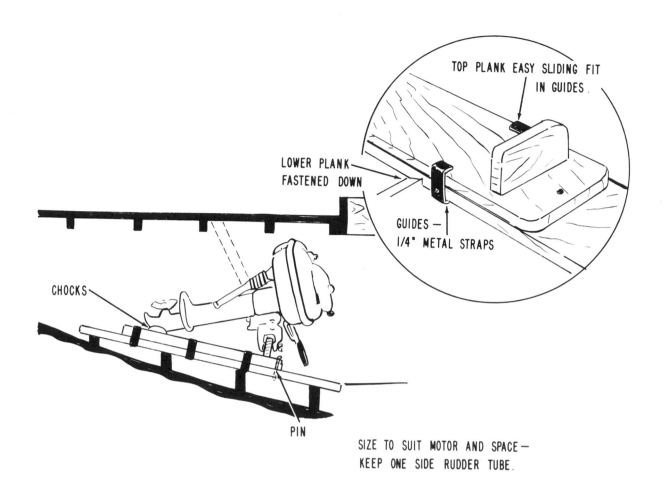

TOP PLANK EASY SLIDING FIT IN GUIDES.

LOWER PLANK FASTENED DOWN

GUIDES — 1/4" METAL STRAPS

CHOCKS

PIN

SIZE TO SUIT MOTOR AND SPACE — KEEP ONE SIDE RUDDER TUBE.

SLIDING MOTOR HOLDER

Anyone who has carried an outboard as auxiliary power will admit that such a motor often can be a problem to stow properly. It is not merely a matter of shoving the motor into an out-of-the-way place and taking a chance on how it will ride there. The motor must be stowed where it will not interfere too much with the working of the boat; the effect of its weight on the boat's trim must also be considered. For the good of the hull and of the motor itself, some way of positioning it properly and securing it against shifting must be worked out.

As good as any is the sliding type of holder shown above, suggested by George Weightman. Some variation of this method probably could be used to slide the motor in and out of any

suitable stowage space. On Mr. Weightman's boat, the lazarette happens to be just right to take the motor, allowing it to rest so that water cannot drain into the cylinders.

Regardless of the location, the idea is to have a permanently fastened lower plank on which an upper plank to hold the motor can slide. The sliding plank should be an easy fit in the metal guides attached to the lower one, and its after corners should be rounded so that they will not catch. A pair of chocks should be fitted to steady the fin of the lower unit. And finally, there should be something, such as the simple pin through the pair of matching holes shown, to hold the slide when it is shoved back.

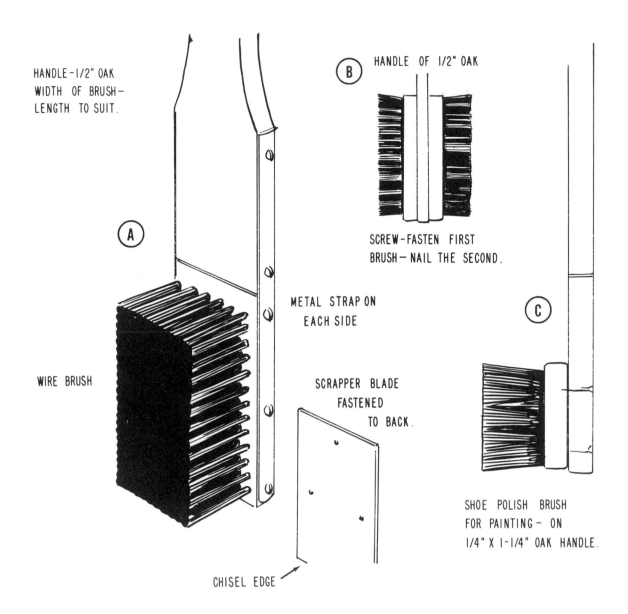

HANDLE—1/2" OAK
WIDTH OF BRUSH—
LENGTH TO SUIT.

Ⓐ

WIRE BRUSH

METAL STRAP ON
EACH SIDE

SCRAPPER BLADE
FASTENED
TO BACK.

CHISEL EDGE

Ⓑ HANDLE OF 1/2" OAK

SCREW-FASTEN FIRST
BRUSH—NAIL THE SECOND.

Ⓒ

SHOE POLISH BRUSH
FOR PAINTING— ON
1/4" X 1-1/4" OAK HANDLE.

CENTERBOARD CASE BRUSH

Here are illustrated the brushes one yard uses for cleaning and painting the wells of sizable centerboard boats. The usual stiff wire brush is too thick to permit fastening an outside handle to get into the average centerboard well, so it is fastened to the end, as shown in A. Another brush (see B), is used for wider wells, the one screw fastened to the handle, and the other secured with finishing nails. A scraper blade might be fastened to the back of brush A to permit scraping off barnacles. C shows the brush used for applying copper paint. It holds more paint and gets into the ends of the well better than the usual swab. This is merely the end of a shoe-polish dauber, removed and attached by screws to a shaped handle. There is now a manufactured centerboard case roller applicator.

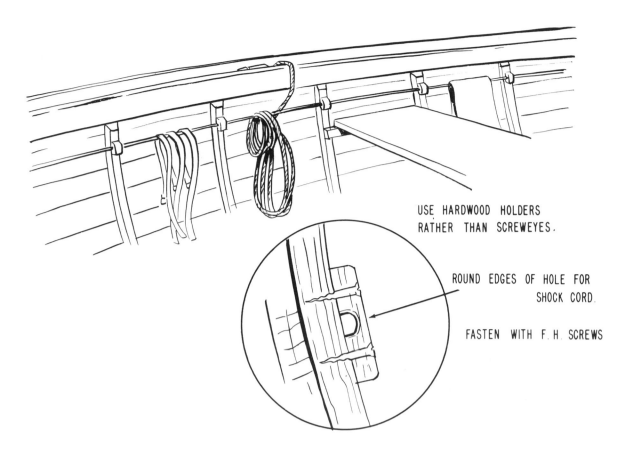

USE HARDWOOD HOLDERS
RATHER THAN SCREWEYES.

ROUND EDGES OF HOLE FOR
SHOCK CORD.

FASTEN WITH F. H. SCREWS

WOODEN SHOCK-CORD HOLDERS

This idea is simple but worthwhile. George Weightman suggested it to me some time back, and recently I came across the same thing on a fairly large open sailboat. In place of the usual screw eyes, oak holders had been installed. The boat's frames were rather far apart, so a holder was screw-fastened to each; then airplane shock cord was threaded through them and stretched fairly taut.

CHAPTER 12

Painting, Maintenance, and Improvements

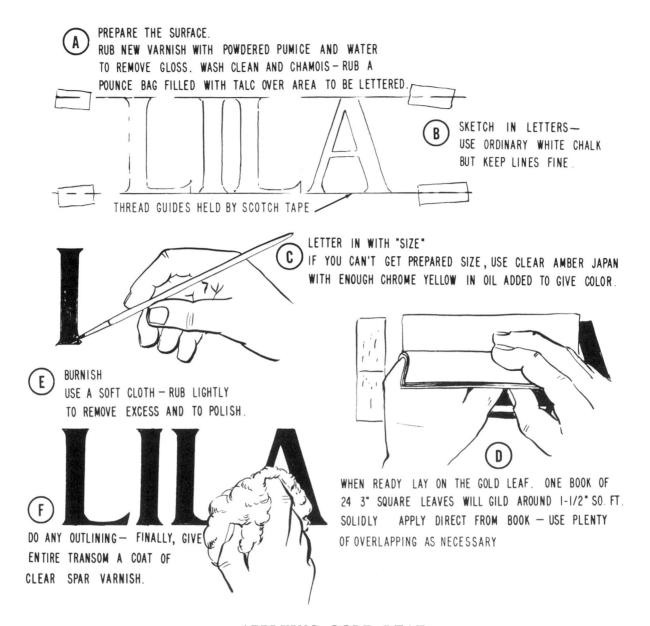

A PREPARE THE SURFACE.
RUB NEW VARNISH WITH POWDERED PUMICE AND WATER
TO REMOVE GLOSS. WASH CLEAN AND CHAMOIS — RUB A
POUNCE BAG FILLED WITH TALC OVER AREA TO BE LETTERED.

B SKETCH IN LETTERS —
USE ORDINARY WHITE CHALK
BUT KEEP LINES FINE.

THREAD GUIDES HELD BY SCOTCH TAPE

C LETTER IN WITH "SIZE"
IF YOU CAN'T GET PREPARED SIZE, USE CLEAR AMBER JAPAN
WITH ENOUGH CHROME YELLOW IN OIL ADDED TO GIVE COLOR.

E BURNISH
USE A SOFT CLOTH — RUB LIGHTLY
TO REMOVE EXCESS AND TO POLISH.

D WHEN READY LAY ON THE GOLD LEAF. ONE BOOK OF
24 3" SQUARE LEAVES WILL GILD AROUND 1-1/2" SQ. FT.
SOLIDLY   APPLY DIRECT FROM BOOK — USE PLENTY
OF OVERLAPPING AS NECESSARY

F DO ANY OUTLINING — FINALLY, GIVE
ENTIRE TRANSOM A COAT OF
CLEAR SPAR VARNISH.

APPLYING GOLD LEAF

Gilding ordinarily is work for a professional sign painter. However, an amateur with some skill at lettering can do a creditable job, if he works carefully and takes his time.

The transom or other surface should have been given its final coat of varnish beforehand. Take the gloss off at least the area to be lettered by rubbing with powdered pumice and water and then washing clean and drying with a chamois. Next, apply pounce, which is talcum powder, French chalk, or even cornstarch in a muslin bag. Rub it over the surface. The letters are then sketched in, usually with ordinary chalk. Prepared size can usually be had, but if not, use clear japan. The touch of chrome yellow added is merely to make your brushing in of the letters show up better. The trick is to know when the letter is ready to receive the leaf. It should be dry enough for you to work but wet enough to have the gold leaf stick properly.

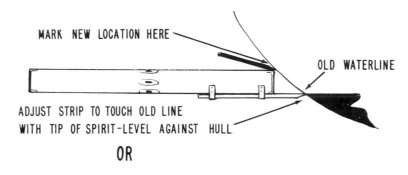

MARK NEW LOCATION HERE

OLD WATERLINE

ADJUST STRIP TO TOUCH OLD LINE
WITH TIP OF SPIRIT-LEVEL AGAINST HULL.

OR

TACK STRIP TO LEVEL TO GIVE HEIGHT
WANTED AND SLIDE MARKER OUT ON IT.

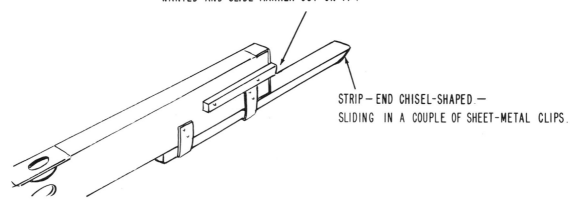

STRIP — END CHISEL-SHAPED. —
SLIDING IN A COUPLE OF SHEET-METAL CLIPS.

RAISING THE WATERLINE

As the accumulation of gear aboard increases, the average cruising boat settles in the water until is becomes advisable to raise the waterline. The rise must be uniform to the eye, 2 or 3 inches along the entire length. While this latter figure may be the width of the band of new paint amidships where the sides are pretty well plumb, it will increase forward, because of the flare of the bows, and may be double the width astern, if there is an appreciable overhang to the counter.

Using a spirit level is one way of getting this right, assuming that your old line is fair and correctly located. To do this, the boat must be hauled out and blocked to be perfectly level athwartships. Its fore-and-aft position does not matter. A masking strip can be held against the bottom of the level; it will be worthwhile to have this a sliding fit. A couple of rough tin or other sheet-metal guides, tacked on as shown, will do. If a rise that is the depth of the level (usually around 3 inches) will be satisfactory,

you can then work with the level, showing its bubble correctly centered. Slide the chisel-shaped end of the strip out to touch the old line and hold the top of the strip against the hull. Using a pencil or a pricker, mark this position. Do this every foot or so, making the marks closest together where the overhang or flare is appreciable. For the entire length of both sides, shift the strip in and out as required and use the pencil or marker always at the same angle. But if this will give too much rise, and you cannot borrow a smaller level, tack a strip the size of the desired rise to the level. Work with a pencil or marker that can be slid straight out on it, for this attached strip will naturally be away from the hull when you are working at the bow and stern. With all the points located, actual striking of the line is a matter of connecting them fairly, either using a limber batten in scribing the line into the planking or snapping a chalk line between the tacks, which can be removed for the actual painting.

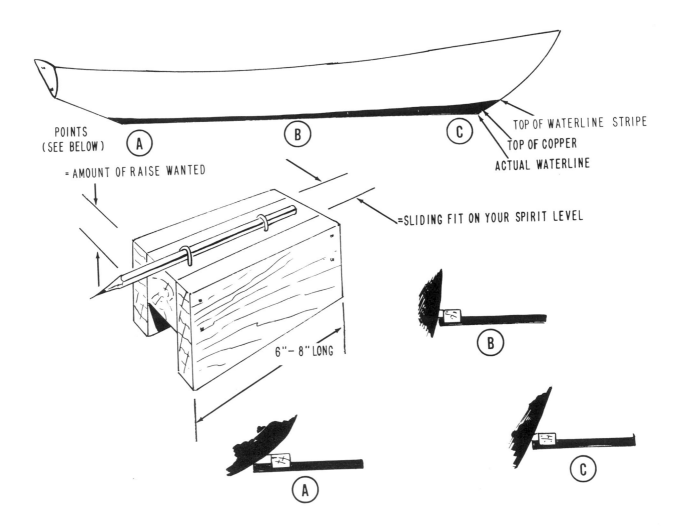

POINTS
(SEE BELOW)

= AMOUNT OF RAISE WANTED

=SLIDING FIT ON YOUR SPIRIT LEVEL

TOP OF WATERLINE STRIPE
TOP OF COPPER
ACTUAL WATERLINE

6" – 8" LONG

Ⓐ Ⓑ Ⓒ

WATERLINE GAUGE

This is a handy tool that I have seen used in several yards. It is generally employed for raising a waterline, something that most boats seem to require eventually. Sometimes, the old one is used for a guide; at other times, tacks are driven carefully on the lines wanted with the boat afloat. Working with a spirit level and the gauge, the corner of the level is held on the old line (or the tack mark,) trued up, and the gauge is slid in or out, as required to have its point prick the hull. This is done in enough places to give points for connecting with a proper batten. The result is that the new line is right to the eye even though the distance between the old and the new will be appreciably more aft, under the overhang of the counter, and slightly more forward.

The waterline stripe, which most people want to have with a sweep up forward and a slight rise aft, is generally done by eye. However, the gauge can help if it is made for the minimum width of the stripe, usually near the cockpit, and if it is used under the counter, particularly to see how much the overhang affects the measurement. The important point is to have a true waterline from which to work. This should be the one marking the top of the copper, or antifouling paint. It should be 2 inches clear of the water, to my mind, and can be made right by using such a gauge.

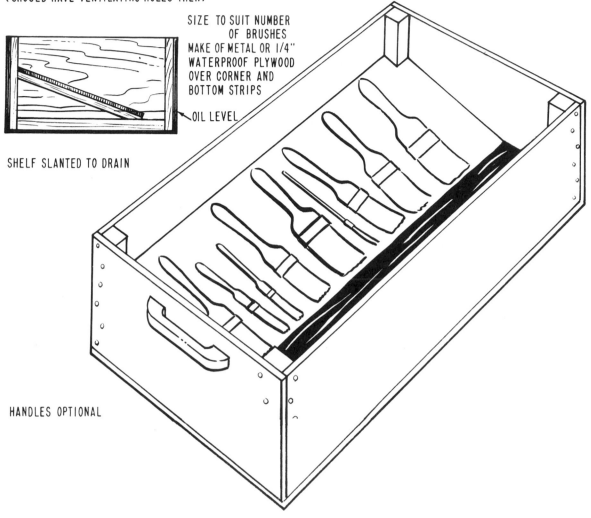

COULD HAVE A COVER TO KEEP DUST OUT
(SHOULD HAVE VENTILATING HOLES THEN)

SIZE TO SUIT NUMBER
OF BRUSHES
MAKE OF METAL OR 1/4"
WATERPROOF PLYWOOD
OVER CORNER AND
BOTTOM STRIPS

OIL LEVEL

SHELF SLANTED TO DRAIN

HANDLES OPTIONAL

BRUSH HOLDER

Those rare fellows who keep their paint and varnish brushes in topnotch shape (and good ones cost enough nowadays to warrant looking after them properly) should be interested in this holder. I saw one of these being used at the Wappoo Marina, across from Charleston, S. C., of which Bill Daniels is manager. The box could be made larger or smaller to suit any number of brushes. The idea is to provide a receptacle for oil with a shelf inclined into it, slanted just enough that the brushes will drain and still not slip down into the oil, unless purposely left submerged. A simple cover to keep the dust

out would be a good idea, but half-a-dozen ⅜-inch holes should then be bored about the upper part of the box to provide ventilation.

Most of us have our favorite kind of oil to use on brushes after cleaning. I think pine oil is good. This is a nondrying oil which has definite paint-penetrating qualities and will effectively prevent that hardening of the heel of the brush which, despite thorough cleaning, can happen in time. Brushes which have been treated with oil should, of course, be washed in mineral spirits before they are used.

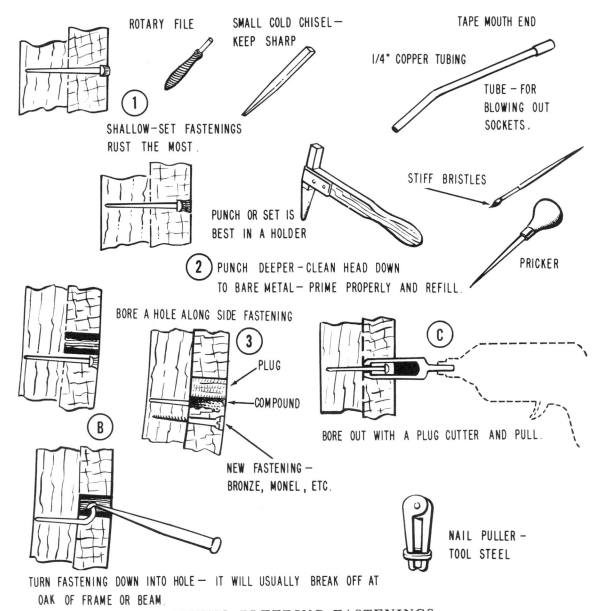

ROTARY FILE

SMALL COLD CHISEL—
KEEP SHARP

TAPE MOUTH END

1/4" COPPER TUBING

TUBE – FOR
BLOWING OUT
SOCKETS.

(1)

SHALLOW-SET FASTENINGS
RUST THE MOST.

STIFF BRISTLES

PUNCH OR SET IS
BEST IN A HOLDER

PRICKER

(2) PUNCH DEEPER — CLEAN HEAD DOWN
TO BARE METAL — PRIME PROPERLY AND REFILL.

BORE A HOLE ALONG SIDE FASTENING

(3)

PLUG

COMPOUND

(C)

BORE OUT WITH A PLUG CUTTER AND PULL.

(B)

NEW FASTENING —
BRONZE, MONEL, ETC.

NAIL PULLER –
TOOL STEEL

TURN FASTENING DOWN INTO HOLE — IT WILL USUALLY BREAK OFF AT
OAK OF FRAME OR BEAM.

FIXING BLEEDING FASTENINGS

Doctoring up bleeding fastenings can get to be a pretty hopeless task. But whatever your pet remedy is, I think it should include, first, driving the fastening deeper. Generally, fastenings that give the most trouble will be found to be set very shallow. The next course of action, to my mind, is to chip the head, getting down to clear, bright metal. From there on, it's a matter of using your pet primer before actually refilling the socket. Your guess here is as good as mine, but there are two remedies— beeswax and a cement such as Duco House-hold—that seem to do as good a job as any. Some people just prime the cleaned head with a couple of coats of the cement and then refill. Or sometimes, the beeswax is used over the primed head in place of the usual compound.

In another case, a shallow filling of beeswax may be applied, with the compound being used to finish it off. The tools shown above help on such a job. A small cold chisel, ground to a narrow sharp end, is best for chipping the head clean of rust. Sometimes, a rotary file used in a hand drill will aid in the final cleaning. The punch or nail set is best held by some sort of handle. A pricker is useful for cleaning out the old filling and exploring the condition of the fastening. For finally blowing the dust out of the socket, it's nice to have a short length of copper tubing with surgical tape wrapped about the mouth end.

It is generally impossible to remove a rusted steel or iron fastening intact. Screws rust worse than nails, the heads soon losing their slots. One thing you can do is break the fastening off deep enough down so that any future rusting will hardly cause concern. A try at one of the fastenings will show what may be expected of the other offending ones. Bore a ⅜- or ½-inch hole as close to the fastening as you can. Then, using a narrow chisel, turn the fastening over into the hole and down, when it will likely break off at the oak of the frame or beam. Coax the broken-off part out and glue a plug into the hole, later filling the space left alongside with compound. Of course, you'll want to finish up by driving a new fastening in the vicinity of

the old one, but use one of bronze or Monel. If it happens that you'll be mixing your metals, and it's a topsides or a deck job, chances are there'll be no bad effect.

Copper rivets are frequently bored out with a plug cutter. The same can be done with an iron nail; you can either break the fastening off or, possibly, pull it. Naturally, the job is hard on the cutter, but it can be resharpened. I've used several nail-pulling devices, but the difficulty seems to be to get one that's strong enough to stand the strain put on it. Most of them are clawlike affairs made something like the one shown. An upward pull on the squared ring clamps the jaw and, in turn, the head of the nail that much tighter. Usually a clawbar or ordinary nail puller is reforged to make for one end that will permit throwing upward pressure on the puller. A piece of metal or hardwood is used under to avoid marring the deck or planking. Naturally, with this way of doing it, the hole that's left must also be plugged and a new fastening driven.

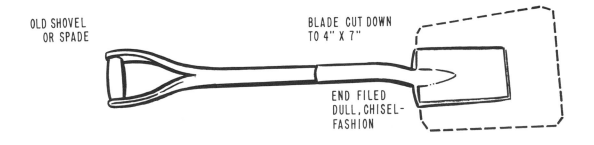

OLD SHOVEL OR SPADE

BLADE CUT DOWN TO 4" X 7"

END FILED DULL, CHISEL-FASHION

YARD SCRAPER

Every yard workman has his own pet type of scraper for removing barnacles. Above is illustrated one made by Joe Harvey of the Fulton Boat Co., Florida, which works out especially well for rough scraping where the bottom is

badly fouled. Joe merely cut an old shovel blade down to about 4 by 7 inches and ground its end or point dull, chisel-fashion. A shovel with a crook to the handle just above the blade works best.

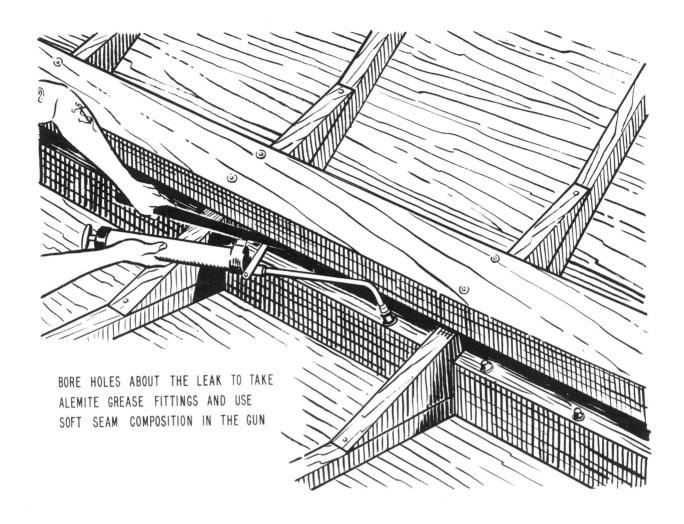

BORE HOLES ABOUT THE LEAK TO TAKE
ALEMITE GREASE FITTINGS AND USE
SOFT SEAM COMPOSITION IN THE GUN

FIXING STUBBORN LEAKS

This is a method I have seen used to cure leaks when other measures could not be employed or had failed. This is a modern version of the old idea of boring holes, filling them with tallow, and then driving plugs in to provide pressure to force the tallow into checks and openings. This method often can be used in hard-to-reach places—where checks in the keel may be causing the leak, or where a shaft log has developed checks, or about the ends of a centerboard case. Bore the holes for the Alemite grease fittings, which naturally must be located according to the fault and be deep enough to do some good. The drier the wood, the better,

but I have seen good results when the boat has been left in the water.

The grease fittings are cheap, so use enough of them. Work from one to the next, finally going back over the lot. Some seam compositions are soft enough to handle in a grease gun, but others must be softened according to directions on the can. Use enough pressure to get the composition into the checks or openings, but do not overdo it; a gun of *any* size can exert enough pressure to force something off. Finally, remove the fittings and fill the holes with dowels or plugs.

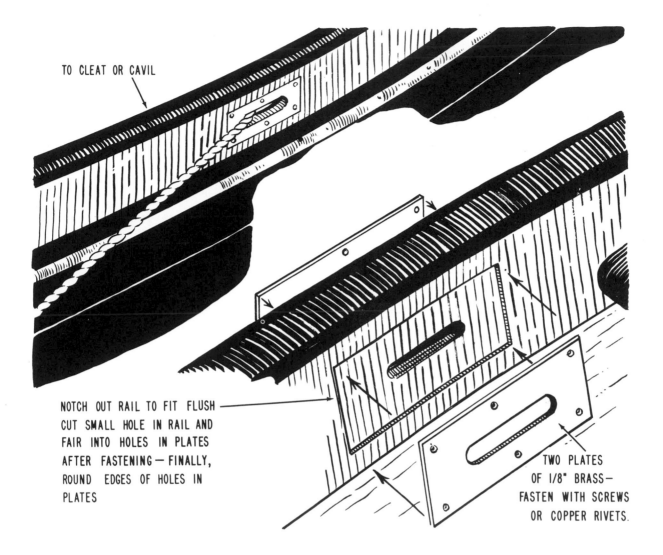

TO CLEAT OR CAVIL

NOTCH OUT RAIL TO FIT FLUSH
CUT SMALL HOLE IN RAIL AND
FAIR INTO HOLES IN PLATES
AFTER FASTENING — FINALLY,
ROUND EDGES OF HOLES IN
PLATES

TWO PLATES
OF 1/8" BRASS —
FASTEN WITH SCREWS
OR COPPER RIVETS.

HAWSE HOLES

Hawse holes for dock lines in a rail of any height look well and can be convenient, if placed right for the lead of line to bitts aft, or for a cleat or cavil on each side about amidships, or at the point of balance for using spring lines. The true-cast type can seldom be had for small boats, but plates used as in the illustration serve the purpose well and are not hard to make or fit. Their actual fitting, of course, must be in keeping with the construction of the rail, but the principle is to cut the hole in the rail considerably smaller than necessary; then, when the plates are let in and fastened, the hole can be enlarged as much as necessary. But be sure its edges are rounded to present a smooth surface to the line of the brass plate. In ordinary use, there will not be so much chafe on the unprotected wood that paint cannot be kept on it, but the rail construction should be such that it will take the strain of the line.

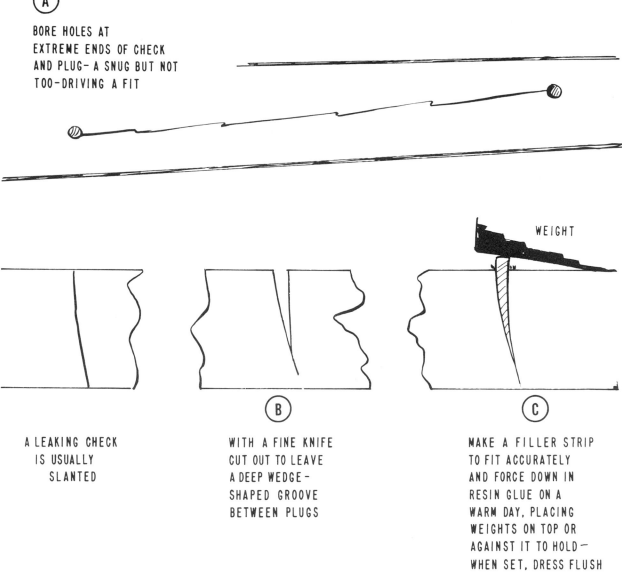

BORE HOLES AT
EXTREME ENDS OF CHECK
AND PLUG— A SNUG BUT NOT
TOO-DRIVING A FIT

WEIGHT

A LEAKING CHECK
IS USUALLY
SLANTED

WITH A FINE KNIFE
CUT OUT TO LEAVE
A DEEP WEDGE -
SHAPED GROOVE
BETWEEN PLUGS

MAKE A FILLER STRIP
TO FIT ACCURATELY
AND FORCE DOWN IN
RESIN GLUE ON A
WARM DAY, PLACING
WEIGHTS ON TOP OR
AGAINST IT TO HOLD—
WHEN SET, DRESS FLUSH

STOPPING A CHECK

Sometimes, a check in a plank in the deck, hull, or cabin side can be harder to keep tight than an ordinary seam. Usually, the fault results from neglect—failure upon first appearance of the check to keep it filled and properly painted or varnished until eventually it continues all the way through. Caulking or filler forced into the opening when the wood is dry usually tends to spread the check because the wood swells when wet and shrinks out again in drying.

When other measures fail, the following treatment is usually a cure: bore a ⅜-inch hole at each end of the check and then drive plugs into the holes, using marine glue to set them tight. With a sharp penknife, cut a wedge-shaped piece from along one side of the check to leave a deep, narrow opening; make a long filler piece to fit this as accurately as possible. Then, on a warm day, with the wood perfectly dry, force the filler piece home in resin glue (the powdered grade now readily obtainable in small cans), keeping a weight on or against the filler until the glue has had a chance to set. Then, the filler can be dressed down and sanded flush.

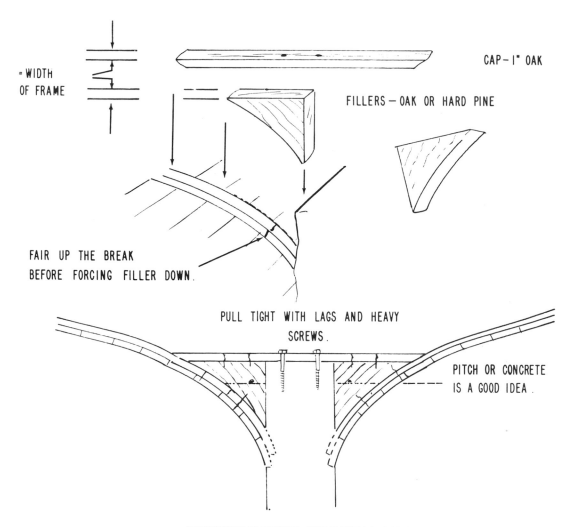

= WIDTH OF FRAME

CAP—1" OAK

FILLERS — OAK OR HARD PINE

FAIR UP THE BREAK
BEFORE FORCING FILLER DOWN.

PULL TIGHT WITH LAGS AND HEAVY
SCREWS.

PITCH OR CONCRETE
IS A GOOD IDEA.

REINFORCING BROKEN FRAMES

Frames which have had to take considerable reverse curvature frequently crack or break completely. One way to fix them is described by John Haines, who did the job a few years ago in his yawl *Candice*. Several pairs of frames in the way of the after deadwood had failed more-or-less completely. He started out by cleaning thoroughly that part of the bilge, with an eye to applying Cuprinol to the wood and putting in pitch. Next, he rasped the broken places smooth enough so that cardboard templates cut for each location hugged the frame face. Oak filler pieces were carefully fitted just high enough so that the cap secured atop each pair forced them down into place over liquid marine glue. Two 4-inch lags were driven into the deadwood or log, and heavy Everdur screws

were put in from outside as well as inside. The pitch which sealed the broken places was not applied until spring, in order to give the preservative a chance to dry thoroughly and for the wood itself to be as dry as possible. As shown, it was flowed in to the level of the limber holes, each pair of fillers acting as a sort of dam to give a series of levels, but all planned to drain properly.

As Mr. Haines explained, the floor timbers in his boat had been put in without being attached to the frames. Thus, the filler pieces could be secured to the floor timbers as well as being capped. The important thing is to place something over the break to strengthen the spot and keep the fault from getting worse.

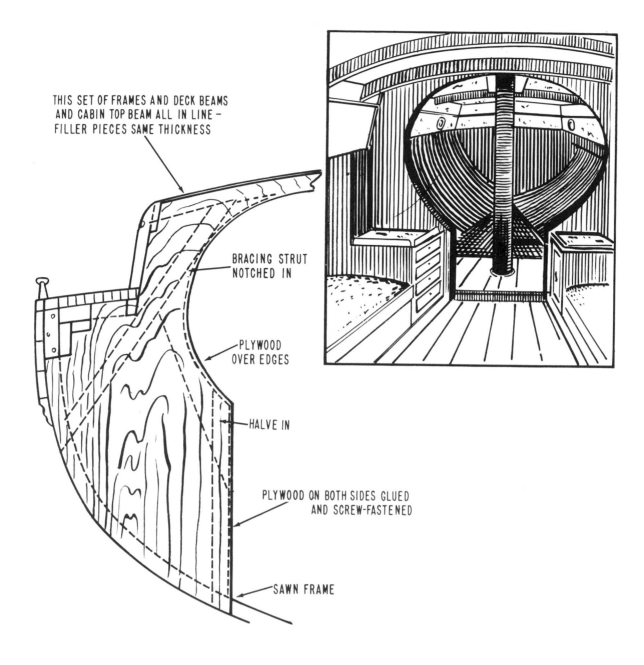

THIS SET OF FRAMES AND DECK BEAMS
AND CABIN TOP BEAM ALL IN LINE —
FILLER PIECES SAME THICKNESS

BRACING STRUT
NOTCHED IN

PLYWOOD
OVER EDGES

HALVE IN

PLYWOOD ON BOTH SIDES GLUED
AND SCREW-FASTENED

SAWN FRAME

STRENGHTENING BULKHEAD

A strengthening bulkhead would seem to be a good idea, where required. A matching set of deck beams and an extra cabin-top beam, all the same thickness, were made up when building. They were kept in line with a pair of sawn frames at the desired location, and a bracing strut notched in each side and filler pieces fitted about as shown. Thin plywood was then fitted and bent in to conceal raw edges, and, finally, panels of hardwood-faced plywood were cut to shape and glued and screw-fastened (screws not shown in the sketch) to both sides, with the joint coming in the center of the cabin beam overhead. In another job where a bilge stringer might interfere, the panels, of course would have to be notched out to fit down over them.

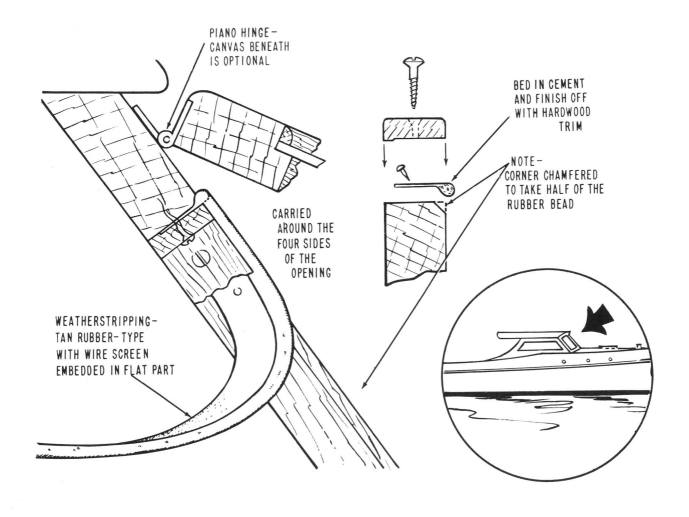

PIANO HINGE-
CANVAS BENEATH
IS OPTIONAL

BED IN CEMENT
AND FINISH OFF
WITH HARDWOOD
TRIM

NOTE-
CORNER CHAMFERED
TO TAKE HALF OF THE
RUBBER BEAD

CARRIED
AROUND THE
FOUR SIDES
OF THE
OPENING

WEATHERSTRIPPING-
TAN RUBBER-TYPE
WITH WIRE SCREEN
EMBEDDED IN FLAT PART

USING WEATHERSTRIPPING

The type of house weatherstripping which is all rubber except for a strip of screen wire embedded in its flat part is handy for many jobs about boats. Its tan color does not look bad and, from what I have seen of it so far, the wire (apparently steel) does not rust because of its rubber covering. However, any cut ends should be bedded in some plastic compound, for the pinpoint ends of the wire are exposed there.

The figure shows how this weatherstripping can be used. Here, about the windshield of a small cruiser, it replaces some rubber which

had never been satisfactory. Note that the trick is to chamfer the corner or edge of the standing part of the construction over which the frame is hinged; ⅛ inch, or enough to take about half of the bead of the stripping, will do when tacking, and the attached trim leaves just enough of the soft rubber protruding to give a gasket. The owner told me that the weight of the frame against this suffices for rain and that taking up on the inside toggles pulls it really tight against flying spray.

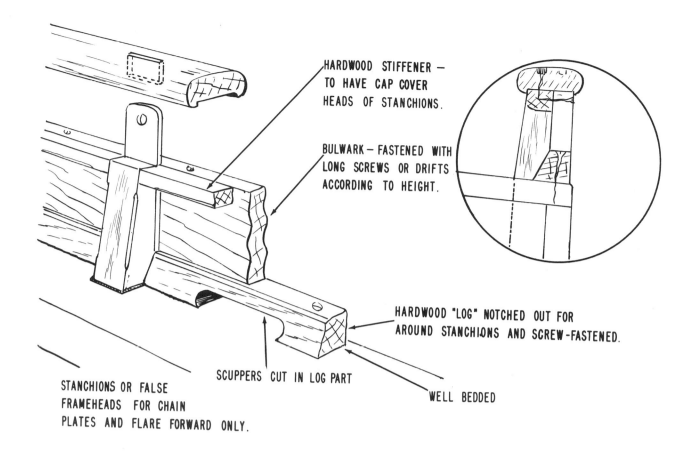

HARDWOOD STIFFENER —
TO HAVE CAP COVER
HEADS OF STANCHIONS.

BULWARK — FASTENED WITH
LONG SCREWS OR DRIFTS
ACCORDING TO HEIGHT.

HARDWOOD "LOG" NOTCHED OUT FOR
AROUND STANCHIONS AND SCREW-FASTENED.

WELL BEDDED

SCUPPERS CUT IN LOG PART

STANCHIONS OR FALSE
FRAMEHEADS FOR CHAIN
PLATES AND FLARE FORWARD ONLY.

ADDING A RAIL

The figure shows what I think is a good way of putting on a fairly high rail or bulwarks. This was used by a yard in Virginia as a replacement job in putting new waterways on a good-sized ketch. Originally these had been pierced by the usual stanchions or timberheads on every other frame, but the owner wanted to get away from such construction as much as possible because signs of rot were beginning to appear.

CHAPTER 13

Hatch Ideas

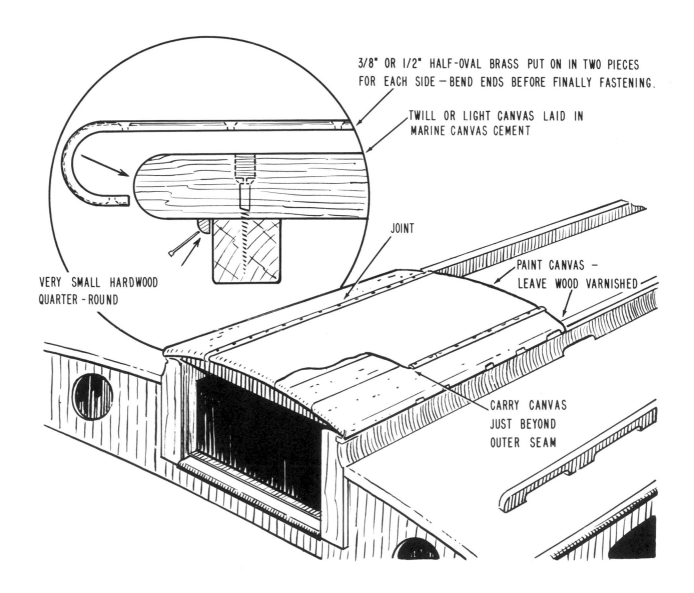

3/8" OR 1/2" HALF-OVAL BRASS PUT ON IN TWO PIECES
FOR EACH SIDE — BEND ENDS BEFORE FINALLY FASTENING.

TWILL OR LIGHT CANVAS LAID IN
MARINE CANVAS CEMENT

VERY SMALL HARDWOOD
QUARTER - ROUND

JOINT

PAINT CANVAS -
LEAVE WOOD VARNISHED

CARRY CANVAS
JUST BEYOND
OUTER SEAM

COVERING A LEAKY HATCH SLIDE

Unless it is made of teak or is of some double-planked construction, a companionway slide that is finished bright will invariably leak in time even to the point of the boatman's having to keep a cover on it, which can be a nuisance. A canvas cover is a real remedy, yet when the companionway is completely covered its looks may not be in keeping with the rest of the boat.

On the other hand, covering, with the canvas painted and the edges left varnished, can look good. The twill or light canvas should be bed-ded in marine canvas cement and carried to just beyond the outer seams and then down beneath the forward and after overhangs. Secure it there with very small quarter-round trim made of the same wood as the slide, for this should be finished bright. The brass trim holding the edges should be half-oval, with the ends bent to go under the overhangs. This usually requires having the strip for each side in two pieces, so that the ends can be bent to fit.

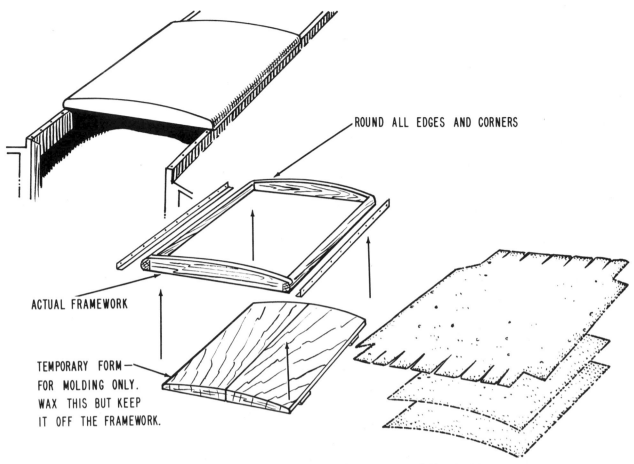

ROUND ALL EDGES AND CORNERS

ACTUAL FRAMEWORK

TEMPORARY FORM—
FOR MOLDING ONLY.
WAX THIS BUT KEEP
IT OFF THE FRAMEWORK.

TWO LAYERS OF CHROME FIBERGLASS CLOTH OVER INSIDE FORM
AND TOP OF FRAME — THEN A FINAL LAYER CARRIED DOWN
OVER THE SIDES AND ENDS.

FIBER GLASS HATCH COVER

I recently saw a molded-plastic hatch slide that seemed to have several advantages over the usual all-wood or canvas-covered type. The sketches show how the molding process was described to me. First, a regular wooden frame was made. A temporary form or filler was then constructed to fit inside the frame for the molding. This was waxed to prevent the glue mix used with the fiber glass from sticking to it. (Care must be taken not to get wax on the frame because the objective is to bond the fiber glass to it.)

Then, working according to the directions from the concern supplying the fiber glass cloth and ingredients for the glue mix, two pieces of the fiber glass cloth were put on, one at a time, to come only far enough over the rounded edges of the four frame members to get a good bond to them. Next, a final layer was tailored to glue down as smooth as possible over these and cover the wood left exposed. After waiting the required length of time, the entire cover was smoothed up, the inside form removed, and the final finish coat of the glue mix applied. This made a quite light and evidently very strong slide with the desired rounded edges.

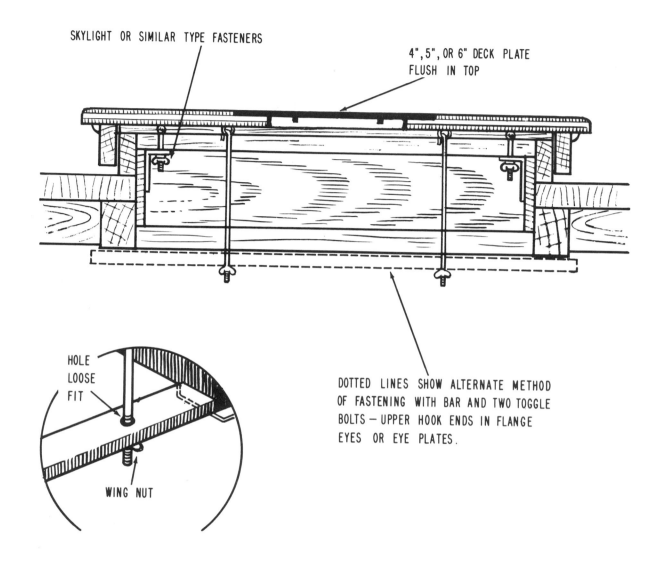

SKYLIGHT OR SIMILAR TYPE FASTENERS

4", 5", OR 6" DECK PLATE FLUSH IN TOP

HOLE LOOSE FIT

WING NUT

DOTTED LINES SHOW ALTERNATE METHOD OF FASTENING WITH BAR AND TWO TOGGLE BOLTS — UPPER HOOK ENDS IN FLANGE EYES OR EYE PLATES.

LOCKING THE HATCH

The cover of a hatch in the afterdeck is invariably difficult to secure well enough to make it watertight and theftproof. One can seldom reach it from beneath, and outside fastenings look cumbersome. A brass deckplate, as illustrated, will usually do the trick. The opening on this deckplate should be just large enough so that you can reach in to get at the type of fasteners used. You'll be safe in considering that anyone being unable to lift the cover will *not* think of opening the plate and feeling below, especially if it has been turned down tight by its key. Or, a couple of simple hooks or other fasteners, as shown, or a bar with toggle bolts, as indicated by dotted lines, may be sufficient. Or, if you are overly pessimistic, a hasp and padlock could be used in addition, although the padlock would have to be placed so that it could be opened with one hand.

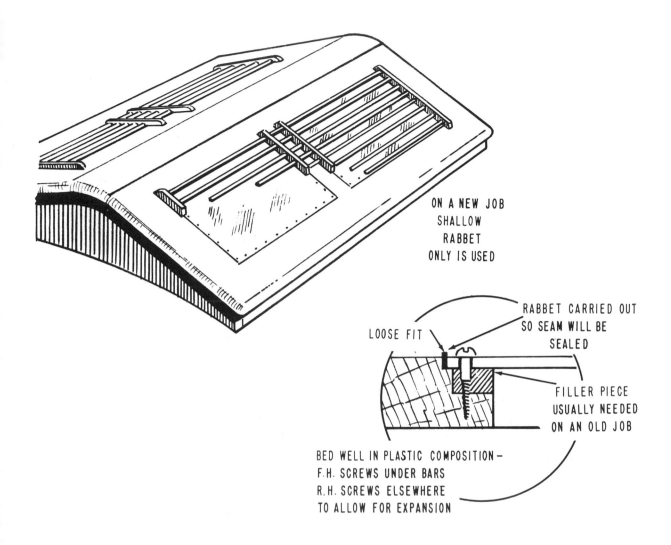

ON A NEW JOB
SHALLOW
RABBET
ONLY IS USED

LOOSE FIT

RABBET CARRIED OUT
SO SEAM WILL BE
SEALED

FILLER PIECE
USUALLY NEEDED
ON AN OLD JOB

BED WELL IN PLASTIC COMPOSITION—
F.H. SCREWS UNDER BARS
R.H. SCREWS ELSEWHERE
TO ALLOW FOR EXPANSION

PLASTIC IN A SKYLIGHT

Wherever I have seen transparent plastic used to take the place of glass in a skylight, it has appeared to be doing its job well, although one owner said the type he used seemed to scratch easily. In one case, it had been used to replace the cracked glass in an old skylight, with an eye to having a perfectly flush surface for each leaf, so that there would be less chance of leaks. The deep rabbets previously taking the panes of glass were accordingly filled with strips bedded in glue, as above, but kept low enough to leave a shallow rabbet for the plastic to bed flush. The plastic was extended slightly beyond the strips to permit sealing and leave a little space for the plastic to work. Accordingly, plenty of composition should be used for the bedding, and the holes for the screw fastenings should be drilled to an easy fit.

Ordinarily, round-head screws, often with washers, are used for holding such plastic, but in this case flat-head ones, might look better.

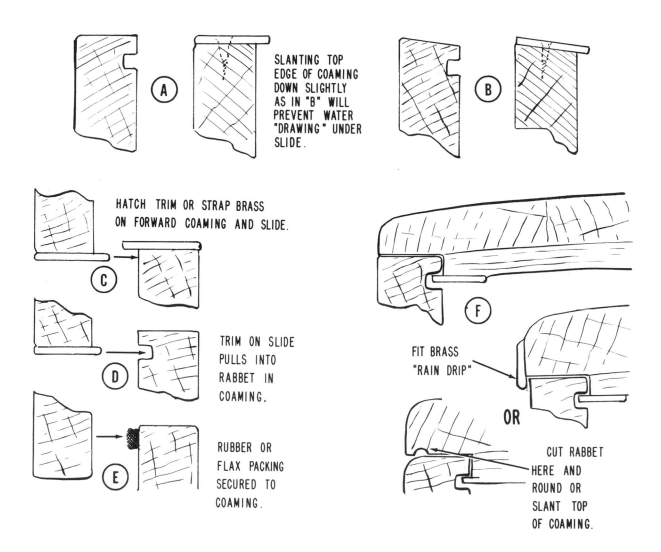

SLANTING TOP EDGE OF COAMING DOWN SLIGHTLY AS IN "B" WILL PREVENT WATER "DRAWING" UNDER SLIDE.

HATCH TRIM OR STRAP BRASS ON FORWARD COAMING AND SLIDE.

TRIM ON SLIDE PULLS INTO RABBET IN COAMING.

RUBBER OR FLAX PACKING SECURED TO COAMING.

FIT BRASS "RAIN DRIP"

OR

CUT RABBET HERE AND ROUND OR SLANT TOP OF COAMING.

CURING HATCH LEAKS

A hatch slide that leaks, even if only across its coamings, can be a nuisance. Some ailments and possible cures are shown above. Often, rain water will draw or drive under the edges of the slide to flow across the tops of the coamings, if they are level, as in *A*, whereas by giving the tops a slant outwards, as in *B*, this can be avoided. If you are building, do not have the coamings or slide runners too level fore and aft; pitch or slant them down forward. This condition is not shown in the sketches, but when they are made too level, water will often follow along the tops to work under the slide itself, despite the fact that everything is kept greased.

C, *D*, and *E* show remedies for where spray or driving rain finds its way up under the forward end of the slide; the first two are real cures for this condition, and *E* is a last resort when none of the others is possible. You will often find a slide fitted somewhat as shown in *F*, when driven rain or spray will surely find its way in. Even in a shower, water is apt to creep or follow across the top of the coaming to drip below. A brass rain drip or guard will avoid this, if the shape or the construction of the slide permits fitting it. Otherwise, cut a rabbet or groove, as shown, and slant or round the top of the coaming; this will probably do the job.

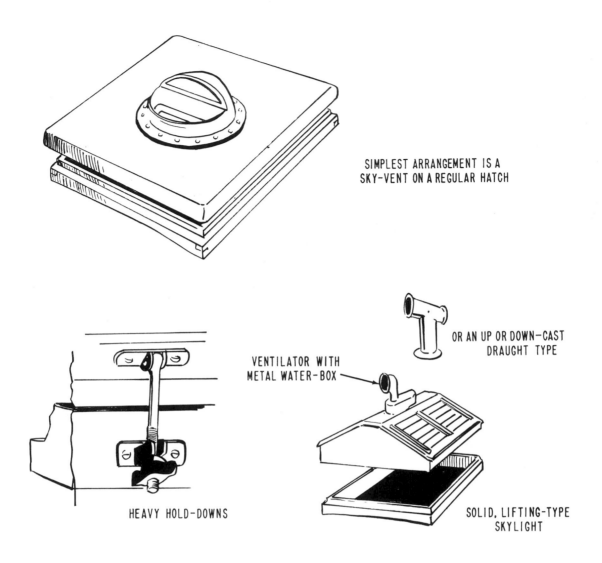

SIMPLEST ARRANGEMENT IS A
SKY-VENT ON A REGULAR HATCH

OR AN UP OR DOWN-CAST
DRAUGHT TYPE

VENTILATOR WITH
METAL WATER-BOX

HEAVY HOLD-DOWNS

SOLID, LIFTING-TYPE
SKYLIGHT

SKYLIGHT HATCH COVER

Any solution to the old problem of letting air in but keeping water out when battened down in rough going is worth listening to. More and more boats are relying on a Sudbury Sky-Vent ventilator mounted on a cabin-top hatch cover. It is a skylight that can be a particular problem though, for, even at best, it is difficult to keep one really tight. So you often end up by having a tailored canvas cover, which naturally shuts out the light when you use it.

One solution is offered by Bill Wells. The sketch is of a skylight he mounted on his sloop's housetop. Actually, it is a hatch cover, made up skylight-fashion, which offers the advantage of glass surfaces to let in some light. Ordinarily, the top is tilted or removed to let in the maximum amount of air. However, for really bad going, it can be fastened down tight. Under such conditions, air is taken in through a Dorade-type ventilator which Bill made, with a metal box instead of the usual wooden one in order to keep the size down to suit the center member of the skylight. Other waterproof ventilators could be used, I suppose—possibly some type that could be removed—and a plate screwed in to close the opening under ordinary conditions.

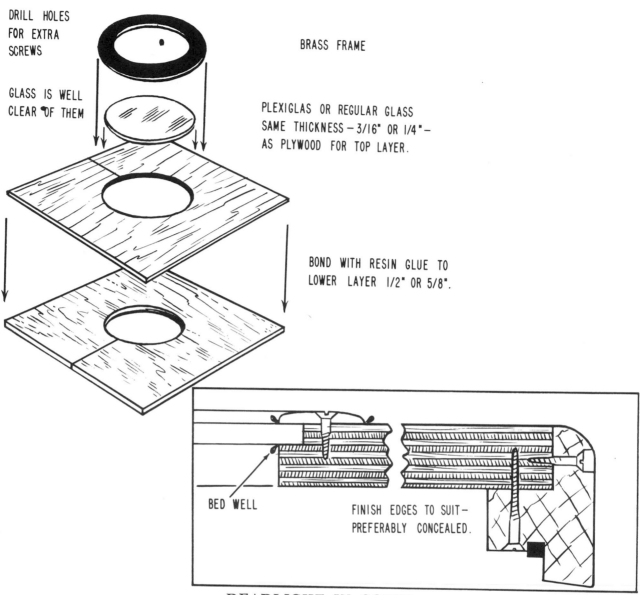

DRILL HOLES FOR EXTRA SCREWS

BRASS FRAME

GLASS IS WELL CLEAR OF THEM

PLEXIGLAS OR REGULAR GLASS SAME THICKNESS — 3/16" OR 1/4" — AS PLYWOOD FOR TOP LAYER.

BOND WITH RESIN GLUE TO LOWER LAYER 1/2" OR 5/8".

BED WELL

FINISH EDGES TO SUIT — PREFERABLY CONCEALED.

DEADLIGHT IN COVER

Where a hatch cover is to have one or more lights of Plexiglas or ordinary glass let into it, the double-layer method shown above has several advantages. Chiefly, it avoids having to rabbet out the edges of the holes to bed the glass properly, something that is difficult to do if plywood is used.

The top plywood and the glass should be the same thickness, preferably 3/16 or ¼ inch, and the hole in this should be cut to an easy fit for the glass used. The diameter of the hole, of course, will be determined by the size of the brass frame to be used.

The under layer should be of heavier plywood, with the hole the same diameter as that of the inside of the frame. Both layers should be large enough to allow for a little edge trimming after the resin glue used for bonding them together has set. The glass can then be set in bedding compound in the rabbet and held down with the frame. Brass frames ordinarily come with four holes for screws, but drilling extra ones to double up on the number of fastenings used will give more uniform pressure on the glass in its bedding.

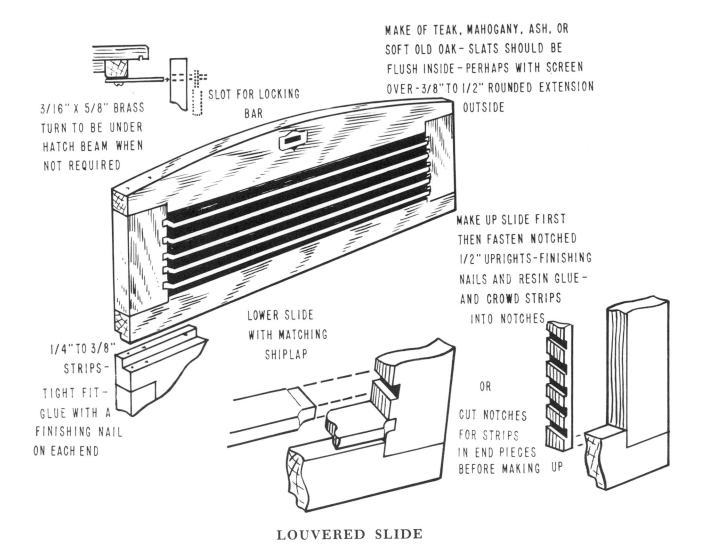

MAKE OF TEAK, MAHOGANY, ASH, OR
SOFT OLD OAK— SLATS SHOULD BE
FLUSH INSIDE— PERHAPS WITH SCREEN
OVER— 3/8" TO 1/2" ROUNDED EXTENSION
OUTSIDE

3/16" X 5/8" BRASS
TURN TO BE UNDER
HATCH BEAM WHEN
NOT REQUIRED

SLOT FOR LOCKING
BAR

MAKE UP SLIDE FIRST
THEN FASTEN NOTCHED
1/2" UPRIGHTS— FINISHING
NAILS AND RESIN GLUE—
AND CROWD STRIPS
INTO NOTCHES

LOWER SLIDE
WITH MATCHING
SHIPLAP

1/4" TO 3/8"
STRIPS—
TIGHT FIT—
GLUE WITH A
FINISHING NAIL
ON EACH END

OR

CUT NOTCHES
FOR STRIPS
IN END PIECES
BEFORE MAKING UP

LOUVERED SLIDE

A louvered, upper lifting door or slide for the companionway is both shippy in appearance and practical; it lets in air but keeps out rain. A simple method of making a louvered lifting door is shown here.

Rather than cutting the door out of one solid board, which is apt to warp and stick in its grooves, make it up of four members, with the two side pieces let into the top and bottom pieces. Assemble with resin glue and fasten each corner with a couple of heavy finishing nails, for which you have drilled holes; or, better still, use wooden dowels.

The louver boards or slats can be let into notches cut into the side pieces; or, the slide can be made up first, the notched uprights glued and fastened in place, and the slats crowded in.

In either case, the notches should be slanted uniformly and should be cut for a tight fit, so that the ends of the slats will have to be slightly tapered in order to get them in. The slats should be made wide enough for them to be dressed off flush on the inside after they have been fastened in place. Their outer edges should be rounded before they are set into the notches, and they should project uniformly about ⅜ or ½ inch on the outside. When making up the slide itself, make it a little wider than necessary, so that the edges can be dressed off to a sliding fit.

If you want the companionway screened, tack copper wire inside and conceal the edges and tack heads with neatly fitted strips or half-round moulding.

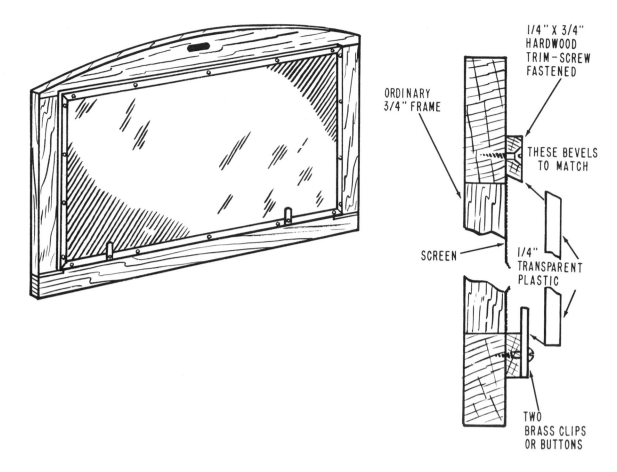

ORDINARY 3/4" FRAME

1/4" X 3/4" HARDWOOD TRIM-SCREW FASTENED

THESE BEVELS TO MATCH

SCREEN

1/4" TRANSPARENT PLASTIC

TWO BRASS CLIPS OR BUTTONS

TRANSPARENT-PLASTIC LIGHT

Anything that can serve a double purpose aboard always helps in solving the storage problem. An example is shown in the illustration, where the companionway screen becomes a solid slide by having its trim made to hold a sheet of transparent plastic. This eliminates the necessity of carrying the usual pair of board slides for cool weather; yet it admits light below. For outside going, I would prefer to have the slides along, but the arrangement shown can be rainproof for ordinary use.

The same idea can be used in connection with a pair of screen doors for the companionway, plastic being used in place of the panels of plywood with which these are often fitted, but held as shown, not with buttons all around, so that water will not be so apt to run inside.

Here, the trim used over the tack heads and raw edges of the screen is made of hardwood and is heavier than usual—say ¾ inch wide—and screw-fastened; ¼-inch-thick transparent plastic will work out better than the ⅛-inch size because it will permit using trim that thickness and will be heavy enough for the top length to afford secure holding. This is simply beveled to take a matching bevel dressed in the upper edge of the plastic, and then the sheet is made a neat but not too-tight fit, with the bottom edge and ends left square to be held by a couple of buttons made of ⅛-inch brass. These should have the hole to take a round-headed screw well toward one end, not in the center; thus, when turned up to hold the plastic, there is no projection below the trim. When not in use, they can be turned lengthwise, with the trim to be out of the way.

CHAPTER 14

Cabin Screens

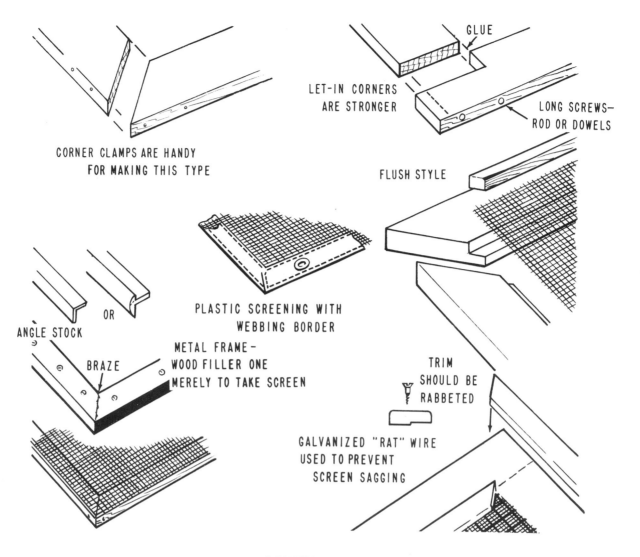

CORNER CLAMPS ARE HANDY
FOR MAKING THIS TYPE

GLUE

LET-IN CORNERS
ARE STRONGER

LONG SCREWS—
ROD OR DOWELS

FLUSH STYLE

ANGLE STOCK — OR

BRAZE

PLASTIC SCREENING WITH
WEBBING BORDER

METAL FRAME—
WOOD FILLER ONE
MERELY TO TAKE SCREEN

TRIM
SHOULD BE
RABBETED

GALVANIZED "RAT" WIRE
USED TO PREVENT
SCREEN SAGGING

SCREENS I

Making screens is always a good winter job. Each boat seems to require her own special size or type. The corners are perhaps the hardest parts to get right and a screen usually shows its first weakness there. A couple of clamps are worth having for their help in getting the corners true and properly fastened. Personally, I like the let-in type of corner because it is strong. I also like the flush-style frame, except that it is difficult to get the wire stretched taut in the rabbet that takes the trim.

A good idea for a screen that will be used flat is to put large mesh wire, often called rat screening, over the netting. Stowable screens—plastic netting held by a webbing frame—are not hard to make and are best for a small boat, or on a large one where the opening to be screened is such that a rigid screen would be impractical. Metal-framed screens are space-saving and strong, but they can be hard on adjacent varnished surfaces.

Frames should be made of good wood—mahogany or teak. Not much wood is required and one only wastes time using a wood that is too soft to hold fastenings well and that will mar and warp. Monel netting is well worth the extra cost, as are Monel fastenings.

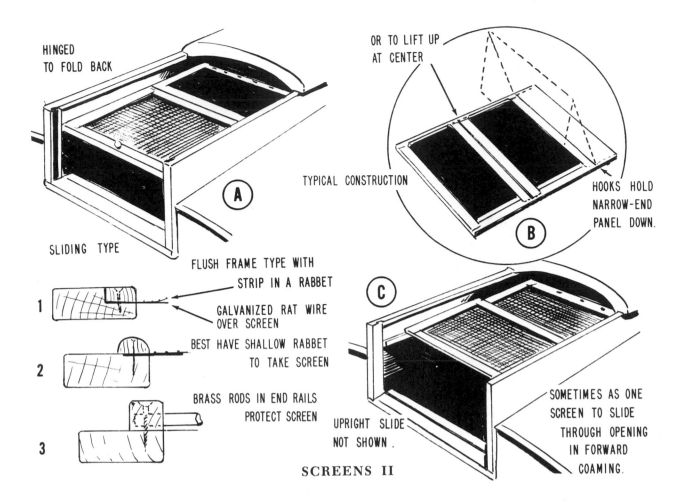

HINGED TO FOLD BACK

OR TO LIFT UP AT CENTER

TYPICAL CONSTRUCTION

HOOKS HOLD NARROW-END PANEL DOWN.

(A)

(B)

SLIDING TYPE

FLUSH FRAME TYPE WITH STRIP IN A RABBET

GALVANIZED RAT WIRE OVER SCREEN

1

BEST HAVE SHALLOW RABBET TO TAKE SCREEN

2

(C)

BRASS RODS IN END RAILS PROTECT SCREEN

3

UPRIGHT SLIDE NOT SHOWN.

SOMETIMES AS ONE SCREEN TO SLIDE THROUGH OPENING IN FORWARD COAMING.

SCREENS II

In addition to keeping insects out, a proper companionway screen should permit easy access or exit and should be of a type that will stow compactly away. A single-section screen doesn't always meet these requirements, except where it is arranged to shove forward—similar to the sliding hatch, but under it. The opening necessary in the forward or cross coaming is apt to allow spray to drive through in a seaway, unless the forward end of the slide has a lip to seal it. Some variation of the two-section type seems to suit most boats best.

A simple arrangement is shown at A, wherein one section, larger than the other, is hinged for lifting up and laying back on the slide. B shows a three-section type, which is a very narrow screen or even a board usually held down by hooks, with two sections hinged to it in such a way as to lift up at the center and jackknife back out of the way. In C, one section simply slides over the other to be really out of the way.

B gives the largest opening; in the other two, the whole thing must be lifted out, if the full opening is wanted. In folded form, these sectional types stow compactly, perhaps in a canvas envelope made to take the screen or screens:

Screen frames are usually made too light. They have to withstand pretty hard use and commence working at their joints. A full 1 inch is not too thick, with corners halved in and fastened in resin glue. Wooden dowels or long screws are best for the average man doing his own work. Galvanized rat wire, about ¼-inch mesh and fastened atop the regular copper screen with separate tacks rather widely spaced, will prevent objectionable sagging of the soft copper screen; or shippier-looking brass rods in end rails can be used, where they don't interfere with hinging back. The thickness of screen and tack heads, especially if you're using rat wire over, should be taken in a very shallow rabbet.

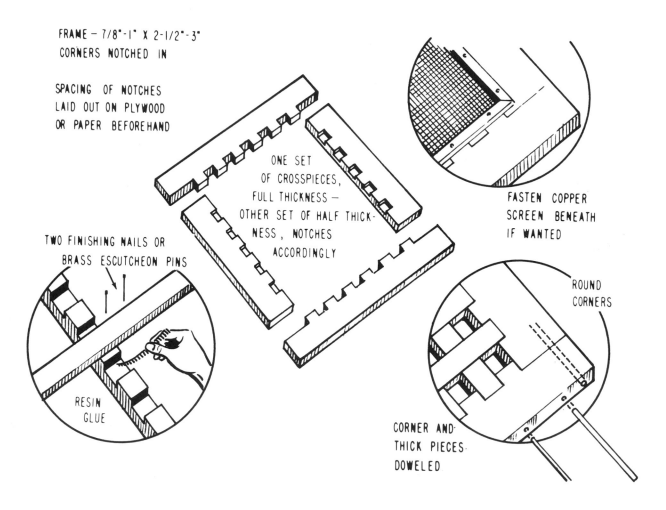

FRAME – 7/8"-1" X 2-1/2"-3"
CORNERS NOTCHED IN

SPACING OF NOTCHES
LAID OUT ON PLYWOOD
OR PAPER BEFOREHAND

ONE SET
OF CROSSPIECES,
FULL THICKNESS –
OTHER SET OF HALF THICK-
NESS, NOTCHES
ACCORDINGLY

TWO FINISHING NAILS OR
BRASS ESCUTCHEON PINS

RESIN
GLUE

FASTEN COPPER
SCREEN BENEATH
IF WANTED

ROUND
CORNERS

CORNER AND
THICK PIECES
DOWELED

HATCH GRATINGS

Here is a let-in type of grating. These are somewhat difficult to make, but are worth the effort. At the start, lay out the shape of the space for the grating on plywood or heavy building paper. Draw in the width of the proposed frame pieces and divide the inner area into an odd number of sections. Teak is the best wood for gratings, but well-seasoned white oak, mahogany, ash, and maple are also suitable. All the woods except teak must be protected with varnish or paint.

Let-in corners can be made without special tools; they also hold well, if dowels of the same wood or long screws, countersunk and plugged, are used. Resin-type glue should be used in making the joints. The frame members should be turned out as pairs, with identical notchings, and assembled on a level surface. Long, adjustable clamps are best used to draw the corners together for fastening.

The crosspieces, two identical sets with notchings to match those in the frame, should be a bit longer than necessary, so that each can be fitted exactly—forcing, but not driving. The frame should remain flat, held by battens secured to the bench to prevent distortion as crosspieces are set in. By careful boring, dowels can be let through into the ends of thick crosspieces. The thin pieces are best held by brass escutcheon pins, the heads of which have been countersunk just enough for filling over with matching composition.

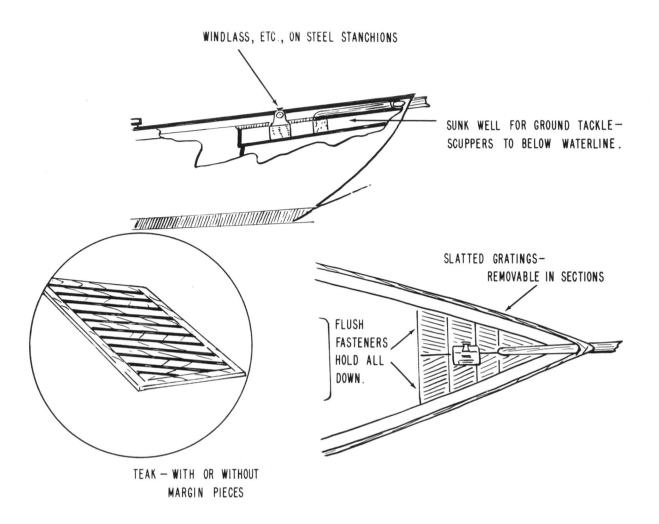

WINDLASS, ETC., ON STEEL STANCHIONS

SUNK WELL FOR GROUND TACKLE-
SCUPPERS TO BELOW WATERLINE.

SLATTED GRATINGS-
REMOVABLE IN SECTIONS

FLUSH
FASTENERS
HOLD ALL
DOWN.

TEAK — WITH OR WITHOUT
MARGIN PIECES

GROUND TACKLE WELL

Harold Mossler's lovely steel ketch *Freedom* has so many unusual and entirely practical features that it is hard to decide which to pass along. What I like best, perhaps, and something over which everyone is enthusiastic, is the sunken deck or well forward for ground tackle and such gear. This is an unusual feature, but it was not difficult to work into a steel hull such as this. If it were designed and built right, it would be equally as practical on a wooden hull. I have shown the ,well approximately as it is, deeper aft than forward in order to give better drainage through the clearing scuppers leading to just below the waterline. The mounting of the windlass and the heel of the bowsprit is merely indicated. Both are bolted atop sup-

ports—I suppose they might be called stanchions —leading up from the backbone of the bow structure and are otherwise strengthened by the watertight bulkhead below.

The slatted teak gratings that close the well to give a flush deck are in sections, as shown. All central and side edges are held in chocks, and there is no flimsiness or looseness apparent in walking on this deck. Extensions on the forward edge of each section engage sockets in the after edge of the section just ahead of it until, when all are in position, a pair of flush fasteners locks them in place.

A modern-style anchor with its chain or cable attached will readily stow beneath the gratings and afford a perfectly clear deck.

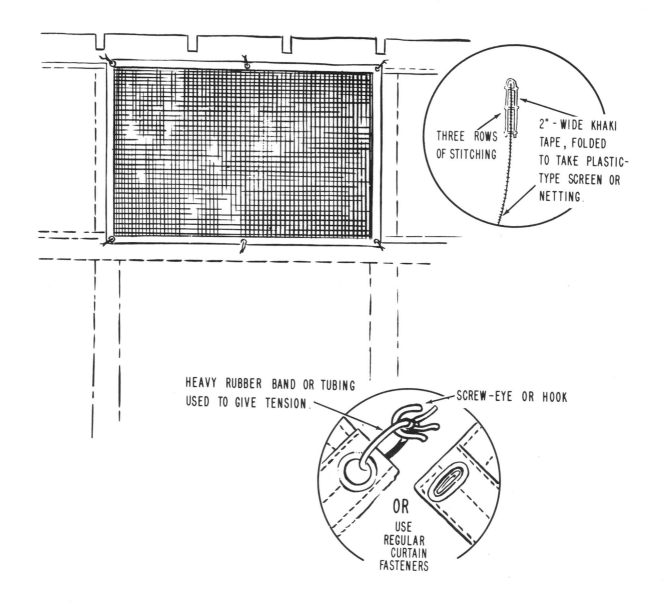

THREE ROWS
OF STITCHING

2"-WIDE KHAKI
TAPE, FOLDED
TO TAKE PLASTIC-
TYPE SCREEN OR
NETTING.

HEAVY RUBBER BAND OR TUBING
USED TO GIVE TENSION.

SCREW-EYE OR HOOK

OR
USE
REGULAR
CURTAIN
FASTENERS

EASILY STOWED SCREENS

Whenever you come across a powerboat owned by a former sailboat man, she is pretty sure to have more than her share of features worked out to make the handling of the boat more convenient and life aboard more comfortable. Dr. Paul Henson's *Uncatena* is a fine example of this. His cutter *Tern* was a well-thought-out boat, and so is his new cruiser, from which I have filched a number of good ideas.

The screens used on the *Uncatena* are shown in the above illustration, and while there may be nothing new about this khaki-tape and plastic-netting type, it is a good one for occasional use. The main advantage, of course, is the small amount of space required to stow these screens, either rolled or flat under a berth cushion. Regular curtain fasteners can be used for the corners. If the screen is large, you can use screw eyes or hooks, perhaps with rubber bands, to stretch the screen taut, or (as does Dr. Henson) lengths of 3/16-inch rubber tubing tied into the grommets to form loops.

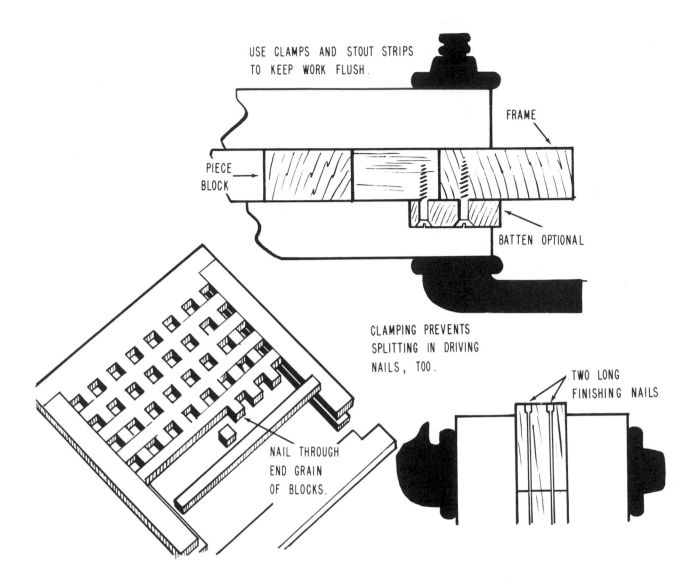

USE CLAMPS AND STOUT STRIPS
TO KEEP WORK FLUSH.

FRAME

PIECE
BLOCK

BATTEN OPTIONAL

CLAMPING PREVENTS
SPLITTING IN DRIVING
NAILS, TOO.

NAIL THROUGH
END GRAIN
OF BLOCKS.

TWO LONG
FINISHING NAILS

BLOCK-TYPE GRATING

A block-type grating is shown here. One end member of the frame is fastened temporarily to maintain the shape; it is taken out after the work has progressed far enough to require its removal for fastening of blocks and then secured finally to tie all together. Each block should be held by a couple of long finishing nails carefully drilled to avoid splitting the wood. Marks should be made on the frame members to insure proper openings; the same spacer should be used, to keep them uniform. If the two reinforcing battens beneath are used as shown, they can be removed when the grating is completed and then be refastened with the same screws and holes, along with two end ones, over bronze or copper screen, since one often wants the grating to serve as a screen as well.

The showing surface of either type should be sanded down flush and smooth in finishing. It is hardly possible to use a plane for other than the roughest dressing because of the opposed grains.

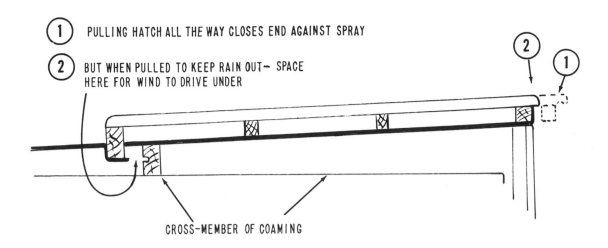

① PULLING HATCH ALL THE WAY CLOSES END AGAINST SPRAY

② BUT WHEN PULLED TO KEEP RAIN OUT— SPACE HERE FOR WIND TO DRIVE UNDER

CROSS-MEMBER OF COAMING

EXTRA-LONG SLIDE

A sliding hatch should be made a couple of inches longer than necessary. It can then be pulled aft just enough to keep rain out of the opening, as shown here. When the hatch is in this position, wind will force itself under the hatch forward and through the opening left there, but rain or spray will seldom come in.

Of course, it can be sealed there by pulling the hatch all the way aft. You will find that it can be kept slightly opened forward in all but the worst weather; and the air that is let in will be most appreciated when running under power in a heavy rain or squall with everything else battened down.

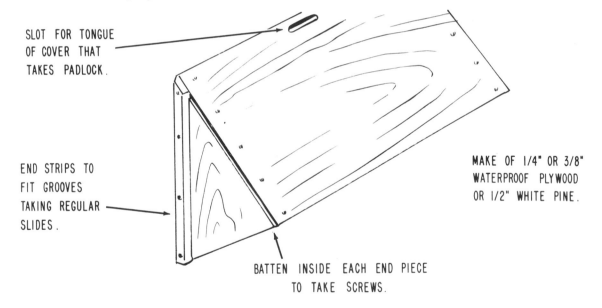

SLOT FOR TONGUE OF COVER THAT TAKES PADLOCK.

END STRIPS TO FIT GROOVES TAKING REGULAR SLIDES.

MAKE OF 1/4" OR 3/8" WATERPROOF PLYWOOD OR 1/2" WHITE PINE.

BATTEN INSIDE EACH END PIECE TO TAKE SCREWS.

VENTILATING SLIDE

The companionway slide illustrated here is used in place of the regular slides or drop doors when leaving the boat, as well as when laying at a dock in weather with the wind astern. In either case it lets air and some light in but keeps rain out. Not shown is an inner screen easily fitted across the bottom or opening to keep insects out.

CHAPTER 15

Shelters,
Docks
and Floats

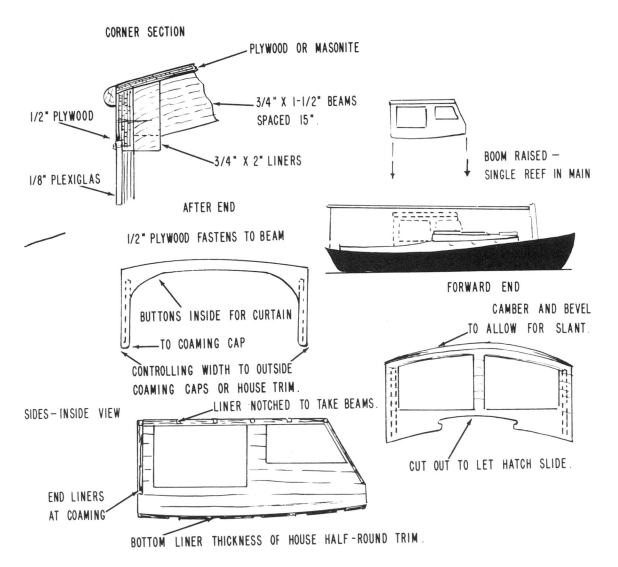

CORNER SECTION

PLYWOOD OR MASONITE

3/4" X 1-1/2" BEAMS
SPACED 15".

1/2" PLYWOOD

3/4" X 2" LINERS

1/8" PLEXIGLAS

BOOM RAISED —
SINGLE REEF IN MAIN

AFTER END

1/2" PLYWOOD FASTENS TO BEAM

BUTTONS INSIDE FOR CURTAIN
TO COAMING CAP

CONTROLLING WIDTH TO OUTSIDE
COAMING CAPS OR HOUSE TRIM.

LINER NOTCHED TO TAKE BEAMS.

SIDES - INSIDE VIEW

FORWARD END

CAMBER AND BEVEL
TO ALLOW FOR SLANT.

CUT OUT TO LET HATCH SLIDE.

END LINERS
AT COAMING

BOTTOM LINER THICKNESS OF HOUSE HALF-ROUND TRIM.

DEMOUNTABLE DECKHOUSE

Owners who have tried a demountable deck-house or shelter are usually enthusiastic over them. Some are of canvas over a framework; some rather like dodgers; others are rigid.

The best example I have seen was on a lovely 24-foot cat of the modern type which was taken South last fall. Naturally, no arrangement will suit all boats, but here are some hints the owner of this boat gave for planning and making a shelter. As he says, it will not be a thing of beauty. You will probably have to raise the boom and use a single reef in the sail. In colder weather, however, winds are apt to be stronger, so power will be used more. The main thing is to shelter the forward end of the cockpit.

Then, the companionway slide can be left open and the additional space allotted to the galley. The two sides and the forward end are best made of ½-inch plywood, with Plexiglas for windows. The top can be of a lighter material.

The work involved will be about halved if the sides are made straight, not curved to suit the house and coamings. And it all should be planned to slip down over them and to be held by a few bolts or even lashings, resting more or less on the deck. There will be spaces left, but this will be no great objection. Plug them with cloth. On this boat, a curtain was buttoned on to close the after end and steering lines were led inside for use under power on cold days.

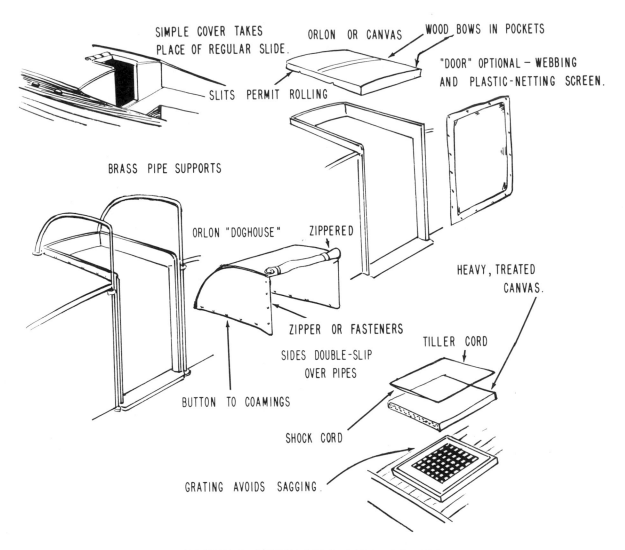

SIMPLE COVER TAKES PLACE OF REGULAR SLIDE.

ORLON OR CANVAS

WOOD BOWS IN POCKETS

"DOOR" OPTIONAL — WEBBING AND PLASTIC-NETTING SCREEN.

SLITS PERMIT ROLLING

BRASS PIPE SUPPORTS

ORLON "DOGHOUSE"

ZIPPERED

HEAVY, TREATED CANVAS.

ZIPPER OR FASTENERS

SIDES DOUBLE-SLIP OVER PIPES

TILLER CORD

BUTTON TO COAMINGS

SHOCK CORD

GRATING AVOIDS SAGGING.

CANVAS SHELTERS AND COVERS

A canvas shelter or cover is quite often handier than the ordinary, solid type. Nowadays, these can be made of Orlon, thus permitting light to pass through. The style shown in the top sketches rolls back to be conpletely out of the way. When needed, it can be quickly buttoned down. Bows of some sort should be fitted in pockets, to prevent sagging and holding water. To have it roll properly, it is generally necessary that there be short slits in the side pieces, as shown.

The doghouse arrangement works out particularly well on a small boat because it provides more headroom where it's apt to be needed most. The top section should be zippered to the sides for a foot or so, in order that the top can be rolled backward. Much of the time the cover can be left off, with the pipe supports remaining in place as hand holds. The shelter can be quickly drawn over the pipes and buttoned to the coamings.

The lower sketch shows an arrangement I have been using for some time. I no longer carry a regular cover for this after hatch, but leave it open, except for the grating, in good weather. The cover is easily stowed and can be as quickly put on. It should be a snug fit. The holding arrangment (simply a length of hard tiller cord with a piece of shock cord secured to its ends to give a band or loop that must be stretched for getting it on) has been entirely satisfactory.

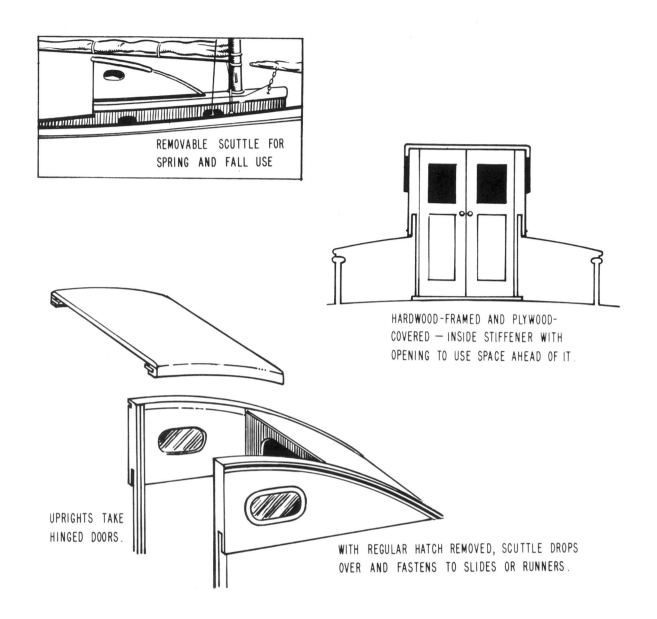

REMOVABLE SCUTTLE FOR SPRING AND FALL USE

HARDWOOD-FRAMED AND PLYWOOD-COVERED — INSIDE STIFFENER WITH OPENING TO USE SPACE AHEAD OF IT.

UPRIGHTS TAKE HINGED DOORS.

WITH REGULAR HATCH REMOVED, SCUTTLE DROPS OVER AND FASTENS TO SLIDES OR RUNNERS.

REMOVABLE DOGHOUSE

Here is a good idea sent in by Bob Harwood. This 26-foot cutter originally had the usual-size companionway hatch, but it was enlarged to give a 2½-foot-square opening, which allows the cook to stand inside when working in the galley at the after end. For warm weather use, it worked well—even in a rain, while the boat was at her mooring or anchored, because a long cockpit fly gave protection. However, Harwood finally made the removable scuttle or doghouse for spring and fall use and says he now would not be without it. The regular slide or companionway hatch cover is taken off, and the scuttle is made to fit over the opening and fastened with a few screws to the slides. Note that the uprights are carried down for fastening, too. They not only stiffen the structure but take the pair of light doors which are used in place of the usual dropboards.

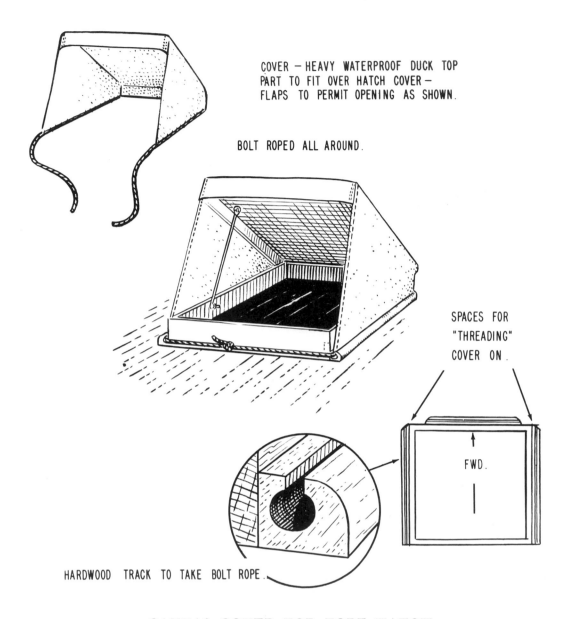

COVER — HEAVY WATERPROOF DUCK TOP
PART TO FIT OVER HATCH COVER —
FLAPS TO PERMIT OPENING AS SHOWN.

BOLT ROPED ALL AROUND.

SPACES FOR
"THREADING"
COVER ON.

FWD.

HARDWOOD TRACK TO TAKE BOLT ROPE.

CANVAS COVER FOR FORE HATCH

Here is a drawing of the fore hatch cover on *Lord Jim*. One of these makes it possible to keep the hatch open, both at sea or at anchor on rainy days. The cover of waterproof duck should fit snugly over the cover of the hatch. The forward edge, or skirt, and the side flaps, or wings, should be long enough so that, with the hatch raised and held firm by a pair of struts, the bolt-roped edges of the canvas cover will fit in the hardwood tracks. These tracks are secured permanently to the deck and base of the hatch coaming. Full-length tracks on the port and starboard sides of the hatch are required, but the forward or third track should be only a partial length, in order to leave spaces at its ends so that the cover can be threaded or started on at either corner. When in place, the cover is held by securing the ends of the track lines aft.

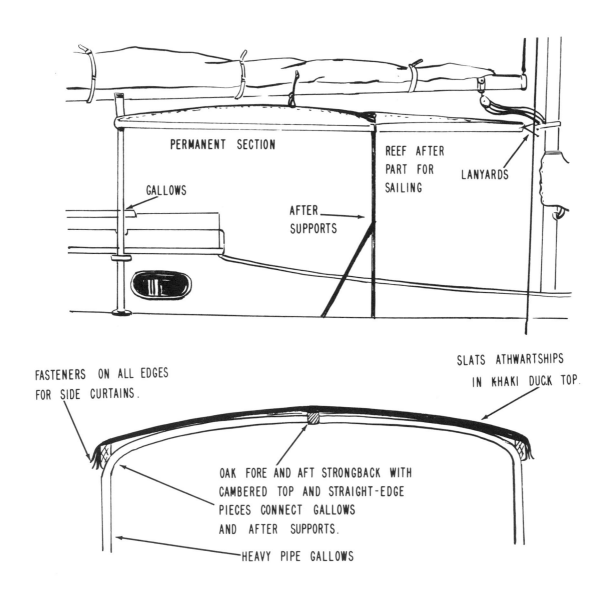

PERMANENT SECTION

GALLOWS

REEF AFTER
PART FOR
SAILING

LANYARDS

AFTER
SUPPORTS

FASTENERS ON ALL EDGES
FOR SIDE CURTAINS.

SLATS ATHWARTSHIPS
IN KHAKI DUCK TOP.

OAK FORE AND AFT STRONGBACK WITH
CAMBERED TOP AND STRAIGHT-EDGE
PIECES CONNECT GALLOWS
AND AFTER SUPPORTS.

HEAVY PIPE GALLOWS

EXTENSION-TYPE COCKPIT SHELTER

The ketch *Canopus* has one of the most practical awning arrangements I have come across. The permanent or standing section covers the companionway and extends well back. The after section is attached to it and rigged in such a way that it can be reefed or rolled up, so that it will not interfere with the mainsheet in sailing and will give the man at the wheel a fairly good view of the sails aloft. A heavy gallows frame of pine extends across the cabin, but is low enough so that the boom clears it when the main is hoisted. This was used for the forward support of the standing section. From it, side pieces and a central member or

strongback, the latter with its top well cambered, extend to the lighter after supports outside the cockpit coamings, and over these the heavy cover of khaki duck is stretched. This has pockets for athwartship battens and is tailored to fit snugly, with the edges brought well down all around and made double with a flap outside. Snap fasteners can be made to take side curtains, if wanted.

The after section has similar flap edges and snap fasteners, in addition to a few athwartship battens and a heavy batten aft, for hauling it out taut to the mizzen and its shrouds.

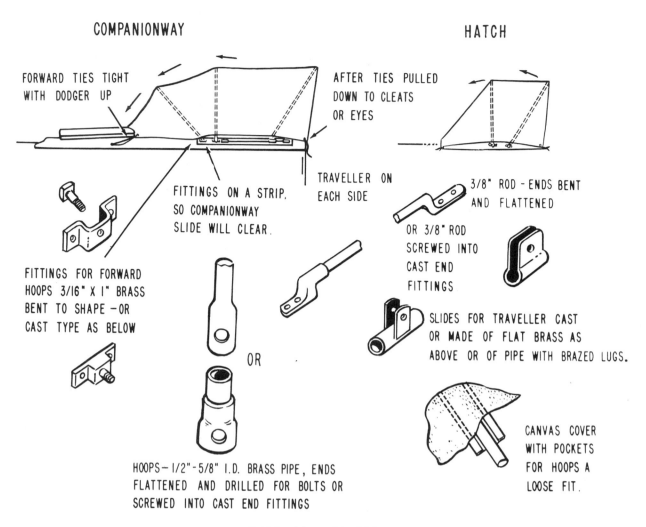

COMPANIONWAY

FORWARD TIES TIGHT
WITH DODGER UP

FITTINGS ON A STRIP,
SO COMPANIONWAY
SLIDE WILL CLEAR.

FITTINGS FOR FORWARD
HOOPS 3/16" X 1" BRASS
BENT TO SHAPE — OR
CAST TYPE AS BELOW

OR

HOOPS — 1/2" - 5/8" I.D. BRASS PIPE, ENDS
FLATTENED AND DRILLED FOR BOLTS OR
SCREWED INTO CAST END FITTINGS

HATCH

AFTER TIES PULLED
DOWN TO CLEATS
OR EYES

TRAVELLER ON
EACH SIDE

3/8" ROD - ENDS BENT
AND FLATTENED

OR 3/8" ROD
SCREWED INTO
CAST END
FITTINGS

SLIDES FOR TRAVELLER CAST
OR MADE OF FLAT BRASS AS
ABOVE OR OF PIPE WITH BRAZED LUGS.

CANVAS COVER
WITH POCKETS
FOR HOOPS A
LOOSE FIT.

CANVAS DODGERS

A canvas dodger over the main companion-way, or even for a hatch in the bridge deck, is as handy to have rigged as its making is difficult to describe. No single plan or set of dimensions will suit more than a few boats. Each must be worked out to give the shelter wanted, depending on the size and nature of the opening and whatever may interfere with the raising and lowering of the dodger.

For the companionway type, three hoops will be required, each flatly U-shaped rather than with corners rounded. The forward two hoops must pivot on fittings attached to the coamings, while the after one should slide on a traveler on each side, so that it can be shoved forward to lower the dodger and pulled back to raise it. Usually, the middle hoop can be a couple of inches higher than the forward one, with the after sliding hoop still another 2 inches higher; 19, 21, and 23 inches are typical heights for a 2-foot-square opening. Perhaps the best way to get the height and shape wanted is to work with three lengths of ¼- or ⅜-inch iron rod, each made to the proper height and bent in the same way to the shape desired; finally, the actual hoops are made according to these. Fittings for their attachment are shown, and all must usually be secured on a hardwood strip on each side fastened to the coamings to bring the hoops out enough to clear the companionway slide.

If you are having the canvas cover made, try to have the person making it take his own measurements.

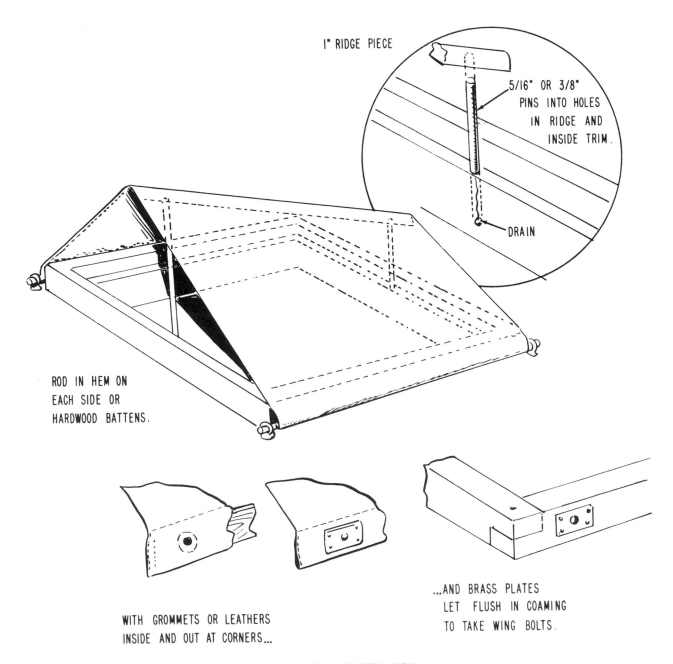

1" RIDGE PIECE

5/16" OR 3/8"
PINS INTO HOLES
IN RIDGE AND
INSIDE TRIM.

DRAIN

ROD IN HEM ON
EACH SIDE OR
HARDWOOD BATTENS.

WITH GROMMETS OR LEATHERS
INSIDE AND OUT AT CORNERS...

...AND BRASS PLATES
LET FLUSH IN COAMING
TO TAKE WING BOLTS.

HATCH SHELTER

I noticed the simple hatch shelter being used on a sizable yawl's afterdeck, where the owner had worked it out chiefly to permit keeping the hatch there open when running under power in the rain or through a squall, because the muffler and after end of his exhaust installation threw off considerable heat. Turned then with the lower end forward, little rain would enter, but it worked out so well that he now uses it at anchor, the higher end facing forward, to force air below. The sides may be held down to lacing eyes on deck or, to avoid such obstructions, each hem can have matching grommets or leathers at the corners to take bolts with wing heads going into plates let flush into the hatch coaming.

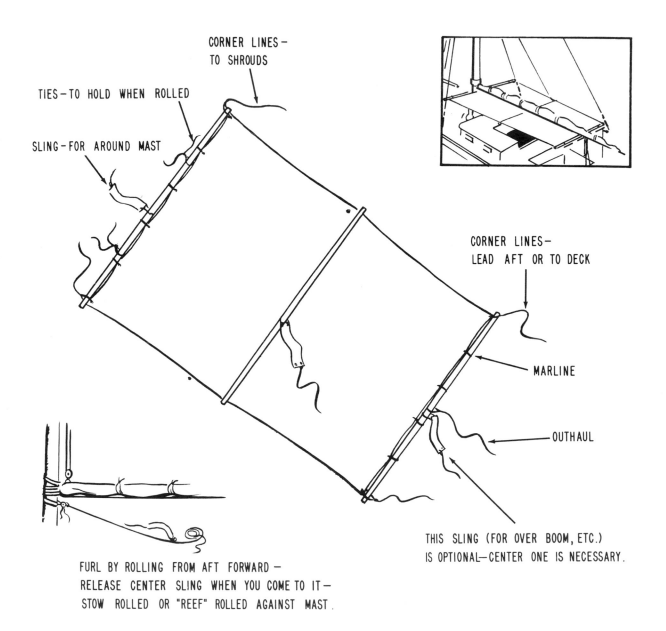

CORNER LINES –
TO SHROUDS

TIES – TO HOLD WHEN ROLLED

SLING – FOR AROUND MAST

CORNER LINES –
LEAD AFT OR TO DECK

MARLINE

OUTHAUL

THIS SLING (FOR OVER BOOM, ETC.)
IS OPTIONAL–CENTER ONE IS NECESSARY.

FURL BY ROLLING FROM AFT FORWARD –
RELEASE CENTER SLING WHEN YOU COME TO IT –
STOW ROLLED OR "REEF" ROLLED AGAINST MAST.

COCKPIT AWNING

This type of awning is fine for a gaff-header or other boat with complicated running rigging, lazyjacks, and lifts, because no lines are disturbed—as, for instance, with an over-the-boom type. Of course, if you can hoist the forward end of the loaded boom a foot or so to make it level, it will improve the headroom and it will set and look better.

Rolled on its poles, it is a handy shape for stowing on the cabintop. To set, leave it rolled while you are securing the sling about the mast and making the corner lines fast to the shrouds. Then, release the ties and unroll it, securing the center sling and finally hauling it taut aft and securing there. Furling is as simple as this, particularly if slippery hitches are used in the securing: merely release the after end and roll tightly about the poles. If you're doing it against a squall, just leave the tied roll secured to the mast and shrouds all ready for resetting.

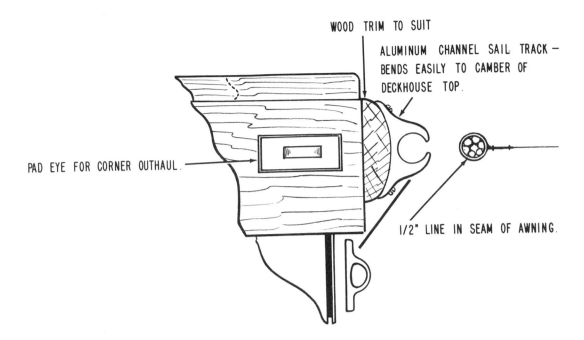

WOOD TRIM TO SUIT

ALUMINUM CHANNEL SAIL TRACK — BENDS EASILY TO CAMBER OF DECKHOUSE TOP.

PAD EYE FOR CORNER OUTHAUL.

1/2" LINE IN SEAM OF AWNING.

LOWER SECTION ON REGULAR SAIL TRACK.

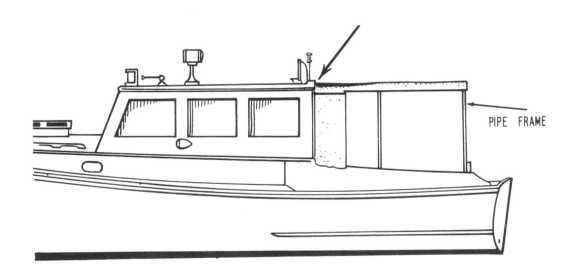

PIPE FRAME

CHANNEL SAIL TRACK

I like Robie Verge's idea of using channel sail track to hold the semi-permanent awning on his *Parametta*. Salvaged from a broken mast, it holds the canvas watertight against the after edge of the deckhouse. The wood trim there required reshaping, Robie says, but in securing the track it took the slight curve nicely. Although the awning is ordinarily left standing, taking it down is merely a matter of freeing the snaps which hold it to the pipe framework and then undoing the forward corner outhauls and drawing the edge out of its track.

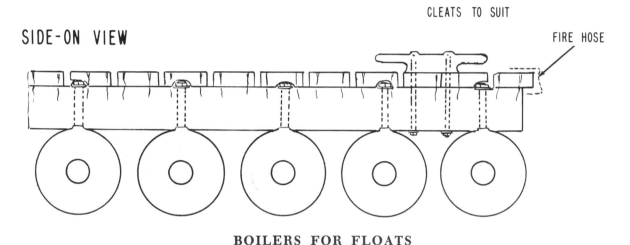

LENGTHS OF I" PIPE SCREWED INTO A PAIR OF THE TAPPING STUDS.
TAKE UP WITH HEAVY WASHERS AND NUTS.

2" X 6"- 8" DECKING

6" X 6" STRINGERS

TAR TANKS FOR LONGER SERVICE OR SALT WATER

END VIEW

USED 30-GAL. HOT-WATER TANKS —
FOR EASY HANDLING MAKE UP AS UNITS OF HALF A DOZEN TANKS—
CHAIN SEVERAL TOGETHER, IF NECESSARY.

CLEATS TO SUIT

SIDE-ON VIEW

FIRE HOSE

BOILERS FOR FLOATS

Old, discarded hot-water boilers or tanks of the usual 30-gallon capacity make an excellent float. They will last longer than oil drums and make a steadier float. Often, an oil drum float, because of its buoyancy, rides too high and dips its end or side too easily.

With the newer insulated heater tank displacing the old-fashioned kind, junk yards generally have plenty of the old ones available for a dollar or so. Half-a-dozen make a handy float that is not too heavy to handle. Or, for a floating raft, chain together as many as are needed.

To get maximum life from the tanks, apply a heavy coat of tar, but use a grade that will set reasonably fast. Good used lumber (6 by 6's and 1½ or 2-inch planks) is generally used for stringers and decking. Each drum, in turn, is secured by threading a couple of lengths of pipe into two tapping studs or openings made on each side of each boiler. These should be of the right length and have both ends threaded to go through holes previously bored in the stringers and to take heavy washers and bolts. Then it is merely a matter of spiking your decking in place and bolting on a couple of stout cleats, possibly nailing old fire hose around the edges as a fender.

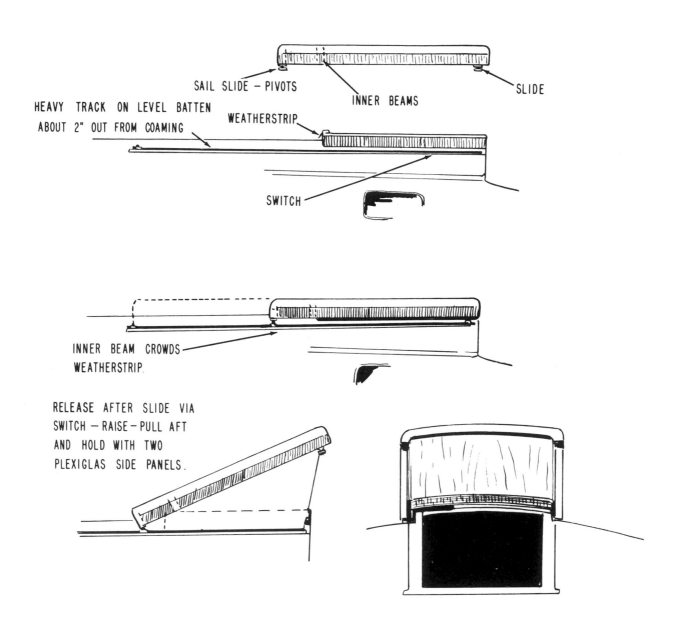

SAIL SLIDE – PIVOTS

INNER BEAMS

SLIDE

HEAVY TRACK ON LEVEL BATTEN
ABOUT 2" OUT FROM COAMING

WEATHERSTRIP

SWITCH

INNER BEAM CROWDS
WEATHERSTRIP.

RELEASE AFTER SLIDE VIA
SWITCH – RAISE – PULL AFT
AND HOLD WITH TWO
PLEXIGLAS SIDE PANELS.

SLIDING HATCH

Here is a way of providing a sliding hatch or cover for the cabin companionway. Note that the sides of the hatch are not carried forward in the usual way as runners; instead, the cover, fitted with two heavy sail slides on each side, travels on matching sail track. It is made longer than necessary and has an extra beam located to bear against the weather stripping on the cross coaming with the hatch closed. The for-ward sail slide on each side should be attached in a way that will permit lifting the after end, after releasing its slides from the track by way of the switch or turnbutton. Then, pull it aft until the forward beam of the cover bears against the coaming, slip in the side panels of Plexiglas, and you have a good wet-weather arrangement.

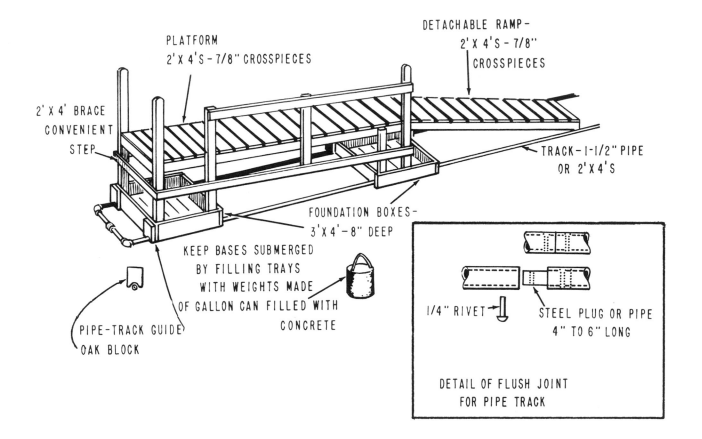

PLATFORM
2' X 4'S - 7/8" CROSSPIECES

DETACHABLE RAMP-
2' X 4'S - 7/8"
CROSSPIECES

2' X 4' BRACE
CONVENIENT
STEP

TRACK-1-1/2" PIPE
OR 2'X 4'S

FOUNDATION BOXES-
3'X 4'- 8" DEEP

KEEP BASES SUBMERGED
BY FILLING TRAYS
WITH WEIGHTS MADE
OF GALLON CAN FILLED WITH
CONCRETE

PIPE-TRACK GUIDE
OAK BLOCK

1/4" RIVET

STEEL PLUG OR PIPE
4" TO 6" LONG

DETAIL OF FLUSH JOINT
FOR PIPE TRACK

PORTABLE DOCK

This portable dock idea was sent in by Frank J. Keating. Both he and his brother-in-law have found this type satisfactory on lakes such as Canandaigua and Seneca in New York State because it can be removed from the water, track and all, late each fall to avoid winter ice damage. With the inshore ramp section removed, the platform part is hauled out on its track by using a tackle or car ashore—usually without having to remove the weights from their boxes.

The track is evidently laid directly on a hard-sand, gravel, or smooth-rock bottom, with a uniform slant of preferably not more than 10 degrees. This track can be made of pipe or angle iron, even of 2 by 4's, with the track guides to suit whatever is used. Any joining necessary is kept flush, as Mr. Keating shows in using pipe. Although only one section of platform is shown (for which Mr. Keating suggests a length of 10 feet and a height above water of around

2 feet), several sections could be used to reach the depth of water desired. The two weight boxes which form the foundation should be made of 2 by 8's with heavy, slatted bottoms; then the platform itself is built on them. The ramp should be hinged to the inshore end of the platform and made detachable, so that it can be handled as a unit.

To hold the boxes and their platform down, weights made by filling gallon-size cans with concrete are suggested, from twelve to eighteen being required for each box. Each should have a handle made by embedding a bent length of rod in the concrete, so that some of the weights can be hauled up, if necessary, to lighten the platform for hauling out. If the slant of the beach is more than 10 degrees, Mr. Keating advises placing a concrete block or other stop at the outer end of the track, in order to keep the guides from sliding off.

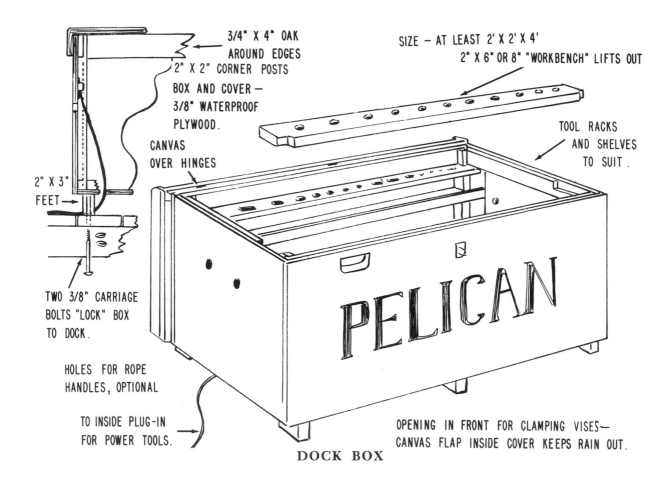

3/4" X 4" OAK AROUND EDGES

2" X 2" CORNER POSTS

BOX AND COVER — 3/8" WATERPROOF PLYWOOD.

CANVAS OVER HINGES

2" X 3" FEET →

TWO 3/8" CARRIAGE BOLTS "LOCK" BOX TO DOCK.

HOLES FOR ROPE HANDLES, OPTIONAL

TO INSIDE PLUG-IN FOR POWER TOOLS.

SIZE — AT LEAST 2' X 2' X 4'

2" X 6" OR 8" "WORKBENCH" LIFTS OUT

TOOL RACKS AND SHELVES TO SUIT.

OPENING IN FRONT FOR CLAMPING VISES— CANVAS FLAP INSIDE COVER KEEPS RAIN OUT.

DOCK BOX

If a boat is kept in a slip, it is best to have a dock box to hold odd gear. Or, if a mooring is used, a box located near where the tender is kept will be almost as handy. Few yards and marinas object to them so long as they are neatly made and painted to be in keeping with the place, for they do tend to keep docks free of loose gear. Some docks even provide one for each slip, for this reason as much as for the convenience of customers.

Usually, however, it is up to the owner to make his own. The box shown here was drawn up after one I saw just recently. It has several worthwhile features for the man who likes to do his own through-the-season work on his boat. The size (2 by 2 by 4 feet) is merely a suggestion—I would say that, if dock space permits, the box should be made definitely longer and possibly wider and deeper, depending on your needs. This one not only has a tool rack across the back with shelves under it, but a plank drops down and hooks into end chocks

to give a sort of workbench which can be used by kneeling. A small vise can be clamped to the front opening. If power tools will be used, an inside electrical socket is a good idea; this is better than merely leading an extension cord (with end fitting removed) through a hole in the bottom of the box, then reattaching the connection with the idea that the cord cannot be removed. The way of fastening the box down, with carriage bolts through the dock decking and the feet and bottom of the box with nuts inside, can hardly be bettered.

Waterproof plywood is usually used for such a box, but it should have corner posts and oak liners inside, at least along the top edges. While the cover should be made watertight against rain, a few drainage holes should be bored in the bottom; but do not have them big enough for mice to slip through. Prime the plywood with a surfacer or preparation for such use before actually painting, and the finish will better withstand exposure.

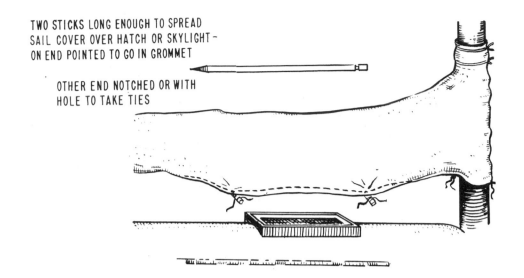

TWO STICKS LONG ENOUGH TO SPREAD
SAIL COVER OVER HATCH OR SKYLIGHT—
ON END POINTED TO GO IN GROMMET

OTHER END NOTCHED OR WITH
HOLE TO TAKE TIES

SAIL COVER SHELTERS HATCH

The idea shown will not always work, but often a sailcover is made full enough to permit spreading an untied part of it over a hatch or small skylight on the cabintop. While this will keep out only a shower or a "straight-down" rain, it will at other times tend to coax a breeze through the hatch. You will only need a couple of stick spreaders, one end of each of which is pointed to slip into a grommet; in each case, the other end is notched or has a hole to take the tie at the opposite side.

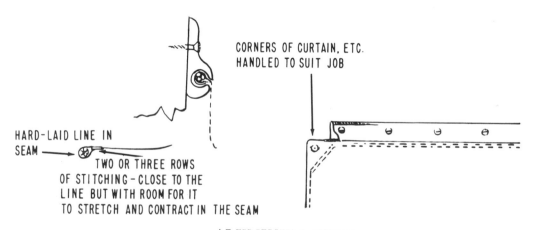

CORNERS OF CURTAIN. ETC.
HANDLED TO SUIT JOB

HARD-LAID LINE IN
SEAM
TWO OR THREE ROWS
OF STITCHING—CLOSE TO THE
LINE BUT WITH ROOM FOR IT
TO STRETCH AND CONTRACT IN THE SEAM

ALUMINUM TRIM

Several shapes of aluminum trim or molding come in handy aboard boats. For example, on the *Maid of Kent* the style shown is used to hold the edges of canvas work on side curtains and a novel canvas sunshade is led out from above windshield windows of the deckhouse. Rather than use boltrope, which does not work out well, a length of hard-laid line is sewn in the seam of the edge to be held, two or three rows of stitching being used, with the inner one close against the line but still allowing it to come and go slightly in its shrinking and stretching. The groove in the aluminum holds this, and the shape is such that water is shed effectively.

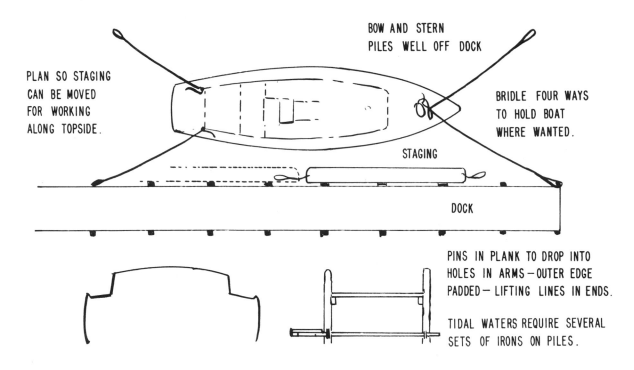

PLAN SO STAGING CAN BE MOVED FOR WORKING ALONG TOPSIDE.

BOW AND STERN PILES WELL OFF DOCK

BRIDLE FOUR WAYS TO HOLD BOAT WHERE WANTED.

STAGING

DOCK

PINS IN PLANK TO DROP INTO HOLES IN ARMS — OUTER EDGE PADDED — LIFTING LINES IN ENDS.

TIDAL WATERS REQUIRE SEVERAL SETS OF IRONS ON PILES.

DOCK STAGING

The figure shows a handy dock arrangement which seems to work out satisfactorily so long as there is not too much rise and fall of tide. Scrap iron (steel wagon tires) was bent and drilled as holders for spiking to the dock's piling, and these take three oak arms a loose fit. These were projected enough to take a staging made of two 10-inch planks, 16 feet long, cleated together, with a number of holes bored so that loose-fitting carriage bolts could be dropped through into holes in the arms to keep staging from shifting. The outer edge of the staging was padded with old fire hose and fitted with ropes for handling.